Formulating Responses in an Egalitarian Age

Formulating Responses in an Egalitarian Age

Edited by
Marc D. Stern

Robert S. Hirt, Series Editor

The Orthodox Forum Series
A Project of the Rabbi Isaac Elchanan Theological Seminary
An Affiliate of Yeshiva University

ROWMAN & LITTLEFIELD PUBLISHERS, INC.
Lanham • Boulder • New York • Toronto • Oxford

ROWMAN & LITTLEFIELD PUBLISHERS, INC.

Published in the United States of America
by Rowman & Littlefield Publishers, Inc.
A wholly owned subsidiary of The Rowman & Littlefield Publishing Group, Inc.
4501 Forbes Boulevard, Suite 200, Lanham, Maryland 20706
www.rowmanlittlefield.com

PO Box 317
Oxford
OX2 9RU, UK

British Library Cataloguing in Publication Information Available

Library of Congress Cataloging-in-Publication Data

Orthodox Forum (13th : 2001 : Congregation Shearith Israel, New York, N.Y.)
Formulating responses in an egalitarian age / edited by Marc D. Stern.
p. cm. -- (The Orthodox Forum)
Proceedings of a conference held at Congregation Shearith Israel, New York, N.Y., March 18-19, 2001.
Includes bibliographical references and index.
ISBN 0-7425-4597-0 (hardcover : alk. paper) -- ISBN 0-7425-4598-9 (pbk. : alk. paper)
1. Equality--Religious aspects--Judaism--Congresses. 2. Orthodox Judaism--Doctrines--Congresses. 3. Women--Legal status, laws, etc. (Jewish law)--Congresses. 4. Gentiles--Legal status, laws, etc. (Jewish law)--Congresses. I. Stern, Marc D. II. Title. III. Series: Orthodox Forum series.
BM645.E85O78 2001
296.3'8–dc22

2005008599

Printed in the United States of America

∞™ The paper used in this publication meets the minimum requirements of American National Standard for Information Sciences—Permanence of Paper for Printed Library Materials, ANSI/NISO Z39.48-1992.

THE ORTHODOX FORUM

The Orthodox Forum, convened by Dr. Norman Lamm, Chancellor of Yeshiva University, meets each year to consider major issues of concern to the Jewish community. Forum participants from throughout the world, including academicians in both Jewish and secular fields, rabbis, *rashei yeshiva*, Jewish educators, and Jewish communal professionals, gather in conference as a think tank to discuss and critique each other's original papers, examining different aspects of a central theme. The purpose of the Forum is to create and disseminate a new and vibrant Torah literature addressing the critical issues facing Jewry today.

The Orthodox Forum
gratefully acknowledges the support
of the Joseph J. and Bertha K. Green Memorial Fund
at the Rabbi Isaac Elchanan Theological Seminary
established by Morris L. Green, of blessed memory.

The Orthodox Forum Series
is a project of the Rabbi Isaac Elchanan Theological Seminary,
an affiliate of Yeshiva University

Rabbinic Authority and Personal Autonomy
edited by
Moshe Z. Sokol

Jewish Tradition and the Non-Traditional Jew
edited by
Jacob J. Schacter

Israel as a Religious Reality
edited by
Chaim I. Waxman

Modern Scholarship in the Study of Torah: Contributions and Limitations
edited by
Shalom Carmy

Tikkun Olam: Social Responsibility in Jewish Thought and Law
edited by
David Shatz, Chaim I. Waxman, and Nathan J. Diament

Engaging Modernity: Rabbinic Leaders and the Challenge of the Twentieth Century
edited by
Moshe Z. Sokol

Jewish Perspectives on the Experience of Suffering
edited by
Shalom Carmy

Jewish Business Ethics: The Firm and Its Stakeholders
edited by
Aaron Levine and Moses Pava

Tolerance, Dissent, and Democracy: Philosophical, Historical and Halakhic Perspectives
edited by
Moshe Z. Sokol

Jewish Spirituality and Divine Law
edited by
Adam Mintz and Lawrence Schiffman

THE ORTHODOX FORUM
THIRTEENTH CONFERENCE

Sunday and Monday, March 18–19, 2001
23–24 Adar 5761
Congregation Shearith Israel
New York City

LIST OF PARTICIPANTS

Rabbi Elchanan Adler, RIETS/Yeshiva University, New York, NY
Dr. Norman Adler, Yeshiva University, New York, NY
Rabbi Assaf Bednarsh, Marsha Stern Talmudical Academy—Yeshiva University High School for Boys, New York, NY
Dr. David Berger, Brooklyn College, New York, NY
Rabbi Gedalyah Berger, Yeshiva University, New York, NY
Prof. Jay Berkovitz, University of Massachusetts, Amherst, MA
Rabbi Ari Berman, The Jewish Center, New York, NY
Rabbi Jack Bieler, Hebrew Academy of Greater Washington, Silver Spring, MD
Dr. Rivkah Blau, Writer and Lecturer, New York, NY
Rabbi Yosef Blau, RIETS/Yeshiva University, New York, NY
Dr. Judith Bleich, Touro College, New York, NY
Prof. Edward Breuer, Loyola University of Chicago, Chicago, IL
Prof. Alan Brill, Yeshiva University, New York, NY
Rabbi Michael Broyde, Emory University, Atlanta, GA
Rabbi Shalom Carmy, Yeshiva University, New York, NY
Rabbi Zevulun Charlop, RIETS/Yeshiva University, New York, NY
Mr. Nathan J. Diament, Orthodox Union, Washington, DC
Rabbi Mark Dratch, Congregation Agudath Sholom, Stamford, CT
Dr. Yaakov Elman, Yeshiva University, New York, NY
Dr. Roberta Farber, Stern College for Women/Yeshiva University, New York, NY
Dr. Carl Feit, Yeshiva University, New York, NY
Rabbi Daniel Feldman, Yeshiva University, New York, NY
Rabbi Hillel Goldberg, Intermountain Jewish News, Denver, CO
Dr. Martin Golding, Duke University, Durham, NC
Rabbi Jay Goldmintz, Ramaz Upper School, New York, NY
Rabbi David Gottlieb, Congregation Shomeri Emunah, Baltimore, MD
Prof. Jonathan Helfand, Brooklyn College, Brooklyn, NY
Rabbi Nathaniel Helfgot, Yeshiva Chovevei Torah, New York, NY
Rabbi Robert S. Hirt, RIETS/Yeshiva University, New York, NY
Prof. Binyamin Ish-Shalom, Beit Morasha, Israel
Rabbi David A. Israel, RIETS/Yeshiva University, New York, NY
Rabbi Moshe Kahn, Yeshiva University, New York, NY

Prof. Ephraim Kanarfogel, Yeshiva University, New York, NY
Rabbi Zvi Kaplan, Yeshiva University, New York, NY
Rabbi Dr. Eugene Korn, Edah Journal, New York, NY
Dr. Norman Lamm, Yeshiva University, New York, NY
Miss Yael Levi, Bruriah High School for Girls, Elizabeth, NJ
Mr. Nathan Lewin, Washington, DC
Rabbi Aharon Lichtenstein, Yeshivat Har Etzion/RIETS, Jerusalem, Israel
Rabbi Dov Linzer, Yeshiva Hovevei Torah, New York, NY
Rabbi Shmuel Marcus, Young Israel of Fair Lawn, Fair Lawn, NJ
Rabbi Shmuel Maybruch, Yeshiva University, New York, NY
Rabbi Eitan Mayer, Efrat, Israel
Mrs. Sally Mayer, Efrat, Israel
Rabbi Adam Mintz, Bildner Center for Jewish Life, Rutgers University, New Brunswick, NJ
Mrs. Sharon Mintz, Jewish Theological Seminary, New York, NY
Rabbi Zev Reichman, East Hill Synagogue, Englewood, NJ
Rabbi Yona Reiss, Beth Din of America, New York, NY
Rabbi Zvi Romm, Yeshiva University, New York, NY
Rabbi Michael Rosensweig, RIETS/Yeshiva University, New York, NY
Prof. Smadar Rosensweig, Touro College, New York, NY
Rabbi Gidon Rothstein, Kollel, HAFTER High School, Cedarhurst, NY
Rabbi Kenneth Schiowitz, The Ramaz School, New York, NY
Dr. David Schnall, Yeshiva University, New York, NY
Rabbi Ezra Schwartz, Yeshiva University, New York, NY
Dr. David Shatz, Yeshiva University, New York, NY
Rabbi Charles Sheer, Jewish Chaplain/Director Emeritus, Columbia University and Barnard College, New York, NY
Dr. Michael Shmidman, Yeshiva University, New York, NY
Rabbi Alan Stadtmauer, Yeshivah of Flatbush High School, Brooklyn, NY
Mr. Marc D. Stern, American Jewish Congress, New York, NY
Prof. Suzanne Last Stone, Cardozo School of Law/Yeshiva University, New York, NY
Rabbi Moshe D. Tendler, RIETS/Yeshiva University, New York, NY
Dr. Jeremiah Unterman, Max Stern Division of Communal Services, RIETS, New York, NY
Dr. Chaim I. Waxman, Rutgers University, New Brunswick, NJ
Rabbi Jeremy Wieder, Yeshiva University, New York, NY
Dr. Joel B. Wolowelsky, Yeshivah of Flatbush High School, Brooklyn, NY
Dr. Walter S. Wurzburger, z"l (deceased), Yeshiva University, New York NY

Contents

Series Editor's Introduction

Robert S. Hirt

Formulating Responses in an Egalitarian Age is the twelfth volume in the Orthodox Forum Series. Marc D. Stern, the volume's editor, has presented us with a broad array of articles spanning a variety of disciplines.

Current sociological and ideological trends encouragingly stress the need for greater sensitivity to human dignity, but at the same time challenge the very structure and sanctity of traditional Jewish norms.

The Contributors in this work explore the issues of particularism and universalism, Jewish legal principles, and moral relativism in a manner that should be of interest to the layman and scholar alike.

The Forum Series provides a valuable and relevant resource, bringing the insights of Jewish thinkers to the fore in a rapidly changing society.

We hope that this work will enrich the knowledge of our readership.

1

Egalitarianism and *Halakha*: An Introduction

Marc D. Stern

There exists a conflict between the fundamental commitment of American society (and Western society generally) to the equal treatment of all people—regardless of race, religion, sex, and, increasingly, sexual orientation—and the different, often non-egalitarian requirements of *halakha*. Although too often unrecognized, but as important in its own right, that conflict also focuses attention on the malleability (or lack thereof) of *halakha* to respond to fundamental social change—should a response be appropriate.

JEWS CHOSE EQUALITY

Shreveport, Louisiana's Sunday Blue Law required stores to close after 9:00 a.m. Sunday. Somewhat atypically for the time (1874),[1] the ordinance exempted storekeepers who kept their stores closed on the Saturday Sabbath. The exemption substantially equalized the position of the observant Jewish shopkeeper with his Christian competitor, who otherwise would have enjoyed a substantial competitive advantage by being open for business on Saturday when his Jewish competitor was closed.

A Jewish storekeeper, Levy, opened his store on both Saturday and Sunday. Fined for violating the Blue Laws, Levy challenged the exemption for Saturday Sabbath observers on the ground that it granted a special privilege to Jews.

The Louisiana Supreme Court agreed, striking the statute as a breach of the constitutional mandate of equal treatment of all citizens. Forty years later, the same court, relying on its earlier decision in *Levy*, held that public schools could not compel Jewish students to participate in Christian religious exercises because such exercises denied them equality with their Christian schoolmates.[2]

Were Jews better off because the court insisted on formal equality of Jews and non-Jews? Did the cost to *shmirat shabbat* outweigh the benefits of a shield against official favoritism toward Christianity? (The economic pressure on Saturday Sabbath observance was in part responsible for the decision of some reformers to "move" *shabbat* to Sunday. It certainly led many American Jews to abandon *shmirat shabbat*.) What about the benefits of an official reaffirmation of Jewish equality at a time when equality was not a highly prized value in the highly Christianized American South? How do we weigh the economic penalty for *shmirat shabbat* against the benefit of not exposing vulnerable and Jewishly illiterate schoolchildren to Christian preaching by their teachers and peers? How should Jews at the time, not blessed as we are with hindsight, have reacted?

Not long ago, a friend was honored for many years of service to the Jewish community. The speaker at the dinner, the former director of the National Jewish Community Relations Council (now the Jewish Council on Public Affairs), recalled in a startling, though perhaps not fully historically accurate, admission that, in the immediate aftermath of World War II, Jews decided to insist on full equality. In taking this decision, he said, Jews knew that the pursuit of equality would increase the likelihood of assimilation. Yet they went ahead anyway.[3]

Should they have acted differently? Should Jews have tolerated inequality in order to forestall assimilation? Should they have left in place quotas limiting their admission to Ivy League schools or left unchallenged restrictive housing covenants that severely restricted their choice of residence? Doing so would (probably) have slowed assimilation and intermarriage. Perhaps, as *Rav* Aharon Lichtenstein tentatively suggested at the Forum, not insisting so insistently on equality would have been a wiser course. It seems safe to say—and several participants at the Forum made the point in response—that at this late date, Jews of all stripes are not willing to turn back the clock.

Should Jews have left intact Christmas celebrations in the schools in order to keep Jewish children uncomfortable and thereby discourage assimilation into hostile surroundings? (Or, perhaps, encourage assimilation as school children conformed to avoid peer hostility?) As early as 1904, the Agudas Harabonim thought not, joining with the Reform rabbinate—naturally not in the same statement—in saying no. Were both groups misguided in challenging Christian practices in the public schools?

Finally, consider, particularly with regard to our community's struggle to respond to the gay community's demand for equality, the debate in the English Parliament over the granting of full citizenship to Jews in 1835. Responding to an opponent of granting Jews equal political citizenship who denied that he sought to persecute Jews or deny them equal economic rights, Lord Macaulay said:[4]

> But why a man should be less fit to exercise [political] powers because he wears a beard, because he does not eat ham, because he goes to the synagogue on Saturday instead of going to a church on Sunday, we cannot conceive.
>
> The points of difference between Christianity and Judaism have much to do with a man's fitness to be a bishop or a rabbi, but they have no more to do with his fitness to be a legislator, or a minister of finance, than with his fitness to be a cobbler. . . . Any man would rather have his shoes mended by a heretical cobbler than by a person who had subscribed to all 39 articles but had never handled an awl. Men act thus, not because they do not value religion, but because they do not see what religion has to do with the mending of shoes. Yet religion has as much to do with the mending of shoes as with the budget and the army estimates.

Few American Jews today would fail to agree with Lord Macaulay that Jews cannot be a little bit equal. Jews would at least be suspicious of a candidate who thought Jews should be equal citizens only in some regards, or that important private institutions should be free to discriminate against them. Agudath Israel publicly supported the so-called Yale 5's claim that they were denied equal access to Yale because it refused to accommodate their objections to gender-integrated student housing.[5] Agudath Israel (and the students) rested their arguments on a claim to equal treatment.[6] How, then, can Orthodox groups seek to deny gays legal protection to equal access to Yale? It is not illegal to advocate a denial of equality for others as one insists on it for oneself; whether such advocacy is compatible with the rules of liberal democracy is another question.

It is important to distinguish equality in the economic and social sphere from approval of gay sexual practices as such. Gay rights laws purport to address only the former, although they inevitably have the effect of removing the stigma of single-sex sexual orientation and practice more generally. Advocates of gay rights advocate anti-discrimination laws not only because they eliminate economic or other discrimination, but because such laws ultimately lead to the erosion of beliefs hostile to gay sexuality.[7] They are right in that expectation, an expectation which compounds the difficulty of shaping an Orthodox response.

THE PROBLEM OF EQUALITY AND ITS DISCONTENTS

The move toward equality has not been without social costs for Orthodox Jews. The feminist movement has done women in general, and Orthodox women in particular, much good. It would be wrong to deny the value of the increased economic, medical, and social opportunities available to women as a result of the feminist movement because that movement also advocates policies and behaviors with which Orthodox Judaism has the most profound of disagreements.

During the course of the 2000 presidential campaign, Senator Joseph Lieberman was asked whether he would allow his child to intermarry and whether he daily recited the blessing "who has not made me a woman." His answers (yes to the first, no to the second) upset many in the Orthodox community.[8] However, it went largely unremarked that these questions probed the candidate's acceptance of the prevailing egalitarian ethos. It is difficult, perhaps impossible, to run for high office and insist that one's fellow citizens (and voters) are unfit to marry one's children, or that women are in some unspecified way inferior to men.

There is no denying that the modern feminist movement has created many difficulties for Orthodoxy. The trend toward equality for women is, in reality, hundreds of years old.[9] Our generation's efforts to grapple with the new set of problems posed by modern feminism can at least draw upon ample *halakhic* precedents.

The *halakha* has in some measure adapted to feminist demands for equality. A generation ago, the *Bat Mitzva* was unheard of among Orthodox Jews. Today it is ubiquitous. Without question, the acceptance of the *Bat Mitzva* is a recognition that the unequal treatment of boys and girls as they became obligated in *mitzvot* was untenable. Today, both boys and girls expect extravagant parties. (Equality, it appears, does not always lead to progress.)

The same cannot easily be said about the social consensus that adherents of all faiths are "equal" before the law or the emerging—though not yet complete—consensus with regard to equal treatment of gays. The problem of religious equality is not a new one, and one for which there are again ample *halakhic* precedents. Here, at least, it is theoretically easy to insist on the difference between equality at law and equality of theological truth. This is, in today's secular society, far less so with regard to sexual preference.

The problem of gay rights is not one on which we have precedents to guide us beyond the fact that the Torah unambiguously condemns (male) same-sex sexual activity. What does the social commitment to equality (coupled with a respect for autonomy in private matters) imply for an Orthodox position toward gay fellow citizens?

Do we try and fashion a little bit (or almost) equal policy, disregarding Lord Macaulay's strictures? If there is no middle ground, must we insist on no quarter at all for gay fellow citizens as a mark of our commitment to the Torah's denunciation of homosexuality? Perhaps we must take a hard-line public position against protecting gays from social and economic discrimination even though the *halakha* as such may not compel a position one way or the other. In contemporary circumstances, lack of opposition might be taken as acquiescence in, or approval of, the underlying sexual behavior. Just how far must we take that concern?

Only if those passing on these questions understand the deep-rooted egalitarian background to these dilemmas, can they reach credible and workable decisions. My impression is that many in the rabbinate regard the clamor for gay rights laws only as an attack on conventional sexual morality, and thus miss a substantial part of the contemporary debate.

One could argue that the commitment to equality applies only to political rights, and that Orthodox Jews do not oppose equal political rights for gay citizens. However, this argument fails. The contemporary commitment to equality extends far beyond political rights. It extends to equal access to important institutions of social, economic, and cultural life.[10] Would Jews be considered equal members of society if they could vote, but not hold government or private sector jobs or seek admission to Harvard or Yale? The Pale of Settlement was based in large measure on economic and social restrictions, including restrictions on marriage. (Today, half of American Jews regard a religious rule against intermarriage as racist.)[11] No American Jew should be prepared to return to the crippling social and economic regime of the Pale for themselves. How, then, can one insist on it for others?

Could we then perhaps draw the line at marriage? Perhaps, and here we for the moment enjoy broad public support for such a limitation, as we do not on protection for gays in the workplace.[12] Nevertheless we cannot avoid grappling with the problem of equality even as to gay marriage. Andrew Sullivan[13] has powerfully argued that, because the state defines marriage and marriage as an institution is so central to American life, gays cannot be truly equal citizens without access to it. Of course, Orthodox Jews cannot accept this argument. The question is how to justify that opposition—and how far to carry it—in a society committed to equality, and in which many economic benefits are dispensed through marriage—for example, medical insurance and pensions.

If we commit ourselves to the full equality of all citizens before the law, are we limited to enforcing the Torah's prohibition only in our personal sexual behavior, perhaps not even allowing those views to be enforced in quasi-public communal institutions (Cardozo Law School) or in our capacities as landlords? Can all or some Orthodox Jewish landlords demand exemption from fair housing laws banning sexual orientation discrimination because those laws violate the landlord's religious obligation not to facilitate a same-sex relationship? Should Jews oppose fair housing laws because they might require such results?[14]

The absence of a commitment to equality in the Orthodox community goes beyond *halakhic* objections. It appears to be a matter of unthinking reflex and deep-seated bigotry. That absence reflects among other things a shameful ignorance of the roots of Jewish acceptance and success in America.

The protection of religious observance in the workplace, for example, would have been impossible without the substantial achievements of the black civil rights movement, the premier egalitarian movement of our time. The relevant legislation protecting Sabbath observers was enacted on the coattails of the 1964 Civil Rights Act. It would not have been enacted standing alone. No group is more loud and assiduous in claiming its rights under this statute than Orthodox Jews. Yet Orthodox Jews are often at best ambivalent about, and often openly hostile to, other manifestations of egalitarianism, including racial equality.

I often encounter open racism among Orthodox Jews. Orthodox Jews are assuredly not the only bigots in the United States. There are racist militias who hate both Blacks and Jews. There are also black bigots and anti-Semites. However, for a group which benefited so greatly from the legal and social changes which made religious discrimination illegal, the persistence of racism among Jews is more than troubling; it is inexcusable. Popular Orthodox attitudes toward Moslems often reflect a similar bigotry.

The tolerance of bigotry in our midst is neither an acceptable political nor moral stance. There is something wrong, seriously wrong, when we are not moved by the suffering of those denied equal access on grounds of race, sex, or national origin to the benefits society has to offer. Yet Orthodox Jews are, it is fair to say, not so moved.

While leaders of Reform, Conservative, and secular Jewry played a visible role in the struggle for civil rights, Orthodox Jews were mostly silent. Can it really be that we had nothing to say—after the Pale and the Holocaust—about the shameful treatment of American Blacks? If adolescent memories can be relied on, many in the Orthodox community mocked the struggle, and certainly the participation of rabbis in it. Few Orthodox Jews actively participated in it.[15]

The problem is not unique to American Orthodoxy. My wife remembers a teacher at her Israeli seminary—a survivor—challenging one of her classmates for expressing concern over the plight of starving people in Biafra.[16] And while much of the Israeli community recently expressed distress over the treatment of Israeli Arabs, the Orthodox community there (and here) appears to have been largely silent. In particular, I do not remember hearing anything from the *gedolei* Yisroel who guide the religious parties in Israel.

Here is the place to notice that an Orthodox response to the challenges of egalitarianism might depend on the reasons why egalitarianism is a binding norm.[17] At least four justifications suggest themselves:

1. Legal: the post–Civil War constitution[18] and numerous civil rights statutes, presumably binding as *dina d'malchuta dina*.
2. Pragmatic: equality advances Jewish interests on the whole. Opposition to equality is likely to be fruitless and generate hostility which is not outweighed by any contrary interest. There may be cases where the interest in some other civic good requires unequal treatment of citizens.
3. Moral: derived either from religious sources (*i.e.*, the story of the creation of man), or, alternatively, from general moral principles not contradicted by religious sources.

4. Empirical: Jews are biologically, psychologically, intellectually, or morally no different than others, and thus have no claim to special treatment.

There are obvious differences between these rationales. If the commitment to equality is merely one of *dina d'malchuta* (and if *dina d'malchuta* extends this far) then there is no obligation to extend the obligation beyond strict requirements of law, and we are free to seek to minimize the scope of such laws through the ordinary democratic processes. We would also have no obligation to teach children of the value of equality or to reprimand them when they express bigotry, except as we might train them to be generally law abiding, or avoid rude behavior likely to impede success.

On the other hand, if the obligation is moral or empirical, the fact that the law might not reach a particular act would not excuse us from seeking to achieve an ethical result beyond that required by law. We surely would not have justification for opposing laws guaranteeing equality. If the arguments for equality are either *dina d'malchuta* or pragmatic there would be little occasion to examine normative religious practices to align them more closely with equality norms. If, however, equality norms are rooted in moral or empirical principles, there might be occasion to do so.

To take but one relatively trivial example: if we have a moral or empirical basis to insist on equality, perhaps we should reject *chumrot* beyond what the *halakha* absolutely requires with regard to the production of kosher wine (*i.e.*, the position that non-Jews should not be permitted to see wine to be used for *kiddush*)[19] or stringencies in *bishul Akum*, which will result in employment discrimination.

EDUCATIONAL DILEMMAS

Whatever our answer to these questions about the substance of public affairs, what do those ideas suggest with regard to the education of children, both in school and home? Are children capable of dealing with anything but black or white positions? Can they accept the idea that Orthodox public policy must, for pragmatic or legal reasons, allow for positions different from what the Torah would require in a perfect Torah society? Or will they see such positions as concessions that the Torah is imperfect and that we really do not mean what we say when we assert a commitment to Torah? Would too great a concern with these possibilities lead to a distortion of Torah in the form of too great a rejection of egalitarian values? What of the danger that without full-throated commitment to equality, children will grow up as bigots, or at least unable to cope with the deeply egalitarian society of which they are part?

How do we tell our children that non-Jews are in some ways our equals and yet our intercourse with them must be limited? Can we inculcate the importance of separateness without also tolerating, even encouraging, raw and ugly bigotry? The *Rav* in *Confrontation* insisted on advancing universal themes while remaining separate, but the evidence (including the widespread refusal to recognize the universalist themes of *Confrontation*) is that this dialectic is not easily maintained.

Scientific advances, underscoring the common genetic heritage of mankind[20] and the fundamental biological commonalities of all humans—Orthodox Jews are not at all reluctant to accept organ transplants from non-Jews[21]—heighten the problem. We can—at least on the present state of the evidence—no longer delude ourselves that Jews are biologically different than other humans.[22] Some in the Orthodox community nevertheless regard the entire non-Jewish world as somehow less than fully human.

All sorts of deleterious behavior is the result. Several years ago, a Jewish funeral home refused to prepare a young Moslem child for burial on the ground that its Jewish clientele would object to the use of premises set aside for Jewish funerals to be used for non-Jews. Of course, this action violated the *halakha* of *darkei shalom,*[23] and it was a *chillul ha-Shem* to boot.[24] But the funeral home correctly gauged popular Orthodox sentiment.

In *kashrut*, the attitude toward non-Jews borders on paranoia—non-Jews are out to trick us into eating *treif*—well beyond what strict *halakha* requires and, as far as I can tell, without any empirical corroboration.

TOO MUCH EQUALITY IS DANGEROUS TOO

If an untutored devotion to the particular is a problem for most of the Orthodox community, untutored devotion to universal values is a problem in other segments of the Orthodox community. Some Orthodox Jews are so anxious to demonstrate their openness of equality that they find it difficult to say no to any overture undertaken in the name of pluralism and equality.

At the height of one recent crisis over religious pluralism in Israel, some prominent American Orthodox Jews tripped all over themselves to demonstrate their religious commitment to religious pluralism. These statements were immensely popular in the Anglo-Jewish press and with a Federation leadership anxious to avoid offending major donors and to demonstrate an institutional commitment to the idea that all forms of Judaism are equally valid. The Orthodox expressions of devotion to religious equality did not reflect any serious effort to grapple with the problem of sustained, intentional, and principled deviations from *halakha*.

Much the same conflict was evident at the advent of the Enlightenment. Some Jews were willing to forego equality to prevent the assimilation which would inevitably follow equality. Others were anxious to demonstrate that Jews shared universal human traits despite predictable results in intermarriage and loss of religious distinctiveness. The Enlightenment was not the first occasion for this, there being precedents in Geonic Babylon and later in Spain.

Much as we must condemn an untutored devotion to universalism, a universalism which sees no special role for Jews except to practice self-sacrifice on the altar of human progress, we must equally and candidly acknowledge that the extreme and too popular vision of Jewish particularity and superiority is also not a viable possibility. This is so not only because we are unwilling to so confine ourselves intellectually and socially. After the events of the last century, including Hitler's Germany, Stalin's Russia, and endless tribal violence in the Balkans and Africa, how can Jews with a straight face and quiet conscience urge their own religious (racial?) superiority as a sufficient justification for mistreating others or ignoring the suffering of "lesser" beings?

Without attempting to deny the non-egalitarian nature of much of *halakha*, it also embodies a fundamental recognition of the common humanity of all, including universal rules against murder and theft, and obligations of mutual support. These elements of the *halakha* are known intellectually. They have not, however, been internalized, and they do not affect behavior or attitudes.

Tainted by years of working for a liberal Jewish organization, I believe in the most fundamental of ways in the fundamental equality of human beings regardless of race, sex, or religion. The clash between egalitarian values and *halakha* is for me not just another clash between passing desire (*i.e.*, for a cheeseburger) and the *halakha* (which demands that I not fulfill that desire). It is between fundamental ethical commitments.

One is reminded of Professor Gerald Blidstein's well-known discussion with the Rav concerning the morally insufficient basis of the *heter* of *mishum aivah* for doctors saving non-Jewish lives on *Shabbat*. The patient probably does not care about the moral problem, so long as he or she is attended to, but we ought to care.[25]

Moral arguments at the level of principle are unattractive and not compelling in our community, convinced at a deep level of its own moral, ethical, and religious superiority. So let me try and make the case at the level of the pragmatic.

Chazal, in a famous passage in Bava Kama,[26] relate that the Romans studied Jewish law to see if it was just. The Roman inspectors concluded it was, except for certain discriminatory rules of tort law which favored Jews over non-Jews. I suspect (I hope wrongly) that more yeshiva students know this *sugya* with regard to its citation by the *Yam Shel Shlomo* to assert an *issur* of *silufa shel Torah*[27] (falsification of Torah) than for what it means for our relations with non-Jews. Characteristically, the *Meiri* notes on the spot that the discriminatory tort rules do not apply to moral non-Jews.[28] *Rashi* in *Eicha* comments that the rules of *Kashrut* which separate Jews and non-Jews in the common human experience of dining engender anti-Semitism, as indeed they did. It is not as if the subject is not raised by rabbinic authors sensitive to its multiple dimensions;[29] it is that their writings are ignored.

The self-censorship of Jewish texts (*i.e.*, with regard to the use of different terms in the *Gemara* as it is printed to refer to non-Jews, or the *Arukh Hashulchan*'s use of the word *mitzri* [Egyptians] to refer to all non-Jews as parties in litigation),[30] is another manifestation of awareness of the problem by rabbinic authorities. Awareness seems not to have touched off any contemporary examination of attitudes toward non-Jews.

It is proper to excuse Jews living from pogrom to pogrom from the charge that they spent insufficient effort worrying about the equality of their oppressors. We do not have that excuse. It is time we stopped acting as if we do. That millions of Jews were murdered by Hitler is no excuse for ignoring the suffering of Biafrans, Rwandans, Cambodians, or Bosnians, for using racist epithets, or for speaking of Arabs as if they were less than human.

If the problem of excessive particularism and the bigotry it engenders were to disappear tomorrow, we would confront the opposite and equally dangerous problem—the openness of our society, and its pervasive equality between members of all religions and none. That openness can lead—and has led—to the total breakdown of any uniquely Jewish sphere. For much of American Jewry, it already has.

Intermarriage, as *Hazal* knew full well, follows from social intercourse with non-Jews as equals. Hence, they insisted on a string of prohibitions regarding food and living patterns—even play patterns—to discourage such mixing. How do we balance that message with the message of intolerance to bigotry?[31] The *Meiri*, who rendered moot many prohibitions of doing business with non-Jews and abrogated rules of legal inequality of non-Jews,[32] left untouched rules against social intercourse. Does this work other than as *halakhic ipse dixit*?

What are we to make of 15th-century Italian Jewry that consumed *stam yeinam*, and so did at least some of German (Czech) Jewry? The *Rama*, who records a series of *kulot* with regard to doing business with non-Jews on their holidays,[33] was not prepared to unambiguously condemn this leniency, much as he sought to discourage it.[34] It would be interesting to know of the assimilation and intermarriage rates of these communities.[35]

Intermarriage is *the* pressing problem for the American Jewish community. Early in my lifetime, a non-*Shomer Shabbos* Jew would have been crushed to have an intermarriage in the family. No longer. According to the latest AJ-Committee study, the change in attitude has even intruded into the Orthodox community (albeit at a lower rate than the general Jewish community).[36] The problem is not just a lack of Jewish content in people's lives or the "Reform movement doing its assimilationist thing" again.

Rather, it is a manifestation of the American commitment to the equality of human beings which makes intermarriage possible. The fact that Jews are no longer regarded as the devil's children, and Judaism is just another way of serving G-d, makes intermarriage acceptable to non-Jews. So far have matters degenerated that the American Jewish Committee found that more than half of American Jews believe it *racist* to condemn intermarriage.[37]

Important segments of Jewish life, not the least of which is the leadership of the Federation movement, are fully prepared to accept intermarriage. Several years ago, Rabbi Shlomo Riskin, the keynote speaker at a Federation annual General Assembly, spoke of the dangers of intermarriage. The speech was poorly received. The published summary of the Assembly ignored the fact that it had been given at all.

The Orthodox community, though at reduced rates, is not immune from intermarriage, particularly for those of our children who attend the "best" secular colleges. My impression (confirmed by several participants in the Orthodox Forum) is that the discovery that non-Jews are fundamentally not different than Jews fuels these occurrences. These are manifestations of the egalitarian principle which graduates of yeshiva high schools are ill-prepared to confront.

Orthodox Jews are not alone in facing this dilemma. Evangelical Christians who overwhelmingly disapprove of homosexuality by equally overwhelming margins support the right of homosexuals to equal employment opportunity.[38] The Catholic Church has struggled to reconcile its refusal to accept homosexuality with its commitment to equality.[39] More recently, it has struggled to reconcile the Church's claim to having a uniquely valuable way to the salvation of souls with its commitment to respecting other faiths. A recent document of the Congregation for the Doctrine of the Faith, *Dominus Jesus: On the Unicity and Salvific Universality of Jesus Christ and the Church*, asserting the Church's unique role in saving souls, has received largely a negative reception among American Catholics[40] because it departs from the notion of the fundamental equality of persons of all faiths. That belief makes it difficult, if not impossible, to accept the corollary that persons outside the Church are doomed to hell.

This idea that all faiths are valuable and largely equal is not purely an egalitarian one—it also reflects a large measure of skepticism about religious truth—but it has unmistakable egalitarian overtones. We are not the only group struggling with conflicting commitments and we could do worse than study how others similarly situated struggle with the problem.

THE NON-EGALITARIAN *HALAKHA*

The corpus of Jewish tradition is not easily reconciled with the thoroughgoing egalitarianism of modern Western society. First and foremost, although the question often gets lost in the buzz over newer questions such as feminism and gay rights, the question is pressing with regard to non-Jews.

Who relishes the thought of explaining the *Kuzari*, with its racialist characterization of non-Jews, to a non-Jewish colleague? Or to explaining why wine touched by a non-Jew (or, for some, even seen by a non-Jew) is no longer kosher?

Not long ago someone showed me an anti-Semitic screed which cited the Talmud, *inter alia*, for the proposition that Jews regard non-Jews as horses. A colleague laughed at the absurdity of such a charge. I cringed because the *Gemara* in *Yevamot* and *Sanhedrin* does just that.[41] Of course, it does so for a *halakhic* purpose (*Rabbeinu* Tam tentatively invoked this source as a way of permitting a Jewish woman who had converted to Christianity and had an adulterous relationship with a non-Jew to return to her Jewish husband when she returned to Judaism), but it does so.

How does one explain why Jews in Williamsburg seek, in violation of fair housing laws, to exclude non-Jews from buildings in the Jewish area of that neighborhood? If there are no moral or pragmatic justifications for Hasidim engaging in such behavior, what is wrong with holding that Arabs may not be excluded from housing on *Keren Kayemet* lands? Can we justify ourselves with no more than a reference to *lo techaninam* (not giving non-Jews a foothold in Israel)?

If the Hasidim in Williamsburg are morally and pragmatically right to do what they do to protect their community's religious cohesion, and for the same reason the Israeli Supreme Court was wrong to insist that Arabs could purchase homes in Jewish neighborhoods, then what was wrong with non-Jews in the town of Airmont, New York, discouraging Jews from moving into "their" town, on the ground that Orthodox Jews were clannish and would not contribute to the existing sense of community? Was the town of Tenafly, New Jersey, right to refuse an Orthodox community permission to build an *eruv* because of the demographic changes the *eruv* would likely bring?[42] My questions, I should add, are not primarily legal; they are moral and practical.[43]

THE SITUATION IN ISRAEL

The problem of egalitarianism is by no means a challenge only in America. Egalitarian notions are deeply ingrained everywhere in the world, even if everywhere imperfectly implemented. Those principles are enshrined in international covenants on human rights to which both Israel and the United States are signatories. They are a part of political discourse everywhere. Listen to what Amnon Rubenstein, a prominent leftist Israeli, has to say on the subject in objecting to *chareidi* (really Orthodox) conceptions of the state of Israel: "Indeed, Israel should be involved in the construction of a different kind of house . . . building a place to live, the home of Jews who will share it in equality with other Jews and non-Jews."[44]

After rehearsing the discriminatory treatment of non-Jews in Jewish law, which he calls "paper vengeance against the non-Jew,"[45] he concludes "[i]t is clear how the Orthodox Rabbinical establishment . . . responded to the Zionist Revolution. They took the anti-Gentile *halakhic* injunctions and sometimes applied them, with even greater intensity, in the state where the Jews represent the majority of the population." He concludes:[46] "[t]he majority of the Jews in the world live as equal citizens in democratic countries, where human rights are respected. But in their own country, Jews are being forced to fight to maintain a democratic system in an atmosphere of soaring nationalism."

Amnon Rubenstein is no fringe figure. We ignore his challenge and his conception of the future of the Jewish state at our peril.

The failure to appreciate the importance of equality as a foundational principle of the modern social order also pervades Israeli discussion of religious pluralism. To judge from afar, much of the Orthodox response to demands for religious pluralism in Israel is premised on the assumption that the problem is purely theological or of church–state relations, thus missing the important dimension of equality.

This same myopic view colors the debate over women's prayer groups at the *kotel*. For the bulk of the Israeli public, the question is one of equal treatment of women and of differing religious views. Talking only about tradition does not answer this perception of the dispute. Fighting the wrong battle—and not even knowing it—is a sure way to lose.

Some years ago, after mass murderer Baruch Goldstein massacred Arabs at prayer, the Israeli education ministry ordered Israeli (Jewish) public school students to meet with their Arab counterparts. The *Mamlachti Dati* schools were thrown into turmoil. Should they participate or not? Would such meetings lead ultimately to intermarriage, if not before peace, then after? Should they have cross-gender meetings? As far as I know, the *Chinch Atzmai* schools did not participate altogether, although it is precisely its students who, one would imagine, have the least idea about how to get along with non-Jews.[47]

It would be wrong to minimize the dilemma Israeli school officials faced. But the dilemma is not one-sided. The problem is not only how to immunize children against the lure of the other. In a modern state, citizens of different faiths must treat each other as equals. Although advocates of diversity regularly exaggerate the need for "diversity education," navigating a pluralistic society remains a skill to be learned, particularly as the Orthodox community becomes ever more insular ideologically and residentially.

Many of the decisions of the Israeli Supreme Court regarding women at the wall, Arabs buying land, lesbian mothers adopting children, punishing hate speech, and the like all stem from the Court's deep-seated egalitarian commitment. In the Orthodox community, there seems no understanding that this salutary motive is in play, let alone any appreciation of the positive value to be placed on equality. Given the Orthodox establishment's blindness toward the importance of equality in contemporary culture, it is hardly surprising that Orthodox causes do so badly in Israel.

Consider the following, which reads as if Amnon Rubenstein wrote it to prove his point. The *Beis Ha-Levi* comments on the verse "save me from my brother, from Eisav" (Genesis 32: 12), that the duplication (Yakov had only one brother, so Eisav need be identified only as his brother or as Eisav) implies that Yakov is concerned both with his brother's enmity and friendship. The *Beis Ha-Levi* then comments, in an obvious reference to Russian *haskalah*,[48] that Jews can be tempted from their faith either by the enmity of non-Jews or too close a relationship with them.

Not particularly unusual. But consider the following expansion of the *Beis Ha-Levi*'s comment from a popular contemporary *sefer* on the *Parshat ha-Shavuah*, *Lekach Tov*: "Gedolei Yisroel in all generations worried always about equal rights that were bestowed on us by the gentiles. Assimilation and following in the paths of the nations, which are a direct result of equal rights, justified their fears."

The editor of the anthology (who appears unaware that Gedolei Yisroel were in fact divided on the question of equal rights, unless opposition to civic equality is now a requirement of *gadlut*) then cites R. Yisroel Salanter's comment that as a punishment for an early (1844) Reform rabbinic conference in Brunswick, Germany,[49] "permitting" intermarriage, the Germans would forbid Jews to marry them. And so it was, the editor reports, 90 years later, a reference to the infamous Nuremberg laws, which the editor acknowledges were "racist" laws.

The editor is opposed not only to intermarriage, but to any attempt by Jews to be accepted by non-Jews. He describes religious persecution as a good thing because it keeps Jews separate. If so, what was wrong with the Nuremberg laws? The irony of bemoaning the loss of religious sanctions against intermarriage and in the same breath condemning the Nuremberg laws escapes the editor.

The debate over equality is not about details at the margins. It goes to the heart of the conflict between those who want a Jewish state and those who want a state of the Jews, or perhaps a secular bi-national state. In the former, equality is not a particularly important principle; a Jewish state does not and cannot afford all citizens perfect equality; a state of the Jews comes much closer; a secular, pluralistic state would insist on full and perfect equality of Jews and non-Jews.

Orthodox Jews want a Jewish state and not a state of the Jews. We must accordingly wrestle with the problem of equality and limit the practical effects of the resulting inequality. But above all, Orthodox Jews and their leaders cannot bury their heads in the sand and pretend the problem of inequality does not exist.

Israel, after all, is a state which at least from its Declaration of Independence (and even before in the debates over the ideas of a pluralist state advanced by Judah Magnes) has wrestled with the problem of being a Jewish state, with a Jewish calendar, Jewish symbols, and a law of return which is the sort of ethnically based immigration law which prevented so many Jews from fleeing Hitler (and which American Jews fought for decades) with guarantees of equality for all citizens, including Arabs.

It is no accident that Palestinian spokesmen repeatedly label the law of return racist and that some Israelis agree. It is this egalitarian assumption which makes the arguments over returning Palestinian refugees to Israel such a powerful public relations argument for the Palestinians and why human rights groups like Human Rights Watch have endorsed it. We may prefer not to think of the problem, but it will not be blinked away.

To be sure, there is an element of religious self-hatred and self-loathing in this commitment to equality. It appears from here in the *Golah*, where the price of those burdens is infinitely less, to be motivated partly by a desire to be rid of the burden of being different. The phenomenon nevertheless cannot be dismissed as simply more assimilation. Much of the movement to strip Israel of its Jewish character that is not simply anti-Semitic is founded in a profound commitment to equality of all human beings.

Kach may think that it can dispense with equal treatment of Arab citizens, treating them as "*hotevei etzim*" and "*sho'avi mayim*" ("hewers of wood" and "drawers of water"), but if Israel were to do so, it would be an outlaw state. American Jews would refuse to support such policies and would not have anything to do with such a state. We are fortunate that *Rav* Herzog, *Rav* Neriah, and others including the *Rav*,[50] insisted on a very different path, but one which has been insufficiently trod in recent decades. To my amazement (and to our community's shame) in most Orthodox *shuls* one is far more likely to hear speakers from *Kach* than *Mamad*.

In *Kadan v. Menahel Mikarkei Yisroel*,[51] in which an Israeli Arab seeking to purchase an apartment in a building standing on *Kerem Kayemet* land, Chief Justice Aharon Barak acknowledged the conflict between a Jewish state and the universalistic claim of justice for all citizens, famously remarking that the claim of the Israeli state to be a Jewish state must be read at the most abstract level, with the particular having to yield to the egalitarian in practice.

Justice Barak's easy universalism and his refusal to give operative weight to the particularistic side of the equation are disturbing. But it will not suffice to complain about it. We must strive for positions which are loyal to tradition, intellectually satisfying, politically practicable, and morally tenable.

The tradition is not implacably hostile to the regnant egalitarianism. There are sources which are sufficiently universal as to give us ground upon which to stand, being careful not to become thoughtless and uncritical egalitarians. We must mine these sources diligently, and insist that they be considered along with (not instead of) particularistic ones.

We must not abandon the field to those who would dehumanize Arabs and other non-Jews, just as we must be diligent not to yield to those who refuse to use their *da'at* to make *havdalot* (distinction) between Jew and non-Jew, men and women, and those who live by the Torah and those who flout it. We face twin, mirror image, dangers. In our determination to fight the one, we must not lose sight of the other.

EQUALITY IS HERE TO STAY: THE EVIDENCE FROM CONSTITUTIONAL LAW

Some social trends are little more than fads, no more lasting than the hula hoop or this year's hem length. If there are those hoping that the egalitarian trends will reverse themselves, and that the Orthodox community need not adjust to those trends, they are certain to be disappointed. Equality of all human beings is a bedrock principle of modern civilized society. It is not going to be displaced anytime soon by some other principle.

American law is typical in this regard. It would be hard to overstate the importance of equality in contemporary American life, although the fact that the Presidency was decided because Florida did not guarantee voters in different counties an equal method of having their votes counted should be an object lesson.[52] A brief survey of constitutional law underscores the point.

Early in the 20th century, Justice Oliver Wendell Holmes, one of the true giants of American law, could, in a case upholding compulsory sterilization of mental defectives, dismiss the equal protection clause of the Fourteenth Amendment as the last refuge of the desperate lawyer.[53] Not today. The struggle for black civil rights culminating in *Brown v. Board of Education*[54] was a struggle for legal equality. Without question, *Brown* was the single most important decision of the past century.

Despite all the defects of that decision as an example of the judicial craft, no one could today get elected to office or confirmed to the federal bench questioning its correctness.[55] The drive for black civil rights spawned movements for women's equality and that of other classes of formerly disfavored groups, including illegitimate children, aliens, the poor, and gays.

For decades, lawyers and others fought over the meaning of the proscription of established religion. Between World War II and roughly 1980, the battle was fought over history. Those seeking to permit a greater government subsidization of religion invoked history. They lost. Then someone had the idea of insisting that the limitations on government aid to religion had the effect of denying religious persons and institutions equality with subsidized secular institutions.

Those claims succeeded, revolutionizing the law of church–state relations. This may be good or bad (the same commitment to equality has led the court to refuse to grant special privileges to religion under the rubric of the Free Exercise Clause),[56] but it is a fact. Free speech law, too, is pervaded with the idea that all speech ought to be treated equally, regardless of viewpoint or subject matter. Federal criminal sentencing has now been reduced to a relatively mechanical process in furtherance of the goal of insuring equal sentences for similar offenses.

Of course, equality is not the only constitutional value. Occasionally, some other value will collide with the national commitment to equality and will trump equality. That was the case with the right of the Boy Scouts to exclude gay scoutmasters, *Dale v. Boy Scouts*.[57]

Dale, an Eagle Scout, was an assistant scoutmaster until he announced that he was gay. Dismissed, he sued under the New Jersey Law against Discrimination, claiming that he was discriminated against on the basis of sexual orientation. The Scouts claimed a constitutional right to not associate with gays. The New Jersey Supreme Court sided with Dale, dismissing the Scouts' claim as, to coin a phrase, bigotry in drag.

A closely divided United States Supreme Court reversed, holding that the right of association trumped. Most Orthodox Jews view this as a welcome result, but it was the product of a 5–4 Supreme Court decision, reversing a unanimous New Jersey Supreme Court. It is not a decision that marks the retreat of the egalitarian hordes.

Editorial comment responding to *Dale* was almost all hostile to the Scouts.[58] Since the decision, many corporations which formerly supported the Scouts have withdrawn their support. Public schools which sponsored the Scouts are in many places withdrawing their support.

Just two terms earlier the Court had invalidated an anti-gay rights referendum in Colorado, on the stated grounds that it discriminated against a class of people in the political process.[59] The opinion comes close to announcing that legislation against gays will be treated as presumptively invalid, just as legislation targeting racial minorities is.

Some think a conservative Court will seriously erode the law's commitment to equality. The evidence is to the contrary. Some of the profoundest changes worked by this Court rest on claims of equality, recasting substantive rights (freedom of religion or speech) as little more than guarantees of equal protection.

The academic commitment to equality also runs deep. Most important constitutional theorists have written about, and from, deep commitments to equality. Defenders of "inequality"' are few and marginal. There are critics of particular egalitarian policies, but not egalitarianism as such.

The commitment to equality is not limited to decisions of the Supreme Court. When Jewish and other defenders of religious liberty sought to provide statutory protection for religious liberty, those efforts ran up against twin objections rooted in equality. First, opponents insisted that by insulating religious observers from neutral laws, government was favoring religion over non-religion, and discriminating against non-believers.

The second obstacle proved insurmountable. It was the charge that such protection would weaken the civil rights laws. That is, citizens could claim under that law that their religion required them to discriminate against some protected class. Not a single Democrat, and only a very few Republicans, were prepared to fight this objection of gay rights groups. No member of Congress was willing to say categorically that equality is not as important a value as religious liberty. Not one.[60]

Almost all non-Orthodox Jewish organizations were horrified, truly horrified, that religious groups would even consider sanctioning discrimination, even if only to the point of asking that the burden on religious practice imposed by civil rights laws be justified. Many of these organizations have only the most ephemeral commitment to religious liberty, but they nevertheless feel obligated to at least go through the motions. But not at the expense of equality.

Dr. Laura's television program was boycotted because she expressed the view that homosexuality is wrong. Many corporate sponsors fell away, and Dr. Laura was compelled to apologize abjectly for her views. Efforts to boycott the many large corporations which offer domestic partnership benefits to gay couples fall flat. Equality is persuasive; inequality is rarely sustainable.

In some ways, the United States, with its tolerance of individualism, remains more tolerant of private inequality than European countries. In the United States, racist groups like the KKK often insist that the law guarantees their racist speech equal treatment with more socially desirable speech.[61] Not so in most of the world, where hate speech is a criminal offense because it undermines the fundamental equality of human beings.

HALAKHIC RESPONSES TO EGALITARIANISM

Religious leaders, like others, can fall prey to the trendy and to the fad *du jour*. When the ecology movement burst onto the scene, Jewish magazines printed articles demonstrating that Judaism was more ecologically minded than Greenpeace. The *halakhic* support for the proposition was often not even weak but it was essential to be seen as up to date. We can do without the trendiness. The Orthodox community must carefully guard against the tendency to sway with every breeze, to pronounce that a crisis is upon us, that the *halakha* is out of date and must be instantly "updated."

Other Jews have gone that route and have little but failure, assimilation, and a Jewish Universalist-Unitarianism to show for it. The conservatism of *halakha* is often frustrating, but that conservatism is an important safeguard against pandering to trendiness, to say nothing of rejecting the most intolerable departures from Torah morality.

The opposite danger is that for much of our community, and especially the rabbinate, being counter-cultural and anti-egalitarian is trendy. That, too, is a trendiness we cannot afford. The motto *chadosh assur min ha-Torah* as a polemical warning against *halakhic* change ascribed to the *Chatam Sofer* has become the all-encompassing norm.

The egalitarian trends *halakhists* confront are not limited to the public sphere. They extend well into the private sphere, and indeed may be more intense there. Here the issues are not those of relations between Jews and non-Jews, but between men and women. The changes in family structure—from the Ozzie and Harriet family of the male breadwinner and female child rearer to the two-income family—is a product not only of economic necessity, but also egalitarian impulses.

These changes resound broadly. How many of our fathers did laundry or changed diapers? How many women today would truly be happy with lives devoted solely to housekeeping and raising children? How do those new demands on men to share equally in household chores square with the special male obligation to learn Torah? Hard questions, all raised by near-universal implementation of a deep egalitarianism.

The profound changes in the education of women were started by a woman, but gained the endorsement of as conservative a religious figure as the Chofetz Chaim. Chassidic girls are now learning more seriously than ever, in some cases actually studying *Chumash* from a text, a change occurring in this generation. Stern College now has an advanced program of textual Talmudic studies for women.

There are many aspects of Orthodox life that have not adjusted to these changes. In all too many communities, *shiurim* for women are infantile outpourings of primitive and unreflective emotion, as if women were incapable of understanding anything complex and reflective, let alone textual. More than one talented woman has been lost to the Orthodox community as they rebel against this infantilization of their gender. Too few *shuls* have been built in the last generation that reflect both a concern for *mechitza* and the ability of women to be full participants in the *davening*.[62]

It is commonplace in the Orthodox community to denounce feminism, but that movement has worked profound positive changes, typically accompanied by denial. It is good that our daughters are better educated than their grandmothers (and, in many cases, their grandfathers). No one, I hope, wishes to return to the days when Jewish women were religiously illiterate. Men have better relationships with their children because they are now involved in their lives. There should be no denying that these changes trace back to feminist impulses. Why, then, would one routinely and unthinkingly denounce feminism?

In some instances, feminism has brought about changes that *halakha* insists upon, but about which it never would have been heard to influence public policy. Are Orthodox Jews for tolerating sexual harassment of women in the workplace? Do we advocate the unrestricted availability of pornography? Substantial progress has been made against these halakhically unacceptable behaviors, not because the *Shulchan Arukh* forbids them, but because feminists challenged them in the name of gender equality.

The attack on sexual harassment would not have been brought about by citing *Even ha-Ezer*, nor the war on pornography won by invoking *hilchot tzniut*. An effort by Agudat Yisroel to remove sexually offensive ads from buses and subways has gone on for years unsuccessfully, running up against cries of censorship and religious imposition. These same objections are credible when cast in terms of equality for women.

No one should oppose these achievements of equality because other manifestations of feminism are irreconcilable with *halakha*. Instead we should ask how to determine what is a permissible accommodation of the demand of women for equal treatment and what is not. And we must ask if it is legitimate to nudge the tradition along.

Chazal long ago recognized that women wanted a fuller and more equal access to ritual observances than would have been the case if they observed only *mitzvot* they were obligated to perform. They accordingly permitted women to perform *s'micha* on sacrifices in order to give satisfaction to women, even though this involved at least some turning a blind eye to a rabbinic prohibition.[63] Yet they are explicit: it was the demand of the women for an active role in the Temple that moved *Chazal*. Yet those same impulses today seem only to generate public rabbinic disdain and condemnation. It may be, however, that private rulings are far more accommodating to the demand for equality,[64] recognizing changed social circumstances. A comparison of polemic with *p'sak* and practice in this area would be desirable.

It does not follow, it bears repeating, that Orthodoxy can accept equality blindly. Some claims of equality are simply contrary to *halakha*. Moreover, equality is a powerful force, and does not easily satisfy itself with less than its full realization. If we increase the level of Torah study for women, we cannot expect women to confine themselves to less than equality with equally (or less) learned men. Have we thought through what will be the career paths of women who study Talmud at an advanced level? If the *halakhic* objections to women's prayer groups are not irrefutable, the impulse to ban such efforts may be justified on the reasonable intuition that the participants in those groups will not long be satisfied with less than full participation in the synagogue. Yet synagogues continue to arrange the *ezrat nashim* in ways which make women feel unequal and unwanted. If we are serious about both *halakha* and equality, why not seek to satisfy both impulses where possible?

Contrary to populist claims, it is not true that where there is a rabbinic will there is a *halakhic* way.[65] Neither is the counter aphorism that "Torah," defined broadly to include all religious practice, is eternal, never changing, true. No one who has learned a serious amount of *Shas* and *Poskim* could easily defend the latter claim. It was a useful shorthand to define the difference between Orthodoxy and non-Orthodox movements, but it is a slogan, not *halakhic* principle.

THE NEW EGALITARIANISM AND *HALAKHIC* CHANGE

This brings me directly to the second question posed at the outset: that of the ways in which *halakha*, and to a lesser extent *aggada* and *hashkafa*, adapt themselves to the sort of profound change which the egalitarian movement represents.

One could write about this subject from a historical point of view, as many have. One can write about the problem jurisprudentially—what devices and limitations does *halakha* employ to respond to changed circumstances?[66] One can write about it theologically—what does *halakhic* change as documented by the historian of *halakha* mean for beliefs in *torah min-ha-shamayim,* the perfection of Torah, or the significance and sanctity of precedent? And one can write about it from a polemical point of view to dispel false notions of the process.

Each has its place, but each should not be allowed to intrude on the role of the other. It would be wrong to allow the historian to *pasken* (decide) a new *shaila* (question) because his historical studies convince him that an earlier, contrary *p'sak* is explainable only by historical circumstances.[67] It would be equally wrong to have the *posek* act upon the polemicist's cry that *halakha* does not change as an excuse for not grappling with changed circumstances where the *halakha*'s own internal methods permit change.

The egalitarian trend which might have been dismissed in the middle of the last century as a fad cannot be so dismissed today. That being so, the question that must be asked is: how should *poskim* take note of this phenomenon in shaping responses to *halakhic* problems presented to them? Some of the ways *poskim* take note of the problem are unremarkable, except perhaps for the matter-of-fact way in which the egalitarian principle is assumed. In considering the ways in which a bank operated by observant Jews could deal with the problem of interest, R. Moshe Feinstein casually dismisses the possibility of charging only non-Jews interest as impossible.[68]

The question of change has a technical aspect. One must distinguish between Torah and Rabbinic laws, and between both and custom, and even customs of different degrees of acceptance. Some *mitzvot deRabbanan* have been allowed to fall into desuetude, for example, the practice of tying or overturning beds and wrapping the head during *shiva,* as well as the special *bentching* for the *beis ha-Aveil.* So too the *t'nai ketubah* of *isur nechasim* is no longer observed and the *ketubah* is collected from personality, not just real property.[69]

Nor should we ignore the number of legal devices used to avoid the harsh effect of Torah laws. The most obvious is *mechirat chometz*, a device made necessary by the Jewish dependence on the trade in liquor, but it is hardly alone. The *shabbos* clock, *prosbul*, the slow cooker, the *heter iska,* and the electric shaver are others. None of these devices cancel or abrogate a Torah law, but the effect is the same. And in each case, one has to be concerned about the impact on the spirit of the law, as R. Moshe Feinstein famously was, apparently without effect, with regard to the *shabbos* clock.[70] The Ashkenazic conception of the Jewish family was changed irrevocably by the *takanot* of *Rabbeinu* Gershom abolishing polygamy and unilateral male divorce.[71] These changes raise not so much *halakhic* problems as theological concerns that need to be forthrightly addressed.

What devices did the Torah confer on *talmidei chachamim* to adjust to changing circumstances? There are legal fictions; *sha'at ha-dechak*; reliance on a *shitat yachid* in cases of need;[72] changed circumstances (such as the practice of levying against personal property instead of real property only in collecting a *ketubah*);[73] impossibility;[74] or compelling public necessity (as with the amelioration of the rabbinic prohibitions against doing business with gentiles on their holidays advanced by the *Ba'alei ha-Tosafot*, changes explicitly resting on economic need).[75] *Rabbeinu* Tam was famously unrepentant when challenged about these leniencies. It was, he said, a *mitzva* to allow Jews to earn a living.[76] It would be ironic if economic realities could effect change in *halakha*, but not moral ones.[77]

The well-known *gemara* in *Beitza*[78] states the general rule that a formally enacted rabbinic rule needs a formal abrogation, even where the reason for the original rule no longer pertains. However, even a cursory study of the rule and its application reveals wide differences of opinion on its scope, some more conservative than others. For example, does the rule apply only where *Chazal* do not state a reason or even where they do? Does it apply only to some rules, and not others?[79] Then too, a *posek* confronted with a rule which seems ill adapted to contemporary circumstances could likely use more general, but less radical, *halakhic* techniques such as narrow interpretation.[80]

The easiest case is that of changed facts or changed scientific understanding. When tobacco reached Europe, some *poskim* prohibited smoking on *Yom Tov* because it was medicinal.[81] No one could conceivably think that today, because our understanding of medicine and the effects of smoking has changed.[82] Similarly, the prohibition against drinking uncovered liquids is no longer generally observed because of changed external circumstances.[83]

The harder case is presented by the cases of social changes or changes in values. They are more problematic both because ascertaining sociological facts or assessing the depth of change in values is a far less precise process than determining whether tobacco causes cancer. The older rule may also represent a different set of values, not changed circumstances.

Just recently, Rabbis Michael Broyde and Avi Wagner published an article in which they insist that it is now permissible to take a hot shower on *Yom Tov*, because in our day a shower is a *davar hashaveh le'kol nefesh* (a universal practice), something which it was not in the time of *Chazal*, or even a hundred years ago.[84] In these cases, the *halakha* could be said to remain the same; external changes, neutral with regard to religion, worked a change in the matrix to which the *halakha* is applied.

Ever since the emergence of the Reform movement, and perhaps more urgently since the rise of the Conservative movement, the question of *halakhic* change has been a sore point. Even where a case for change could be made using standard *halakhic* principles, *poskim* are properly concerned that those changes would give rise to the notion that where there was a will there was a way. Rabbi Shimon Schwab once argued against *eruvin* in large cities not because he thought they were invalid, but because he thought they would give rise to the view among poorly educated American Jews that any prohibition could be circumvented by the rabbinate if only it wished to do so.[85] But taken too far, the prevailing *halakhic* conservatism threatens to leave Orthodoxy incapable of responding to real needs and even to abuses of *halakha*.

To the best of my knowledge, no one has attempted a serious and comprehensive study of the problem of *halakhic* change, one which is both theologically acceptable and historically tenable. It made sense to pass over the problem in the 1950s when Orthodoxy came close to being swept away by Reform and Conservative Judaism. But now that Orthodoxy's place is secure, a refusal to confront new problems and new conditions leads to impossible difficulties. Real people pay a real price for persevering in fighting a long-ago won battle. What is said of generals is equally true of rabbis—too many are fighting the last war.

In the 1950s, Orthodox rabbis rejected a suggestion to solve the problem of the *aguna* with an amendment to the *Ketubah*. The particular formulation may have been problematic, but the idea of confronting the problem of *aguna* with a voluntary agreement is hardly radical (the *Nachlat Shiva*, a *talmid* of the *Taz*, suggested the text of such an agreement). It is what the Orthodox Caucus proposed in the form of the prenuptial agreement prepared by Rabbi Mordecai Willig.

The reason the prenuptial agreement is not embodied in the *ketubah*, where all would have to accept it, is the need to differentiate it from the Conservative agreement embodied in their *ketubah*. It should not have taken 40 years to be confident that the Orthodox version would not be mistaken for the Conservative one. How many *agunot* are an acceptable price for that differentiation?

The Orthodox Caucus prenuptial agreement contains a provision that allows the parties to insist on equitable division of property in the event of divorce. This provision has met far more social resistance than the rest of the agreement, and not on *halakhic* grounds. This resistance stems from a refusal to take into consideration changes in both marital and economic facts (wives now contribute substantially to the household economy and net worth of a household than they did a generation or two ago) favoring gender equality in marital property division.

Although the standard form *ketubah* recites admissions about dowry, the fact is that these are theoretical statements, not reflecting reality. But they once did, and the real force of *ketubah* then had the effect of protecting women against capricious divorce and disinheritance. The form *ketubah* used today does no such thing. On the contrary, if the *ketubah* were routinely enforced men would be *encouraged* to divorce their wives.

The form *ketubah* now in use reflects changes to protect women and overcome several *halakhot* which treated them unequally. Women do not inherit their husbands according to *halakha*, so 13th- and 14th-century German Jewish men, whose wives' contributions to the household were great, wrote *ketubot* far in excess of their net worth to insure that their wives would in practice inherit their estates.[86]

This was not the only change adopted to protect women in ways greater than the *halakha* itself provided. Daughters could not inherit, so men lavished large dowries on their daughters and wrote *shtarei hazi zachar* and gave *matnot bari* (*inter vivos* gifts) and *shechiv me Rah* (deathbed gifts) to equalize the treatment of sons and daughters.[87] *Poskim* seem not to have objected, even though the efficacy of each of these procedures had the effect of minimizing the default rule the Torah laid down. If we take the default rule as laying down an ideal division of property,[88] *poskim* should not have accepted and facilitated these practices. They, however, did just that.

The *gemara* prohibits men from doing business with married women on the ground that what they sell might be stolen from their husbands. Already the *R'avan*[89] rejected the no-business-with-women rule as not reflecting contemporary reality. Presumably only in knowing reliance on the *R'avan*, dress stores in Boro Park and Monsey sell expensive dresses to married women.

These sources and others do not require that *poskim* enlist themselves as willing warriors in the egalitarian revolution in an unthinking fashion. The *halakha* should not be rewritten willy-nilly so that we are fashionable or trendy or up to date, or even to avoid any conflict with the government or the *zeitgeist*. Not every egalitarian value is morally, religiously, or practically sound. Neither should it be assumed that a principle which rests ultimately on the assumption of every human being a reflection of his or her Maker is a deadly danger. To do so is to cast doubt on the wisdom of the *borei olam* who created all humans (and not just Jewish men) in His image.

* * *

I do not have a fully thought out program to respond to the challenges described. Some things appear obvious. A concerted effort is urgently needed to simultaneously purge the community of crude bigotry, yet reinforce its separateness.

Jews must stop thinking of themselves as eternal victims, doomed everywhere to being perpetually hated (a de-emphasis on the Holocaust as the paradigm of Jewish history would help). Jewish history should be taught in conjunction with world history, so that students have some sense that Jews are often not alone and share much in common with others. Texts which address these problems such as the *Rav's Confrontation* and R' Ahron Soloveichik's *Jew and Jew, Jew and Non-Jew* should be required reading in day schools and *Yeshivot*. So should an explication of the boundaries and limits of relations with non-Jews, and the need to maintain Jewish distinctiveness.

Educators and rabbis must emphasize those ways in which Jews must remain apart, and, more importantly, why they must do so. The centrist community has not devoted enough energy to this problem, as more separatist Orthodox Jews have devoted insufficient attention and energy to universal obligations. Every egalitarian development is not a clear and present danger to *Yahadut*. Neither does egalitarianism usher in the Messiah.

No one should be able to complete years in yeshiva without a serious introduction to *responsa*, in which *poskim* grapple with application of law to a kaleidoscope of new problems and changed conditions. More emphasis needs to be paid to the rules by which *halakhic* decisions are made. A serious effort must be made to explain the limits of change, including not only a study of the relevant general rules such as the *Rambam*'s controversial formulation in the second chapter of *Hilkhot Mamrim,* but as applied by *poskim* throughout the *Shulchan Arukh*.

More generally, Orthodox Jews must stop fearing ambiguity. We can neither cast out our fate as *gerim* nor repudiate our responsibilities as *toshavim*.[90] It is far easier to be one or the other. It is our lot to be both.

NOTES

Marc D. Stern is assistant executive director of American Jewish Congress. The views expressed are obviously his own and not those of AJCongress.

1. *See* M. Borden, *Jews, Turks and Infidels* (1984); N. W. Cohen, *Jews in Christian America: The Pursuit of Religious Equality* (1992).

2. The Blue Law case is *City of Shreveport v. Levy*, 26 La.Ann. 671, 21 Am.Rep. 553 (1874). The prayer case is *Herold v. Parish Bd.*, 136 La. 1034, 68 So. 116 (1915).

3. T. Sullivan, "Judge Wagner Honored at Greater Hartford JCRC Annual Meeting," *Connecticut Jewish Ledger*, June 2, 2000, at 1.

4. The quote is from T. B. Macaulay, *Miscellaneous Essays and Poems*, 598, 599–600 (New York); I came across it in A. Sullivan, *The Case for Gay Marriage* (1999). Sullivan (far more tolerant of people who for religious reasons cannot accept gays than most gay rights advocates) asks whether and how one can distinguish the present-day political and social situation of gays from the situation of the 19th-century English Jews. One could argue on the basis of revelation, but that argument will not persuade in public arenas.

5. The Union of Orthodox Jewish Congregations in America, whose members are far more likely than adherents of Agudath Israel to send their children to Yale, was silent. I assume that the silence was due to a desire not to make Yale reluctant to accept Orthodox students. It is a fair question whether the desire to send children to Yale and similar schools reflects an insufficient weighing of the danger of the egalitarian ethos prevailing at that and similar institutions. *See* Rabbi J. B. Soleveitchik, *Al Ha-Teshuva* 64 (6th printing, 1995).

6. *See* M. Stern, "God and Man at Yale: Orthodox Style," 65 *Congress Monthly* No. 1 at 6 (Jan. 1998). The final decision rejecting the students' challenge to Yale's dorm policy is *Hack v. President and Fellows of Yale College*, 237 F.3d 81 (2d Cir. 2000).

7. A recent Gallup Poll (February 19, 2002) shows that the trend toward acceptance of homosexuality as an acceptable lifestyle is growing, particularly among the young. Just over half of all Americans accept that proposition, but 62 percent of young adults do.

8. The intermarriage remark also caused a storm in the non-Orthodox Jewish community. Senator Lieberman acknowledged later that he had misspoken on the question of intermarriage.

9. Historians point to a substantial improvement in the condition of women in 12th- and 13th-century Christian Europe. R. Fossier, *The Structuring of Society* in *The Cambridge Illustrated History of the Middle Ages*, p. 338–39 (R. Fossier, ed. 1997). Is it mere coincidence that at that time and place, *Rabbeinu* Tam justifies women performing *miztvoth* which are time bound with a *bracha* (against the contrary position of the *Rambam*), the *Ravan* limits restrictions on women's economic activity, and the *Ravyah* insists that all women are *chashuvot* when it comes to *heseibah* on *Pesach*?

10. M. Stern, *Is Religion Compatible with Liberal Democracy?* (Trinity College, 1999), available online at Trinity's website.

11. American Jewish Committee, *Responding to Intermarriage: Survey, Analysis & Policy* (2000) at 19.

12. *See* John C. Green, "Religion and Politics in the 1990's: Confrontation and Coalitions" in M. Silk (ed.), *Religion and American Politics: The 2000 Elections in Context* (2001).

13. A. Sullivan, *The Case for Gay Marriage* (1999).

14. Equality is not the only idea at work in the struggle over gay rights. The gay rights movement also has substantial roots in individual autonomy and limited communal enforcement of moral norms which do not prevent harm to others. Without denying the importance of those strands of the gay rights movement, I think it is true

that today notions of equality are more dominant and persuasive in the public debate. *See* Professor S. L. Stone's contribution in this volume.

15. However, *see* Rabbi J. B. Soloveitchik, *Confrontation* (1964), reprinted in *A Treasury Tradition* at 55, 79 (citing civil rights as a project on which Jews and non-Jews should work together). The *Rav* was not a very orthodox Orthodox rabbi.

16. Contrast Rabbi Hershel Billet's recollection (in a personal communication) of *Rav* Aharon Lichtenstein wanting his *shiur* to attend a rally calling attention to starvation in Biafra. He arranged an early *minyan*, gave *shiur*, and then led the class to the rally, where they were the only whites in attendance.

17. Dr. David Shatz suggested this taxonomy.

18. The Thirteenth, Fourteenth, and Fifteenth Amendments (racial equality); Nineteenth Amendment (granting women the right to vote); the Twenty-Sixth Amendment (giving 18-year-olds the right to vote), all sound in equality. One might well argue the same about the Sixteenth Amendment, allowing for an income tax, and the Seventeenth Amendment, calling for direct election of senators (instead of elitist election by legislators). The Twenty-Third, giving residents of the District of Columbia the right to vote for president, and the Twenty-Fourth Amendment abolishing the poll tax are also about equality. Almost half of the Amendments adopted since the Bill of Rights enhance equality.

19. For a collection of sources, *see* B. Goldberg, *Bein Yisroel le-Nochri-Inyonei Y.D.*, 23:12, n. 26 (1995).

20. *Compare Rav* Kook's *Teshuvot* on autopsies *Da'at Kohen*, #199, 383, in which he argues that autopsies should be performed only on non-Jewish cadavers which have "less holiness" than Jewish bodies. *Rav* Kook seems to have thought that non-Jews would have no difficulty accepting this notion. For a discussion of *Rav* Kook's view, and those of his critics, *see* Michael Z. Nehorai, "Halakkah, Metahalakha and the Redemption of Israel: Reflections on the Rabbinic Rulings of Rav Kook" in L. J. Kaplan and D. Shatz, *Rabbi Abraham Issac Kook and Jewish Spirituality* (1995) at 120, 14–48.

21. In a communication with the author, Rabbi Reuven Bulka pointed out—correctly—that the willingness of Jews to accept organs and blood from non-Jews, without accepting a reciprocal obligation to donate, is a scandalous *chillul ha-Shem*.

22. My son Gedalia called my attention to the Responsa *Chatam Sofer*, Y.D. 336, which rejects claims of biological (but not spiritual) differences between Jews and non-Jews.

23. Gittin 619; *Shulchan Arukh* Y.D. 367:1. *See* Shach, *ad loc, s.v. Kovrim*; *Beit Hillel, ad loc, s.v. Kovrim*.

24. More than once, my children have been taught by bigoted and ignorant *limudei kodesh* teachers that the *mitzva* of *chillul ha-Shem* is relevant only to how Jews perceive their conduct, non-Jews not counting. I cannot even begin to count the number of remarks denigrating non-Jews they have heard in classes taught by supposedly "frum" teachers.

25. *Compare Mishna Brura*, 330:2; *Piskei Teshuvot, id.*

26. T.B. B. Kama 38a.

27. Paradoxically or not, the *Yam Shel Shlomo* to this *sugya* serves as a springboard for the condemnation of women's prayer groups in Rabbi H. Schachter, *et al.*, *Tzei Lach be'Ikvei ha'Tzon*.

28. *See* Professor David Berger's article in this volume.

29. *See, e.g.*, in addition to Professor Berger's article in this volume, R. Yoel Schwartz's *Am Segulah* (1981), 43–62, which devotes an entire chapter to "*Bechirat Yisrael ve'Torat ha-Geza*"—the Choseness of Israel and the Torah of Race. His discussion is surprisingly moderate. I am indebted to R. Yona Reiss for the reference. *See also* M. D. Gross, *Da Ma Sh'Tashiv* (1908). I am indebted to R. Elchanan Adler for this reference. *See also* J. D. Bleich, "Tikkun Olam: Jewish Obligations to Non-Jewish Society" in D. Schatz, *et al.* (ed.), *Tikkun Olam* (1997).

30. *Choshen Mishpat* 28:84.

31. How does one teach a *Rashi* such as that found in Pesachim 22a, *s.v.* "oto", suggesting that a dog is more deserving of honor than a non-Jew? The position is ultimately rejected, *see Sfas Emes, ad loc*, but the educational problem remains.

32. The *Meiri*, of course, has so far had little impact on the *halakha* in this regard. Perhaps this was simply because he lacked the *mazal* that even the *sefer* Torah in the *heichal* needs, but perhaps it is also because Jews had the intuition that, under the circumstances, acceptance of the *Meiri*'s views would have inevitably led to assimilation. In Renaissance Italy, where the prohibition on non-Jewish wine was not widely observed, intermarriage was indeed a problem. *See* E. Horowitz, "Families and Their Fortunes: The Jews of Early Modern Italy" in D. Biale (ed.), *Culture of the Jews: A New History* (2002) at 576–82.

33. For a contemporary summary of these laws, which, on my unsystematic study, generally takes a stringent view, see a *sefer* written (apparently) for *chareidei* Jewry in Israel, B. Goldberg, *Bein Yisroel le-Nochri* (1995). It is interesting and revealing that the author believes that a stringent approach is possible and desirable on the theory that, since Jews in Israel are not dependent on non-Jews for a livelihood, as were Jews in the *Rama*'s Poland or the *Tosafos'* France, the leniencies these authorities introduced are of questionable continuing validity. It is interesting that both the *Rama*'s *teshuva*, condemning the use of non-Kosher wine and that of R. Yossef Kolon's Responsa 82 (Oraysoh1988), limiting the scope of *chukat ha-goyim* (imitating pagan practice), were not printed in all editions of those works. *See* the comments of the editors of the modern editions of these Responsa. *Compare* the "Oraysoh" edition of the *Maharik* with an earlier photo offset edition published in Williamsburg, New York, in which a *teshuva* expressing leniencies with regard to imitating secular non-Jewish practices is listed in the index, but is not reproduced.

34. *See Teshuvot Rama* (Siev, ed.) 124; Responsa, Maharam Padua, 76.

35. *See* note 11, *supra*.

36. The AJCommittee's 2000 *Annual Study of American Jewish Opinion* dealing with intermarriage reports that only 84 percent of American Orthodox Jews would be pained if their children intermarried. Only 80 percent of Orthodox Jews believe that Rabbis should not perform intermarriages. The authors of the AJCommittee study correctly regard the Orthodox community's opposition to intermarriage as an anomaly since the rest of the Jewish community holds far more tolerant views. True enough, but I am struck by the number of Orthodox Jews who would not be pained by a child's intermarriage and that almost a fifth of American Orthodox Jews are prepared to see their clergy officiate at such ceremonies. This may be nothing more than a painful acknowledgment of the reality of intermarriage, but it also may reflect the assimilation of egalitarian norms into the Orthodox community.

37. *See* note 11, *supra*.

38. John C. Green, "Religion and Politics in the 1990's: Confrontations and Coalitions" in M. Silk (ed.), *Religion and American Politics: The 2000 Election in Context* (2001), at 29 (three-quarters of "traditional" evangelicals would support legislation protecting gays from employment discrimination even though the same percentage thought gay sex unacceptable). A Harris poll, noted in a Reuters report of February 8, 2000, indicated that 56 percent of Americans favored a ban on job bias against gays, but only 15 percent favored gay marriage. I know of no study of Orthodox Jewish opinion on this subject.

39. *See Some Considerations Concerning the Catholic Response to Legislative Proposals on the Non-Discrimination of Homosexual Persons*, a Vatican document available at listserv.american.edu/catholic/church/vatican/gay.pastoral; *Declaration on Certain Questions Concerning Sexual Ethics* at listserv.american.edu/catholic/church/vatican/cdfsex.txt.

40. *See* G. Niebuhr, "Keeping Friends and the Faith," *New York Times* (Week in Review), September 17, 2000, at 5, col. 1. *See* D. R. Hoover, "Rome, Relativism and Reaction," *Religion in the News* (Fall 2000) (surveying responses to the letter). For a Jewish response to *Dominus Jesus*, see D. Berger, "On Dominus Jesus and the Jews," 185 *America*, 7–12 (September 27, 2001). It will be reprinted in *Encountering Dominus Jesus* (forthcoming). Note, too, that the Pope, while endorsing *Dominus Jesus*, simultaneously undercut it by restating the Church's commitment to treating other faiths with respect. There has been speculation that the document *Dominus Jesus* is a manifestation of an internal struggle between cosmopolitans and parochials within the Catholic Church. The analogy to our own community's struggles with ecumenicism is intriguing.

41. Yevamot 98a; *cf.* Sanhedrin 74b, and Tosefot *ad loc. s.v.* v'ha.

42. *Tenafly Eruv Association v. Borough of Tenafly*, 309 F.3d 144 (3rd Cir. 2002).

43. It is possible to justify special protection for minority religious groups on the ground that the community has an interest in preserving a small culture from destruction. Those wishing to accept this notion must be prepared to accept Afrocentric or gay-only university dorms.

44. A. Rubenstein, *From Herzl to Rabin: The Changing Image of Zionism* (2000), at p. 265. An artistic exhibit in Tel Aviv presented artworks challenging the very notion of a Jewish state. *New York Times*, January 18, 2001, A-4, col. 3.

45. Rubenstein, *id.* at 268.

46. *Id.* at 271.

47. Israel is not alone in facing the problem. A recent study on race relations in the United Kingdom proposed that publicly supported faith schools be required to admit 25 percent of their pupils from faiths other than that of the sponsor. *Report of the Community Cohesion Report Team* at 37 (2001). (The report is available on the Home Office's website.)

48. *See* I. Etkes, "*Parashat Haskalah me'Taam ve-ha-Temurah be'maad T'nuat ha-Haskalah bRusia*," in I. Etkes (ed.), *ha'Da'at ve-ha-Chayim* (1993), at 167.

49. *See* M. A. Meyer, *Response to Modernity* (1988), at 134–35.

50. It requires investigation whether these figures were egalitarian on moral or pragmatic grounds. For a discussion, *see* the various articles in 2 *Techumim* (1981) under the title "*Bein Yisroel le-Amim*" (167–232).

51. Israeli Supreme Court, 6698/95 (1998).

52. *Bush v. Gore*, 531 U.S. 98 (2000).

53. *Buck v. Bell*, 274 U.S. 200, 208 (1927).

54. 344 U.S. 1 (1954).

55. *Cf.* Trent Lott. For a critical discussion of the *Brown* decision, *see* H. Wechsler, *Towards Neutral Principles of Constitutional Law*, 73 HARV. L. REV. 1 (1959). Chief Justice William Rehnquist, then a law clerk, apparently authored a memo defending segregation, a memo he was at great pains to disavow as his own at subsequent confirmation hearings. The obvious point that a memo written by a young man in the early 1950s would not necessarily reflect the Chief Justice's more mature views in the 1980s was not a politically sufficient answer.

56. Justice John Paul Stevens explained that soldiers in uniform should not be permitted to wear yarmulkes because the armed forces cannot accommodate every religious practice. Equality, he thought, demanded that the armed services accommodate all or none, *Goldman v. Weinberger*, 475 U.S. 503 (1986). Justice Brennan, it is true, would have been satisfied with the highest possible degree of accommodation, but Justice Brennan also opposed aid to parochial schools.

57. 530 U.S. 640 (2000).

58. *See* M. Stern, "Discriminating Bodies," 2 *Religion in the News* # 3 (Trinity College, Fall 1999).

59. *Romer v. Evans*, 517 U.S. 620 (1996).

60. Similarly, the most potent political arguments against the President's faith-based initiative are those about funding institutions which discriminate on the basis of religion in employment.

61. *RAV v. St. Paul*, 505 U.S. 377 (1992). *See,* more recently, *Cuffley v. Mickles*, 208 F.3d 702 (8th Cir. 2000) (Klan seeks equal access to adopt-a-highway program). The Court is examining the issue again this term in *Black v. Commonwealth*, 262 Va. 764, 553 S.E.2d 748 (2001), *cert. granted* (2002).

62. About a decade ago, my wife and I attended the dedication of a yeshiva's new building. When the time came for the formal ceremony to begin, the Rosh Yeshiva's wife turned to mine and said "let us go upstairs to our prison." There is something amiss when even a woman of undoubted orthodoxy feels this way.

63. *Hagiga* 16b; *Eruvin* 96a, *Tosafos ad loc., s.v. Michal.*

64. *See Arukh ha-Shulchan*, O.C. 437:7 (recognizing diligence of contemporary women in cleaning for the Passover holiday, acknowledging change from Talmudic times). *See also* the broadly accepted departure from the refusal to permit remarriages in cases of persons lost in "*mayim she'ein la-hem sof*" due to the availability of modern means of communication. *See* Rabbi S. Masash, "*Aguna she-Baala Ne'elam be-Mapolei Niagra*, 22 *Tehumim*, 184–86 (2002) (collecting sources).

65. Probably nothing has so slowed genuine grappling with difficult and pressing problems than the idea that "where there is a rabbinic will, there is a *halakhic* way."

66. *See,* for example, the *Rambam*'s view in *Hilchot Mamrim*, 2:1 that any *Beit Din* can change a *p'sak* derived from the 13 interpretive principles if it believes it has a better way of applying them. The dispute between *Rambam* and *Ravad*, *id.* about the validity of a rabbinic decree where its *raison d'être* has become obsolete is surely relevant here. *See also chidushai ha-Meiri* to T.B. Beitza 5a.

67. Several years ago the United States Supreme Court was considering a case involving the immunity of states from lawsuits. *Seminole Tribe v. Florida*, 517 U.S. 44

(1996). It adopted a broad reading of state immunity under the Eleventh Amendment, pointing to some early 19th-century cases which read the Amendment in that way. The dissenters, *id.* at 120–21, objected that those decisions reflected unique political pressures on the Court and should not be taken as authoritative. The dissent's history was surely correct, but there is much force to the majority's response that legal precedents cannot be so dismissed. *Id.* at 88.

68. *Iggrot Moshe*, Y.D. (2), # 63.

69. *See Tosafot Ketubot*, 51a, *s.v. me-mekarkai.* The *ketuba b'nin dichrin* is also not observed today. *Rama, Even ha-Ezer* 111:16. The suspension of this condition dates to the period of Geonim. *Otzar ha-Geonim Ketubot* at 139–40. Similarly, *Tosafot* sanctioned ignoring Chazal's strictures against the marriage of minors in light of the economic and social circumstances of their day. *See* A. Grossman, *Chasidot v'Mordot: Nashim Yehudiyot B'Eropa B'ymei ha-Beinyim*, 63–87 (2001). But consider the remarks of R. Menashe Klein quoted in 22 *Tehumin* (2002).

70. *Iggrot Moshe*, O.C. (4) 60. *See,* generally, 2 *ha-Chasmal B'Halakha* 68–77 (1981).

71. Something needs to be written reconciling these adaptations (and the principle of *lo Masra ha-Katuv ela le-Hachamim*) and the concept of *Torat ha-Shem temimah.*

72. *See Eduyot* 1:5 *Tosafot Yom Tov, ad loc.*; *Tiferet Yisroel ad loc.* # 28. For a discussion, *see* N. Helfgot, "*Shaat ha-Dechak k'gorem Halakha*" in *Divrei B'racha v'-Moed* (2002), 145–52.

73. *See Ramban*, *Hilchot Ishut*, 16:7. Another well-known example is that the ban on clapping and dancing is no longer enforced because it was intended to forestall repairs on musical instruments, a fear no longer applicable because most people no longer know how to repair musical instruments. *Shulchan Arukh* O.C. 339:3.

74. *See Shulchan Arukh* Y.D. 119:15, and *Taz, ad loc.*, quoting the *Maharshal.*

75. *Kesef Mishna*, *Hilchot Terumot* 1:11, reports on a *Cherem* imposed on a scholar who insisted on a stringency with a firm basis in the Talmud over the contrary lenient (but textually difficult) ruling of the *Rambam*, accepted in his time in the land of Israel. The reliance on the *Rambam* is said by the *Kesef Mishna* to rest in large part on financial considerations. It is doubtful that even the *Beit Yosef*'s considerable authority could today enforce a *cherem* against a *chumra.*

76. Quoted in Responsa of R. Meir (of Rothenburg) 796. For additional sources, *see* A. A. Auerbach, *Baalei Ha-Tosafot* 57, n. 24–25 (1st ed. 1968).

77. I am aware of the *midrash* rebuking Shaul for worrying about the morality of wiping out Amalek. Wherever the Torah itself commands discrimination, we are stuck. It is a different matter to suggest that where *halakha* itself allows wriggle room, we ought not to wriggle.

78. 5a.

79. For a general discussion, which is far from comprehensive, *see* 6 *Encyclopedia Talmudit* 698 *s.v. Davar she-be-minyan. See also* the *Bach to Tur*, Y.D. 123:1 for a discussion of this principle with regard to *stam yeinam. See also Arukh ha-Shulchan* Y.D. 115:5–6 (discussing the prohibition on non-Jewish milk where there is no likelihood of adulteration), insisting that even where the Talmud states a reason for a rabbinic prohibition—a reason which becomes obsolete—the rule remains binding. *See* the disagreement between Rabbi Y. Neuwirth, *Shmirat Shabbat K'hilchata* and

R. Menashe Klein concerning the continued validity of the decree of Ezra requiring clothes to be washed on Thursday, not Friday, in light of the advent of washing machines. 3 *Piskei Teshuvot* 242:3. Rabbi Klein's position appears to depend on the rule being a *siyag*, as opposed to a *takana*. It is, however, called a *takanah* by the Talmud. This may be an instance of the impulse to *halakhic* conservatism leading to *halakhic* error.

80. *See* generally, for example, J. Jakobovits, *Jewish Medical Ethics* (1975), p. 281–83.

81. *See Biur Halakha* to *Shulchan Arukh* O.C. 328:41, and *Mishna Berura, ad loc.*

82. *Poskim* are generally insistent that *Chazal*'s views on medicine are to be disregarded where the reliance on *Chazal* might endanger life. *See also Chiddushei Chatam Sofer to Nidda* 18 (refusing to explain a view of Rashi and Tosofot which, he says, modern medicine disproves).

83. *See* 6 *Encyclopedia Talmudit* 71, *s.v. gilui*. I am grateful to my son Gedalia for the reference.

84. M. Broyde and A. Wagner, *J. Halakha and Contemporary Society* # 29, p. 51 (2000). For a view that no change has occurred, *see* Responsa *Even Yashfe* #15 (quoting Rabbi S. Elyashiv). For a change in *halakha* with regard to smoking, *see Biur Halakha* to *Orach Chaim* 511:4.

85. *See, Ma'ayan Beis ha-Sho'eivah*, 231–34 (1994). *But see, Teshuvot ha-Rosh* (21:8), forcefully rejecting *halakhic* objections to an *eruv* and threatening to put an objecting *Rav* in *Cherem* if he persisted in opposing the *eruv*. The Rosh points out that the *eruv* saves many people from *chilul shabbat*. Here, as elsewhere, we are forced to engage in cost/benefit analysis, analysis which will not necessarily lead to the same result in all cases.

86. Yisroel Yacov Yuval, "*ha-Hesderim ha-Kaspiyim shel Nisuim be'Ashkenaz be-y'mei ha-Beinayim*" in *Da'at v'Kalkala* (1995) (M. Ben-Sassoon, ed.) at 191.

87. A. Grossman, "*ha-Zikah bein Kalkala Ve'ma'amad ha-Isha ha-Yehudit be-Ashkenaz ha-Keduma*" in *Da'at v'Kalkala, supra*, note 86, at 139, n. 90.

88. Along the lines of *histakel be'Oraitha u'Bari alma*. A study of the uses of this saying of the *Zohar* (not the *Gemara*!) is urgently needed.

89. His view is codified (through the Mordechai) in *Shulchan Arukh*, C.M. 62:1. *But see* Y.D. 248:4. For a discussion of this view in connection with a woman selling an *etrog* for use on the first day of *Yom Tov*, *see Mishna Brurah*, 558:2 (#9) and *Sh'aar ha-tziun, ad loc. But see Aruk'h ha-Shulchan, id.*, dismissing this concern.

90. Rabbi J. B. Soloveitchik, *Confrontation* (1965).

2

Formulating Responses in an Egalitarian Age: An Overview

Aharon Lichtenstein

This year's Orthodox Forum, convened under the rubric, "Formulating Responses in an Egalitarian Age," stands in marked contrast to its recent predecessors. They generally dealt with phenomena whose value and whose place in the world of tradition is clearly acknowledged, but whose specific Jewish character as well as their relation to other elements required analysis and definition. No one questions the importance of spirituality as a universal category or its concomitant position within *yahadut*. Similarly, we all recognize the immanent character of toleration and its limits as an issue to be confronted and explored. Discussion of the conceptual approach to Jewish learning, more of an "insider topic," focused upon an area which is not only relevant to Jewish life but stands at its epicenter. Elucidation of the perception and parameters of authority is endemic to our understanding of any religious community. In all of these instances, we found ourselves coping with spiritual and intellectual problems whose resolution, inherently and a priori, would be part of any agenda to formulate a serious and comprehensive *hashkafah*.

If my antennae not deceive me, I sense that this is not quite our situation this year. Both the heading proper and some of the accompanying material convey the impression that we are confronted by a phenomenon, ideology and movement both, which somehow casts a pall over our world and its values; which is inimical to the traditional order and constitutes a potential threat to its stability and viability; which has a subversive and corrosive impact upon the ideational content and the institutional fabric of Orthodox Jewish life.

Conjoined to the first, one notes a second difference. Forum discussion has, generally, been just that—the exchange of knowledge and ideas related to selected major themes, governed and coordinated in accordance with a freely chosen agenda. "Response" takes some of the edge off the internal dynamic and largely presupposes a stance vis-à-vis some external stimulus. That stance may of course be positive or negative, affirmative appreciation or heated rejoinder; but it is, in either case, somewhat imposed. And what is most to our purpose, it may be manifested in two distinct areas: discourse and action. At the theoretical plane, we shall forge an ideological response by engaging in familiar intellectual dialogue. In addition, however, we shall evidently strive to suggest and develop a pragmatic and possibly programmatic response, as we assess the present impact of egalitarianism upon Jewish life and seek to influence their prospective interaction. Response at that plane may of course vary markedly, and may include condescendingly benign stonewalling, vehemently combative opposition, or empathetic openness on the road to reorientation and reappraisal. Whatever one's position, however, whether adamant rejection or progressive adaptation, we shall find ourselves entering the lists more than is our wont. The "free play of the mind," so admired by Arnold, will, in all likelihood, be conjoined to the formulation of policy as well as the mapping of strategy.

Personally, together with Professor Stone, I have been charged with focusing upon two questions. The first reads: "How do we distinguish between ordinary Halakhic processes responding to new stimuli and calls for direct revision of a divinely inspired, permanently fixed, Torah?" This question can conceivably be understood in two distinct senses. We may distinguish between two entities, creatively, by establishing difference and relating variously to them, whether through the innovation of whole categories or through the introduction of nuanced criteria which transmute superficial similarity into a distinction with a difference. Where others see no reason for differentiation, even when they note disparate characteristics, a fertile mind will seize upon previously unappreciated dissimilarity as a basis for apprehending contrast and for acting on that apprehension.

Alternatively, we may distinguish, passively, when categories and parameters are already well defined but we must yet address ourselves to the task of recognizing under which rubric to classify a given entity—and this, not by drawing the conceptual lines of the class but, rather, by examining the content and contours of the unit. Here, we engage primarily in observation and perception, as we strive to discern the character of a phenomenon and to fasten upon its definitive qualities.

Distinguishing in both senses is, of course, standard intellectual fare, the bread-and-butter of denizens of the *beit hamidrash*—and not only of the Brisker strain. They are, however, clearly different, and I should presumably clarify which is the mandate which has been thrust upon me—or, whether, perhaps, both are included. I do not pretend to plumb the depths of authorial intent, but I hazard the assumption that the question posed relates to distinguishing in the latter sense. Presumably, a committed Jew understands how to relate differentially, in attitude and in practice, to initiatives which seek to implement Torah, on the one hand, or to eviscerate it, on the other. He may not be familiar with the wording of the ninth of the Rambam's thirteen *ikkarim*—

> And the ninth principle is that of [non] nullification; that is, that this Torah of Moses will not be nullified, and there will not come in its place a substitute Torah from G-d; there will be nothing added, nor diminished, from it, not in writing and not in explanation, as it says, "do not add to it or detract from it" or its equivalent in *Mishneh Torah*;[1] and he may not have a catechetical mindset altogether. But, his ignorance of theology notwithstanding, he knows in his guts what has been the backbone of Jewish faith.[2]

That faith in the abiding character of Torah as binding is the core of *emunah*, simple or sophisticated. There is, of course, discussion in Hazal as to whether any element of Torah can be preempted, whether "it is in the power of the Rabbis to uproot a biblical matter." This should mislead no one, however. At no point does the *gemara*, Bavli or Yerushalmi,[3] entertain the possibility that whole sections of the Torah can be nullified—in order to relieve societal needs, to conform to the *Zeitgeist*, or even to stimulate religious experience. Such a contention does not even qualify, Halakhically, as error, worthy of requiring an expiatory sacrifice:

> The Court is not liable [for a sin offering] until they adjudicate a matter that the Sadducees do not concede; but as to a matter [ruling] to which [even] the Sadducees accept, they are exempt. What is the reason? Such [a point] is known to every school child.[4]

The discussion rather centers upon the limited authority to prescribe regulations with respect to detail which, in certain circumstances, will lead to practical conclusions different from those mandated by primal Torah regulations. At a theoretical plane, the situation is different with respect to interpretations of Hazal and, a fortiori, of later links in the *mesorah*. The Rambam held that, in this area, direct revision by properly constituted authority was indeed a legitimate and viable possibility:

> The Great Court, which interpreted the Torah casuistically with one of the [received] methods [of interpretation] as it seems to them; and they ruled accordingly, and later another court arose and it saw reason to contradict [the interpretation of the first court] this is permissible, and it [the second court] judges as it sees fit, as it says "To the judge who will be in those days"—you are obligated to follow the court which [exists] in your generation.[5]

But the committed Jew, instinctively and intuitively, knows how steadfast has been the historical fealty of *knesset Israel* to Hazal; and, if he knows of this *pesak* of the Rambam at all, rightly senses that, inasmuch as the right to revise is restricted to a later *sanhedrin*, its exercise is of millennial moment, of no immediate practical application.

Distinction in the first sense, seems, therefore, fairly clear. Questions will obviously arise with respect to detail, but the broad outlines should be almost self-evident; and I doubt that it is to this task that we have assembled to address ourselves. Perceiving difference is, however, a subtler and trickier undertaking. While grosser contrasts pose no challenge, nicer nuances very often do. I know of no litmus test, simple or comprehensive, which could invariably give us satisfactory guidance, nor can I conceive of one. Primary general directions can, however, be pointed; and this, by analogy to a similar dilemma.

With respect to problematic prophecy, the Torah itself hypothesizes a quandary: "And if you will say in your heart—how will we know that which G-d did not speak?" And it goes on to posit a definitive criterion: "That which the prophet will speak in G-d's name and that [predicted] event does not occur, that is the thing G-d did not speak; with malice that prophet has spoken, and do not fear him."[6]

This test relates to the substance of the prophecy. That being the case, however, it only covers a limited class of situations. As Rashi noted:

> And if you say: this is so of one who prophesies concerning the future. What if he [the prophet] comes and says do such and such and from the Holy One, Blessed Is He I speak, they [*i.e.*, his listeners] have already been commanded that if he comes to subvert one from [observing] any of the mitzvot, do not listen to him, unless he is known to you as completely righteous, such as Elijah on Mt. Carmel who offered a sacrifice at the time when altars [other than that of the Temple] were forbidden, in order to correct Israel, all according to the need of the time, and to fill the gap [in observance]. Therefore it says, "Hashem unto him."[7]

The solution which Rashi offers, focused upon the personality of the prophet, is grounded upon the conclusion of a brief discussion in the *gemara*: "Those cases in which he is recognized are different, for if you will not say so, Abraham at Mt. Moriah, how did Isaac obey him; Elijah on Mt. Carmel, how did [the Jews] rely on him to offer sacrifices [outside the Temple]; but where he is recognized [the case] is different."[8] The *gemara* does not specify with regard to which qualities one is to be validated as *muhzak*. As we saw, Rashi's comment on the *pasuk* singles out piety "that he is totally righteous." The Ramban is critical of this emphasis: "This seems to me incorrect. The ratification is not to the effect that he is totally righteous but, rather, that he is a true prophet, recognized by all, inasmuch as he has foretold future events which have then occurred; and this is his sign as is mentioned in this section, or if he performed a wonder in our presence. And this is, [generally], the certification of prophets."[9]

On his view, it is the veracity of past prophecy which is crucial. And indeed, in his *perush* on the *gemara*, Rashi cites two areas: "That he is a righteous and a true prophet."[10] The individual upon whom one relies to the point of accepting his authoritative decision to deviate temporarily from a Halakhic norm must both be marked, generally, by saintly religious character and, specifically, have a track record as a prophet.

This dual focus is distinctively relevant for the Rambam. Given his view that a prophet cannot merely be a vehicle for conveying messages, and his insistence upon the highest standards of moral rectitude, intellectual excellence, and religious intensity and depth as preconditions for prophecy, there is great coincidence between the personal and the functional aspects of the *muhzak*. Signs and wonders are not a sufficient condition to establish one's status as a prophet or to require others to heed his message:

> Only a person of whom we knew beforehand, by his wisdom and his actions, in which he transcended all his peers, and he conducted himself in the ways of prophecy, and its sanctity and asceticism, who then came and performed a sign and a wonder, and stated that G-d sent him—with regard to him we are commanded to listen to him as it is written "Harken unto him." And it is possible that a sign or a wonder is performed by someone who is not a prophet, the signs having some arcane basis. Nevertheless, we are commanded to listen to him, inasmuch as he is a great and wise person, and qualified for prophecy, we predicate his legitimacy.[11]

The acceptance of *nevu'ah* is grounded upon recognition of the *navi*.

For the Rambam, this is true of response to all claims to prophecy; but it is doubly crucial when, as in the instances cited in the *gemara* in *Sanhedrin*, one is confronted by prophecy which is innovative and, in a sense, even deviationist. The same may be posited with regard to our question. "How do we distinguish between ordinary Halakhic processes responding to new stimuli, and calls for direct revision of a divinely inspired, permanently fixed Torah?" In two ways. At one plane, we test the substance of suggested innovations. The Halakhic universe was not created yesterday. It has a long history, in the course of which methodology was refined, canons of interpretation established, modes of evidence limned, a corpus of relevant sources and their hierarchy defined. Some of these were set down formally, as, for instance, the thirteen *middot* of the *Torat Kohanim* or the thirty-two of Rabbi Eliezer ben Rabbi Yossi Hagelili. Other elements, more fluid in nature, evolved more flexibly; but these, too, within certain parameters. Knowledge of where the frontiers lie and sensitivity to their violation is, partly, acquired through theoretical formulation and analysis. Primarily, however, it is imbibed through reverential immersion in the tradition, whether through existential relation to its texts or, better still, through immediate exposure to its current masters. The aphorism "Its apprenticeship is greater than its study"[12] is not confined to *pesak*. It is, however, surely crucial with respect to that sensitive area—as regards the examination of *pesakim* no less than their formulation.

The second test concerns the *posek*—and this, with reference to both his learning and his spiritual persona. Unquestionably, some *pesakim* of Rav Moshe Feinstein or Rav Shlomo Zalman Auerbach z.t.l. (not all of which found their way into print), had they come from Rabbi X or Y, would have raised eyebrows and possibly incited protest. Is this discriminatory? Superficially, yes; in a deeper sense, categorically not. With regard to such giants, one knows that a decision issues out of a mastery of the Halakhic corpus, imbedded in their bones no less than in their heads; that is anchored in a nuanced intuition of the Halakhic process and of how it balances normative mandates with human needs. Primarily, one knows that it issues from a person of profound faith and abiding belief in the absolute truth of Torah; one of overriding responsibility to the Halakhic tradition and its texts; one in whom the interpretation of Halakhah and its implementation unfolds within a context of pure submissive "Acceptance of the yoke of the kingdom of heaven" and "Acceptance of the yoke of mitzvoth." One can securely respond affirmatively, "Listen to him," when one is fully confident of both the modality and the motivation of any innovative initiative.

Without casting any personal aspersions, this dual test is not met by promulgators of clarion calls for "direct revision" of basic Halakhic norms. Substantively, these often do not spring out of the tradition and its processes but contravene them—at times, in the name of progressive revelation, explicitly pressing for a drastic restructuring of the whole Halakhic order, and not just for rescinding particular directives. Moreover, their impact is not cushioned by assuaging reassurance about the motivation. The calls, while at times issuing from persons fundamentally committed to the truth of Torah, and whose sincerity I have no desire to challenge, are nevertheless often fueled by extraneous concerns and the felt need—admittedly, perhaps moral and religious, no less than societal—to conform to current philosophic vogue. At the very least, one is left with unease about the ideological and axiological basis of the balance between the permanent and the contemporary. Indeed, "Muhzak (recognized) is different—that he is a righteous and a true prophet."

At this juncture, the reader may very well ask: All well and good, but what has this to do with egalitarianism? The modality of evaluation is presumably relevant to any problematic phenomenon. Indeed, I confess I am slightly perplexed myself. Could not the litmus tests suggested for distinguishing between varied responses in an egalitarian age be equally applicable to responses formulated in an agnostic or hedonistic age? Perhaps, I answer, what is anticipated is not a set of guidelines for distinguishing between others' responses, but, rather, a response of my own to egalitarianism which should, in some way, allow for adopting some of its contentions, through the modus operandi of ordinary Halakhic processes, while yet steering clear of heresy. And yet, the question persists. Could not the same criteria, to be presumably postulated on this score—consistency with acknowledged methodology, consonance with the authoritative corpus, concern for values as well as norms—likewise direct any traditional response to hedonism?

They certainly could. If, nonetheless, our assignment confronts us as it does, I suspect it is because we are, collectively, attracted, philosophically and pragmatically, by egalitarianism while sybaritic libertinism leaves us cold. We leave *carpe diem* to the Latins, but in the Declaration of Human Rights we find universal moral import. Hence, in this area, the critical task of winnowing the chaff from the wheat, when we consider that here may be wheat worthy of *menahot*, assumes significant dimensions. We are therefore called upon to define, however briefly, our relation to contemporary egalitarianism, at the level of cardinal tenets and basic *hashkafah*.

As I perceive it, egalitarian thought is characterized by three major themes, although these need not appear in conjunction. The first, and most fundamental, is the metaphysical uniformity of man. For secularists, this conception is virtually axiomatic, deriving from the nature of their total worldview. Secularism is a leveling force. Metaphysically, it regards, and must regard, all places, all times, all objects, and all persons as inherently of a piece, as there is no basis and no source for radical differentiation. Disparity can only be functional and artificial, of a purely secondary order. For the religious egalitarian, uniformity is not a priori necessary, but he assumes its existence nonetheless as an article of faith, faith in the catholic brotherhood of man under the impartial fatherhood of God.

A second, less pervasive, theme, familiar from other contexts as well, is that of moral relativism. Radically expressed, this would entail the rejection of any ethical absolute whatsoever. In a more moderate vein, it would deny the concept of natural law, reduce mores to social convention, and leave, at most, a few overarching virtues such as love or justice, as ultimate values. Closely related, third, is the assertion of personal autonomy, with the individual firmly ensconced as the primary, if not the sole, arbiter of right and wrong.

These basic philosophic premises militate, at the social and political plane, against preferential status for any person or priority for any ethos. They are the linchpins of an ideology which translates, in practice, into movement toward their implementation through pressure for social and political changes. Some of these changes are separable as independent initiatives, each with its local impetus. They are much reinforced, however, by a comprehensive systematic conceptual framework, whose adherents—over and above their concern with the pragmatic ramifications of perceived inequality and their quest for universal entitlement—regard the bare fact of discrimination, regardless of its utilitarian consequences, as an outrageous spiritual abomination.

While egalitarianism is not exclusively, reciprocally, and inextricably bound to these premises—one could certainly conceive of an absolute, divinely revealed system which should be egalitarian in character and content—the presently prevalent strain is, I believe, very much grounded in them. If we ask ourselves where does *yahadut* stand with regard to them, the answer is self-evident. Recognition of the uniqueness of man is central to our religious humanism; but so is the sense of metaphysical distinction. It inheres in the concept of *kedushah*—of place, time, object, and, above all, of *knesset Israel*. That *kedushat Israel* is grounded in chosenness, the fusion of privilege and responsibility which underlies Jewish distinctiveness; and, it is, from our perspective, decidedly metaphysical. Even if one should side with those who contend, in the face of assorted *midrashim* that *behirat Israel* was not, *ab initio*, part of a providential scenario but, rather, the fruit of historical development, we nevertheless acknowledge that the choice, having been determined, broke fresh ground and created a distinctive level of intrinsic metaphysical status. Moreover, there are additional levels of *kedushah* within *knesset Israel* proper, particular chosenness having been accorded *shevet Levi* and *kohanim*; and while merit can, for certain purposes, supersede them, "A bastard who is a scholar takes precedence over a high priest who is an ignoramus,"[13] the categories are very much part of the Halakhic order.

Premises concerning ethical and religious relativism or ultimate personal autonomy are, if anything, even less palatable. Normative absolutes are the essence of Torah and our status as commanded spiritual beings the bedrock of our relation to the Ribbono Shel Olam.

Consequently, in relating to egalitarian ideology, there is no alternative to clearly recognizing and candidly asserting that, as a system, it is, for us, wholly untenable. However we may view certain specific initiatives, we cannot countenance the philosophic framework. In practice, where Halakhically feasible and axiologically desirable, nuanced revisions, in the direction of either stringency or latitude, may lie in store. The frontiers of what, in this area, the Torah world regards, attitudinally and pragmatically, as acceptable or even preferable, may be tested anew, as the substantive significance of modes of conduct and our collective relation to them is altered contextually. Ideologically, however, we cannot encounter egalitarianism on its turf but, regardless of what is currently politically correct, must rather confront it with our own truth. Where it exists, we may note and even stress our own affinity with certain universal elements and egalitarian values; and we should explain the nature of *behirat Israel* and its demands. But we have neither the right nor the desire—nor, for that matter, the ability—to sweep cardinal tenets under the rug. Halakhah does not regard every inequality as an inequity.[14]

I believe that this account of our stance and mind-set is reasonably accurate. I would, concurrently, submit, however, that it is possibly too one-sided. Unquestionably, total egalitarianism—radical and comprehensive, ideology as well as lifestyle—constitutes a philosophy and an ethic we categorically abjure. It strikes at the heart of cardinal tenets regarding the given reality and the ideal desideratum of personal Torah life and of communal Jewish polity. However, as a component of our spiritual universe, the motif of "I am a creature and my fellow is a creature" strikes a responsive chord; and this, not only because we are humanly sensitive to "the tears of the oppressed, lacking all comforter"—the outcry of the disadvantaged, disenfranchised, and discriminated against—but because, at some plane, the prospect of the brotherhood of man under the fatherland of God resonates, beyond our ethical consciousness, in our religious sensibility. Hence, rather than dismiss the egalitarian impulse cavalierly, we need—striking a balance between the universal and the particularistic, between hierarchy and leveling—to assess its place within our overall *hashkafah*.

Still, our fundamental stance should be clear, to ourselves and to our audience. In discussions of the issue, one occasionally catches traces of an attitude which accepts egalitarianism as an ultimate desideratum and, then, confronted with its apparent inconsonance and inconsistency with Halakhic data, strives to find modes of innovation or improvisation which might enable its implementation within the constraints of Torah. There may, indeed, be areas of Halakhah—the tragedy-ridden reality of *mamzerut* is a prime instance—which, in practice, *poskim* seek to circumscribe and even circumvent. Egalitarianism, as a whole, is not, however, among them; and our relation to its cardinal issues ought not be tainted by apologetics.

In one area, the principled *hashkafic* rejection of egalitarian ideology admittedly leaves us open, morally and politically, to the charge of egocentric inconsistency. Since the Emancipation, Western Jews have traditionally pressed for full civil and political rights. That pressure has, in large measure, been fueled by egalitarian impulses and theory; and, to some, it seems palpably unfair that Jews should not seek to enlarge the bounds of others' equality. The argument is not without appeal, but it is fundamentally specious. Despite the often aggressive claims of its proponents, equality need be neither total nor comprehensive. The rejection of one criterion does not militate for the abandonment of all. The extent to which moral standards ought to be translated into legal sanctions has of course been widely debated. In dealing with it, however, we can hardly resolve the issue by equating the right to vote or to attend a university with the right to terminate incipient fetal life. Similarly, within the Jewish community, affinity with the civil rights movement does not entail the social acceptance of the rupture of Jewish identity often attendant upon intermarriage.

The issue is exacerbated by a comparison of the respective American and Israeli scenes. How would we relate, we might be asked, to a local equivalent of *hok hashevut*, which would admit Christians indiscriminately but impose barriers before Jews, Moslems, or atheists? As the answer is self-evident, we stand exposed to the sarcasm of Macaulay's lampooning representation of a particularist's assertion that others are duty-bound to tolerate him as he is right and they are wrong, while the reverse does not obtain. Some might suggest that the gap in consistency could be reduced if Diaspora Jews would forgo some of their entitlement; but as this is a most unlikely prospect, we must look to more salient considerations. Probably the most relevant is the conventional argument that weight needs to be assigned to self-definition. The United States is, socially, a predominantly Christian country but is not formally so, while Israel was conceived and founded as a Jewish state. Hence, as applied to *hok hashevut*, for instance, every prospective Jewish *oleh*, while not yet a citizen of *medinat Israel*, is already a member of *knesset Israel*; and, thus, is admitted to the national home of the Jewish polity, as a returning American expatriate need not apply for a "green card." On this reading, we presumably would not cavil at an Indonesian immigration law which would be tilted in favor of Moslems. The contention is valid, and it obviates many specific objections. I doubt, however, that it answers all; and I think we should recognize that it is entirely conceivable that the conjunction of the pursuit of certain interests in the Diaspora with adherence to the principle of chosenness and to ethnic identity in Israel may indeed issue in a measure of disparity to which we need to be sensitive.

If we noted a mix of the theoretical and the pragmatic in dealing with our first question, it is even more marked as we relate to the second: "How should we respond to changes in society which are motivated by a combination of both positive factors of equal respect for all persons as a manifestation of *zelem E-lohim* and negative factors (tolerance of sexual practices beyond Halakhic norms)?" Any serious answer must take into consideration two kinds of factors. There are, first, issues of principle. To what extent are we obligated or permitted, Halakhically and morally, to stake out a position, ranging from revulsion to support, with respect to such changes? Second, there are matters of interests—not, I trust, material and personal, but spiritual and communal. What impact will a given stance, or its absence, have upon the moral climate of our environment—upon our institutions, upon our youth, upon ourselves? And of course we need to wrestle with these concerns with an eye to a more general dilemma, regarding the balance of principle and interests. To what extent do we have the right or the duty to sharpen or modify what might have been our optimal response in light of possible fallout? I am not so naive as to reject this factor entirely, but determination of how much weight should be assigned to it requires careful deliberation.

In part, these issues would obviously confront us even if we were dealing with change impelled by purely negative or wholly positive factors. With respect to them, too, we would have to weigh, apart from the content of response, whether to respond at all—and if so, in which vein. We can distinguish between at least three strains of response. There is, first, attitude and sensibility. Even when we in no way enter the lists for or against a given phenomenon, we may still, personally and intimately, react to it, with recoil or enthusiasm. Secondly, we may engage it, verbally and forensically, with individual or collective expressions of encouragement or opposition. Finally, we may encounter it actively by seeking to direct the course of events, as regards both society and state, whether through initiatives in the private sector or by promoting governmental involvement to advance or inhibit a particular change. And all of this, again, with respect to monochromatic change. Unquestionably, however, the situation is more complex when we confront a mixed impulse, and, in answering the question posed to me, I shall try to bear this factor in mind.

Whether, confronted by an egalitarianism twinned to a non-judgmental moral stance, we shall respond at all, will surely depend on how much we care, and on how we prioritize our energies and resources. That we ought to care can, I hope, be taken for granted—at the very least, at the level of personal reaction; and this, not only because our own community may become infected, but out of concern for the possible contamination of the broader society per se. The insularity of much of the Torah world in this respect is an educational disaster. Abortion on demand is a moral abomination, whoever the fetus may be. We have much to learn from the late Lubavitcher Rebbe, who took up the cudgels for a modicum of prayer in the public schools. Unquestionably, we shall be far more concerned if and when our own are involved—caring about Israel more than elsewhere, and about Diaspora Jewish communities more than about their ambience. We are not so universalistic as to disregard national ties; and modern history has amply demonstrated that felt ethnicism generates more concern than abstract pronouncements about global fraternity. Insouciance is, however, out of the question.

To care, morally, is, in all likelihood, to judge. I am not at all certain that those who advocate a non-judgmental stance practice what they preach. They tend to be quite intolerant of intolerance—i.e., of the violation of what they regard as a value; and if they are indeed non-judgmental about homosexuality or abortion, it is because they regard these as morally neutral. *Yahadut*, however, does not preach ethical distance at all. As a system, grounded in Halakhah and general morality, it rejects, as previously noted, the relativism upon which much of the abdication of judgment rests; and, hence, it clearly encourages the individual Jew or Jewess to adopt a position vis-à-vis developments in the world around them.

An attitudinal response is, then, certainly in order. One might of course question whether this should translate into personal judgment, with respect to an individual or a group. On the one hand, the *pasuk* enjoins, "Judge your fellow justly."[15] The *Torat Kohanim*, cited by Rashi, offers two explanations of this charge, addressed to authorized judges or to the ordinary person, respectively: "That one should not speak as long as he needs, and to the other you [the judge] say abridge your words, or that one [party] stands and the other sits. . . . Another explanation: judge your neighbor righteously; judge all men favorably."[16]

The latter charge, considerably amplified in a *sugya* in *Shabbat* and *Aboth d'Rabbi Nathan*, and emphasized by the *Sh'iltot*,[17] need not relate to anything expressed to one's fellow; it may simply include private evaluation. It does, however, make allowance for judgment, even if it mandates its quality and perspective. On the other hand, Hillel's equally familiar dictum, "Do not judge your friend until you stand in his place,"[18] appears to discourage judgment altogether. However, it should be obvious that this counsel, too, does not advocate the acceptance of alternative mores. It rather urges empathy and humility in perceiving and interpreting how and why deviation from normative conduct has occurred. We are all familiar with the exchange between Rabbi Meir and Beruryah: "There were thugs who lived in R' Meir's neighborhood who greatly disturbed him; R' Meir prayed that they should die. His wife said to him, Why is this your opinion—because [the verse says] 'sinners should be destroyed.' Does it say sinners (written plene)? No, it says 'sin should be destroyed.'"[19] And I assume most would today be inclined to adopt her softer position, sparing personal criticism even with respect to changes we might find objectionable. That, too, however, is a far cry from what the movers of such changes seek.

As to the substance of response, we need to pay particular attention to the mixed roots of the changes under consideration. In this respect, we are confronted by a quality endemic to much of modern culture. It has often been remarked that while, in medieval and Renaissance literature, one could tell the saints from the sinners without a scorecard, the modern scene is far murkier. Shakespeare has been highly praised for the creative diversity which could humanize a Iago as well as a Desdemona, but even in his plays we are hard put to find a whisky priest or a Raskolnikov. This spiritual chiaroscuro confronts us with a challenge. The Hazon Ish is reputed to have asked, how could one expect meaningful dialogue between the secular and the religious communities when the same act is valued by the former as an expression of love and classified by the latter under *hayvei keritut*?

Nevertheless, at the conceptual plane, the challenge ought not be insuperable. Avoiding the genetic fallacy, we may, in the spirit of the fabled angelic missive of the *Kuzari*, appreciate motives while decrying results: "Your intentions are desirable in G-d's eyes but your actions are not."[20] Moreover, we may distinguish between various strains of the motivation proper. By way of precedent, in this respect, one might cite a remarkable *gemara*. Addressing himself to the narrative regarding the daughters of Lot, who had intoxicated their father and then had sexual relations with him, Rabbi Hiyyah bar Abba in the name of Rabbi Yehoshua ben Korhah derives a striking moral: "A person should always leap at [the opportunity to fulfill] a mitzvah. As a result of the one night that [Lot's eldest daughter] preceded her [younger sister], [her descendants] preceded to enter the Jewish people by four generations—Obed, Yishai, David and Solomon—while [the descendants of the younger one] delayed until Rahavam as it says 'his mother's name was Naama the Ammonite.'"[21]

Whether, from a technical standpoint, this sexual liaison was, to a non-Jew, Halakhically proscribed as incest, was debated in another *gemara*,[22] and the Rambam and the Meiri differed as to the *pesak*.[23] But that the entire scenario of duped sexuality was reprehensible seems reasonably clear. Several lines earlier, the selfsame Rabbi Hiyyah bar Abba contrasts the relative modesty of the younger daughter who, unlike her elder sister, in naming her child, concealed Lot's paternity; and Rashi, analogously, castigates the latter for having initiated the *zenut* (fornication).[24] And yet, on the assumption that the motivation was, at least in part—there was an altruistic aspect of rehabilitating a scorched world, but, surely, a selfish moment as well—admirable, Hazal could appreciate the positive component, and speak of a *devar mizvah* in this context, to boot.

Even at the attitudinal plane, however, such a discriminating approach should no doubt be implemented with selective care—depending, in large measure, on the weight of the positive and negative elements, respectively. I have little difficulty in applying it to the Hazon Ish's case of a wedded couple which does not observe *taharat hamishpahah*. I am not only unwilling but unable, however, to react similarly to romantic love which issues in intermarriage. The magnitude of the transgression, as both a violation of a basic Halakhic norm and as a general apostasy, "They betrayed G-d, as they gave birth to foreign children," is such that it effectively overshadows everything else. Yet, the basic principle of axiological discrimination should be borne in mind.

This last distinction is of relevance to the specific question confronting me. The term "changes in society" has two distinct, albeit linked, referents—one, sociological, the other, ideological; and they differ in motivation no less than in content. In practice, abortion may be impelled by convenience or distress. The theoretical claim to a right to abort, in contrast, is probably fueled by philosophic assumptions regarding personal autonomy. The homosexual is driven by a psycho-physiological urge, his advocates by a sociocultural manifesto. And, of course, the specific gravity of the sociological trends themselves varies widely. We can hardly regard intermarriage and gay unions equally. In ferreting wheat from chaff, we need to observe which is the grain at hand, and steer our course accordingly.

These considerations relate to response as attitude. To them, in dealing with verbal and with active response, must obviously be added pragmatic factors. These focus upon results—the fallout of acquiescence, of affirmation, of antagonism, or any blend of the three. Clearly, decisions regarding such responses will entail a plethora of specific judgments, but the overall thrust of planning response should, almost a priori, be manifest. We are guided by two primary concerns: (a) commitment to the cause of *avodat hashem* and its advance; (b) sensitivity to human personality and its welfare. The need to assess how best to promote each of these, separately and jointly, and what kind of balance to strike when they are in apparent conflict, is the alpha and omega of any meaningful and effective spiritual strategy—whether in private counseling, in educational endeavor, in institutional initiative, or in communal enterprise.

These twin concerns are distinct, and yet, reciprocally intertwined; and this, in several senses. First, sensitivity to those whom we challenge enhances the prospect that they will heed our message. When Hazal counseled, "always, even as the left hand rejects, let the right hand attract,"[25] they were not only concerned with the value of respecting an interlocutor's dignity, but with the prospect of enhancing his sanctity. Secondly and conversely, appreciation of *zelem E-lohim*—or, at another plane, of personal *kedushat Israel*—is itself part of the world of *avodat Hashem* we are striving to enhance.

And yet, divergence and even conflict there will probably be, and we need, thirdly, to give thought to optimal balance. I do not think, for a moment, that a single answer is in order. We may lean towards one orientation or another, but the exigencies of a given historical reality must always be considered. Whichever concern is in relative neglect requires special counterbalancing sustenance. This formula almost assures a kind of perennial unpopularity, but it is what spiritual responsibility demands.

How such an approach will reflect itself in a response to the current trends of egalitarianism should probably be better determined by those much closer than myself to the vortex of this ideology and its manifestations. My own assessment is that within the hard core of the Torah world, the human aspect requires greater emphasis than it is currently receiving, while the reverse is true of the broader Jewish community. But I may be wrong. With respect to both venues, however, we should be careful to embrace both values, even as the educational and tactical nuances shift; and we should not compromise authenticity in the quest for acceptability. The maintenance of standards should take precedence over the enhancement of rating.

In determining policy in this area, axiological considerations should certainly be primary. Nevertheless, they do not stand alone. Some place in the planning of response, with an eye to particular present historical circumstances—what F. H. Bradley called, "my station and its duties"—will obviously be accorded purely tactical factors. Of these, several familiar elements may be singled out for special mention. The first—most directly related to the *mizvah* of reproachful *tokhahah*, but pregnant with far broader ramifications—concerns likely reaction to a prospective initiative. We recall Rabbi Elazar ben Rabbi Shimon's directive, "Just as it is a mitzvah to say something which will be heeded, so it is a mitzvah to refrain from saying something which will not be heeded: R' Abba says 'it is obligatory, as it says "Don't rebuke a fool [scoffer?] lest he hate you; rebuke the wise and he will love you."'"[26]

But we also recall the qualification of many *rishonim* who asserted that, at the public plane, this counsel could not always be heeded, as it had to be balanced by the need to stake out Torah positions and sustain principles.

In a related vein, we will obviously need to evaluate how a given course, heeded or not, will inhibit problematic "egalitarian" trends—and at what cost. Consider the worst: intermarriage. Unquestionably, as the non-Orthodox community realized belatedly, this plague needs to be confronted, first and foremost, educationally; and this, not only by an ethnocentric appeal for Jewish continuity but by inculcating a positive sense of the meaning of chosenness and the uniqueness of *kedushat Israel*. Concurrently, however, some will advocate severe social sanctions in the hope that prospective ostracism will serve as an effective deterrent. I take no issue with this, on principle. An individual who has crossed the line should not be surprised to find himself beyond the pale; and, as I have indicated, I do not view this as an issue with regard to which respect for the underlying involvement of *zelem E-lohim* should counterbalance the gravity of the deviation. Several years ago, a group of Orthodox rabbis floated a suggestion that, given the scope of the phenomenon, the view of those who "marry out" as pariahs should be ameliorated, so that they could continue to feel and function as members of the Jewish community, with all that this could imply for their own and their children's future. In short order, the suggestion evoked vehement protests—in part, on the grounds that its proponents were too soft on the phenomenon, and, in part, out of concern that a more understanding attitude would dilute the deterrent effect of the traditionally tougher stance. The first contention certainly deserves to be weighed on its merits; but, as to the second, both the current force of deterrence and the cost, human as well as Jewish, at which it is attained, requires assessment.

In considering the last point, a partial analogy might be helpful. Rabbenu Gershom was asked whether a *kohen*, who had converted to Christianity and then repented, should be stripped of his prerogatives. The discussion in his *teshuvah* revolves, in part, around the formal Halakhic questions—much debated by earlier *geonim* and subsequent *rishonim*, on the basis of a *sugya* in *Menahot*[27]—as to whether a person who had worshipped *avodah zarah*, perhaps even under duress,[28] could perform *avodah* for the Ribbono Shel Olam, and as to whether the sanctity of *kehunah* is vitiated by apostasy.[29]

Rabbenu Gershom argues for leniency with regard to these issues; but then adds further elements to his decision:

> "Therefore, we have no proof from Scripture or the Mishna to invalidate him; on the contrary, we have proofs from Scripture and Mishna not to invalidate him as it says 'one shall not oppress his compatriot.' With regard to verbal oppression the verse is speaking. How? If he [a person] is a *ba'al teshuva* one should not say to him remember your earlier deeds. And if one will say, this priest should not go up to the [platform] and he should [not be called first to the Torah] there is no greater oppression than this. Moreover, one [undermines] ba'alei teshuva, and it is not proper to do so, as R' Yochanan said 'whoever says Menashe is a sinner, has no portion in the world to come because he [undermines] ba'alei teshuva.'"[30]

This concern, lest the *kohen* be affronted, on the one hand, and with possibly discouraging recantation, on the other, introduces a new dimension to the discussion; and it is one which may have wider application. We should of course note that the *kohen* in question may have converted in a climate of intimidation, if not of outright duress, in the first place; and, most critically, that he has repented. These elements are generally absent in the contemporary case of intermarriage. Nevertheless, at least as a basis of comparison with respect to the weight assigned to deterrence, the analogy may be instructive.

Thirdly, at a totally different level, we need to consider what has popularly become known as "the slippery slope"—the concern that acceptance of certain innovations, even if they are Halakhically tenable, may invite pressures for further progressive change, resulting, incrementally, in the erosion of traditional sensibility or even outright Halakhic violation. This issue has been raised most vigorously with respect to various initiatives concerning the role of women. Within the Torah world and the rabbinic establishment, response to these has been widely divergent. Some have contended that whatever the *Shulhan Arukh* does not proscribe could be regarded with favor. Others have rejected this premise as a general approach; and they have further resisted any innovation, particularly if fueled by feminist ideology, on the grounds that it might lead to further demands or trigger a domino effect. And, there is, of course, a spectrum of intermediate responses.

Here again, we need to maintain a dual watch. The concern about the slippery slope is, in principle, both legitimate and genuine. It is firmly rooted in Hazal, who anchored many *gezerot* upon it, as graphically illustrated in the Rambam's explanation as to the basis of the prohibition against fowl cooked with milk:

> But if it [i.e., the court] says: "The meat of the fowl is permitted by the Torah, and we (a) shall forbid it; and we shall inform the people that this is a Rabbinic

> [precautionary] injunction, so that no liability derive therefrom, [as would occur] if they were [inclined] to say—fowl meat is permitted, because it is not explicitly prohibited, so the flesh of a wild animal is permitted because it is not explicitly forbidden; and someone else will also say even the flesh of a [domestic] animal is permitted except for the flesh of a goat; and (b) someone also will say even the meat of a goat is permitted with the milk of a cow or sheep, as only the [goat's] mother is explicityly prohibited; and someone else will say that even with the milk of any goat but the mother it is permitted, as only the mother's is explicityly prohibited; therefore we shall prohibit even the fowl meat, it [i.e., the court] is not adding [to the Torah] but making a fence around the Torah and so it is with similar matters.[31]

In this case, one encounters outright *d'oraitha* violation early in the chain. The principle is in force, however, even when that is not the case.

Yet, in applying the principle, two factors need to be weighed. We shall have to evaluate, first, the likely course of events. How truly slippery is the slope? What innovation is likely, and how likely, to generate which kind of pressures? Second, we shall need to examine at what cost—whether in the form of possible alienation of certain constituencies or in the impairment or dilution of the quality of spiritual life—the presumed security of an ultra-conservative stance is being attained. This last factor will itself require dual consideration, as we strive both to perceive the prospects of various alternative scenarios on the ground and to determine how much weight to assign this particular concern.

As for myself, I presume that, with respect to both the women's issues, specifically, and the fear of the slippery slope, generally, I find myself somewhere in the middle—enthusiastically supportive of some changes, resistant to others, and ambivalent about many; but I take it that this is not the venue for dealing with the details of various agendas. I feel strongly, however, in conclusion, that none of us can be content with a middling position with regard to a corollary issue. If we cannot countenance egalitarianism as a total ideology, and we cannot rally behind its comprehensive platform, we need to labor to assure that its positive component, respect for *zelem E-lohim*, be properly internalized and inculcated. The formulation of my question notwithstanding, that concept does not mandate, for us, "equal respect for all persons." It demands that all, equally, be regarded with respect, but its quality may differ. We subscribe to both parts of Rabbi Akiva's familiar formulation. At one plane, "Beloved is man because he was created in His image"; additionally, however, "Beloved is Israel who are called the children [of G-d]."[32] And what is true of affection, translates into esteem. While a balance between the ethnic and the universal is variously struck in some of our most fundamental and familiar sources—in *pesukei d'zimrah*, for instance, in one sense, and, most notably, in the opening of *shema*, in another—that balance is often insufficiently appreciated and inculcated within our Torah community.

Its neglect is, however, spiritually unconscionable and pragmatically foolhardy. We need to ascertain that, as we insist that the universal element not effectively neutralize the particularistic, we be equally insistent that the reverse not occur. If our response to the egalitarian manifesto is resistant, we are charged with the moral, religious, and educational responsibility to find compensatory means to assure that Ben Azzai's overarching principle, "'This is the book of the generations of man'—this is a greater rule than this one,"[33] attain—in our homes, in our schools, in our hearts—the position it deserves. That we owe not just to the other—in Milton's phrase, "the human face divine." That we owe to the Ribbono Shel Olam, and to ourselves.

NOTES

1. See *Teshuvah* 3:8.
2. *Perush Hamishnayot*, preface to ch. 10 of *Sanhedrin*, tr. Rav Y. D. Kapah (Jerusalem, 1965), p. 144. In his notes, Rav Kapah addresses a parallel text from *Mishneh Torah*, *Melakhim* 11:6, which due to censorship, has been omitted from most of the printed editions.
3. See *Yebamot* 89b–90b, and *Gittin* 4:2, respectively.
4. *Horayot* 4a; cf. *Sanhedrin* 33b.
5. *Mamrim* 2:1. Inasmuch as the Rambam does not qualify, as he does in the next *halakhah*, that only a greater *beit din* is authorized to reverse its predecessor's decision, it seems clear that even a lesser one is entitled to do so.
6. *Dev.* 18:21–22.
7. *Ad locum*, 18:22.
8. *Sanhedrin* 89b.
9. *Dev.* 18:21.
10. *Sanhedrin* 89b, s.v. *heikha*.
11. *Yesodei Hatorah*, 7:7; and cf. ch. 8, *passim*, and 10:1–3.
12. *Berakhot* 7b; and cf. *Tosafot*, *Ketubot* 17a, s.v. *mevatlin*.
13. *Horayot* 13a.
14. To the trio of themes previously cited might be added: the quest for parity within relationships. This has particularly come to the fore in the context of feminism, with respect to marriage. The issue is important, but here I have largely skirted it; inasmuch as I believe that feminism is qualitatively different from other manifestations of egalitarianism cited. Conceptually, its claims are less radical and more limited in scope. Practically, despite some confrontations with the prevailing social order, generally, and the world of Halakhah, specifically, its challenge to tradition is hardly of a piece with intermarriage or abortion, and should be dealt with independently. Neither the challenge nor the response to it revolves around levels of *kedushah* or personal autonomy, although, admittedly, some conceptual links and certain operational alliances do exist. I am inclined to think that the linkage is greater within the broader sociological context than within our specific Jewish community. I grant, however, that this assessment—with respect to the American scene, largely the per-

ception of an outsider—is open to challenge. In any event, the fuller treatment the issue deserves lies beyond my present scope.

15. *Vay.* 19:15.

16. *Kedoshim*, 4:3.

17. *Shabbat* 127a–b, *A.d.R.N.*, 8:7–8, and *Sh'iltot d'Rabbi Ahai Gaon*, *Sh'ilta* 40, respectively.

18. *Abot*, 2:4.

19. *Berakhot* 10a. Of course, at the level of pure *peshat*, the word *chataim*, with the *dagesh* in the *tet*, is the *nomen agentis* for sinners. The *derash* relates to the use of this unusual form which resembles the plural of sins.

20. "Introduction" in Yehudah Even Shmuel's translation. Of course, as reflected in the concluding coda, part of the thrust of the work is the undermining of this thesis, by way of stressing the need for conjoined action and intention.

21. *Baba Kama* 38b, *Nazir* 23b, *Horayot* 10b.

22. See *Sanhedrin* 58b.

23. *Issurei Bi'ah* 14:10 and *Bet Habehirah*, *Sanhedrin* 58b, respectively.

24. See the *gemarot* previously cited and Rashi, *Ber.* 19:33, respectively. The Ramban, however, focusing upon their longing for progeny—and, probably, upon midrashic statement—takes a much more positive view of their motivation, and even of the initiative proper: And perhaps [it might be suggested] that they said let us do that deed which is appropriate for us, and perhaps G-d will have mercy and we will give birth to a male and female children, and the world will be preserved through them, as "the world will be built on kindness" (Psalms 89,3). Not for nothing did G-d save us. And behold that they were modest, and did not wish to say to their father that they should marry them, even though Noachites are permitted to marry their daughters. Perhaps (the act) was most repulsive in the eyes of the generation and it had not been done ever (m'olom).

25. *Sotah* 47a.

26. *Yebamot* 65b.

27. See *Menahot* 109a, and *Tosafot*, s.v. *lo*; *Tosafot*, *Sotah* 39a, s.v. *vekhi*; *Shibbolei Haleket*, sec. 33; Rambam, *Nessiat Kapayim*, 15:3.

28. *Bet Yosef*, *Orah Haym*, 128, assumed that the controversy was confined to a *kohen* who had converted willingly, but that if the conversion was coerced, all would agree that his status as a *kohen* remained intact; and, in *Shulhan Arukh*, *O.H.*, 128:37, he decided accordingly. However, as noted in *Bedek Habayit*'s comment on the *Bet Yosef*, the Rambam clearly appears to have disqualified even in the case of duress.

29. These are two separate factors. The first would only disqualify the *kohen* from *nessiat kapayim*, the second from priority in *keriat hatorah*, as well.

30. Cited in *Mahzor Vitry*, sec. 125.

31. *Mamrim* 2:9.

32. *Abot* 3:14.

33. *Torat Kohanim*, *Kedoshim* 7:4:12.

3

Formulating Responses in an Egalitarian Age: An Overview

Suzanne Last Stone

The modern ideal of human equality reverses the long-standing trend of societies to discriminate between human beings on ontological, racial, sexual, or religious grounds. Whether or not the pattern of human history displays a steady progression toward equality, egalitarianism is certainly the pervasive spirit of our age. Those who are imbued with the egalitarian ideal view equality not only as a basic corollary of fairness, which demands symmetry of treatment within human relations, but also as a crucial means to avoid humiliation of others and to promote collective bonds of affection within the political community.

The premises of egalitarianism are in tension with central aspects of Judaism, beginning with Judaism's relationship to others. The basic themes of Jewish distinctiveness, chosenness, and separation find expression not only in Jewish theology but also in Jewish law. The religio-legal obligations of Jews differ from those of non-Jews and non-Jews do not enjoy equality of treatment under Jewish civil and criminal law. Jews owe less obligations of solidarity to non-Jews than they do to their fellow Jews. Segregative rules extend well beyond the prohibition on intermarriage. Moreover, the discriminatory rules of the *halakhah*, the idea of chosenness, as well as older patterns of distrust stemming from a long history of persecution, combine to foster an unfortunate attitude of disdain toward and even denigration of non-Jews.

Jewish particularity is not the sole issue. Traditional Jewish society is organized on non-egalitarian terms, as evidenced by the differential obligations, and therefore rights, of Jewish men and women. Moreover, religious objections to certain forms of conduct, such as homosexual activity or abortions, affect Orthodox Jewish attitudes toward the pursuit of equality in civil society. Some Orthodox Jews fear that the pursuit of equality in contemporary America not only threatens to undermine the basic social organization of Judaism but also is undermining the moral quality of the larger political community. Religious objections to homosexual activity and abortions have caused some within the Orthodox community to oppose equal rights for gays and women even within non-Jewish society.

Yet many modern Orthodox Jews are increasingly discomforted by the discriminatory rules of the *halakhah* and especially by the persisting pattern within orthodoxy of denigrating others. This discomfort is not solely attributable to the penetration of general societal attitudes into modern orthodoxy. First, the contemporary setting of Judaism in America differs from prior historical settings in ways that profoundly affect Jewish attitudes toward equality. American egalitarianism finds expression not only through abstract devotion to the principle of equality. It is concretely expressed through the unparalleled grant of opportunities to religious Jews to participate in society, even to lead it (as the 2000 election dramatized). Traditional Jews who are sympathetic to civic equality as a political ideal and to norms of mutuality and respect between groups as ethical ideals are impelled not only by considerations of abstract principle but also by feelings of gratitude and the laudatory human desire to reciprocate beneficence. One critical question raised in this volume is whether reciprocity is a halakhic value, one that should be recognized and affirmed in a new age characterized by the creation of just societies, and evidenced specifically by the decent treatment of Jews.

Second, the ideal of human equality that is at the core of egalitarianism is rooted in a view of humans that comports with the universalist dimension of biblical and rabbinic thought. Egalitarianism rests on a vision of man captured by the biblical assertion that all humans are created in the image of God. The idea of human creation in God's image implies that all people share a basic similitude and worth, despite differences of race, gender, and religion. A second critical question addressed in this volume is whether the concept of creation *be'tzelem*, which until now has played a muted role in rabbinic thought, can provide a basis for increased openness and sensitivity within the *halakhah* to modern ideas about equality and tolerance.

In this overview, I have been invited to address two questions. The first is as follows: "How should we respond" to societal changes ushered in by the egalitarian age that "are motivated by a combination of both positive factors of equal respect for all persons as a manifestation of *tzelem Elohim* and negative factors (for example, tolerance of sexual practices beyond halakhic norms)"? In evaluating what form of response best comports with halakhic norms, ethical aspirations, and communal needs, we may expect to find that the halakhic, ethical, and pragmatic implications of egalitarianism will be in some tension with one another. This raises the sensitive question whether ethical ideals and practical concerns may shape or even alter halakhic norms. Accordingly, I also have been asked to address how one distinguishes "between ordinary halakhic processes responding to new stimuli, and calls for direct revision of a divinely inspired, permanently fixed Torah." Although the transcendental nature of Torah sharpens the wish to clarify and maintain this distinction, all legal systems struggle with defining the difference between the application of legal norms in light of new conditions in society and direct revision of a permanent law. I shall offer here my own views on this distinction, drawing both on rabbinic sources and parallel discussions in American law.

I

There are several ways to structure the relationship of *halakhah* to a new historical age or social phenomenon. Current social settings may simply be treated as neutral background facts that are largely irrelevant to the application of halakhic norms to concrete questions except insofar as they make new questions possible or remove prior questions from the table. Often, however, in the course of *p'sak*, a historical age itself must be contextualized and understood in order to determine how to fashion an appropriate halakhic response.

What then is meant by the "egalitarian age"? The choice of the term "the age of egalitarianism" for this volume, rather than "the age of equality," is intended to capture both the positive and negative aspects of the pursuit of equality in contemporary American culture. The constitutional protection of abortions, private homosexual activity, and potentially gay marriage on equality grounds within general society, as well as the increasing breakdown of the historic attitude against intermarriage within Jewish society, have led some to associate egalitarianism with moral relativism and devotion to personal autonomy, both clearly problematic from a halakhic perspective. As a result, the genuine ethical passion for equality that underlies the egalitarian ethos is all too often slighted. It is important, therefore, to define and distinguish the variety of related, yet distinct, ideals and ideologies that characterize our age: equality, personal autonomy, liberal toleration, identity politics, and the acceptance of morally diverse ways of life.

Egalitarianism, strictly speaking, concerns only "the story of equality."[1] How it emerged and what functions it performs in American society are critical to its evaluation. The political roots of egalitarianism lie in the rise of nationalism. In the West, national identity is conceived in political terms. With the French Revolution, the modern terms of national identity were set. National identity is achieved by re-organizing former corporate groups, such as Jews, into equal, rights-bearing individuals as the price of citizenship. While individuals can be full members of traditional societies without possessing the same status, entitlements, or duties as other members, in modern pluralistic nations membership is defined by equality. Discrimination on the basis of race, religion, national origin, sex, and the like is viewed as denying full membership in the national community. This understanding of national identity reaches its pinnacle in the United States. America lacks a common culture of ethnicity, religion, or language to give it a national identity. Instead, national identity is defined by and consists of a small set of shared civic values, chief among them equality.[2] Equal rights bond citizens together as members of the nation and promote a collective bond of affection and loyalty.

Beneath the political roots of egalitarianism is a set of philosophical and religious ideas that have transformed the way Western societies envision divisions between humans. Egalitarianism's near philosophical root is probably in Kant's philosophical anthropology. Kant views equality as a corollary of fairness, of "symmetry or parity of treatment" in human relations, and he joins this with "a vision of man in which our real identity is tied to something identical in all of us—our rationality." All other differentiations between humans are "relegated to a morally inferior realm . . . the realm of mere appearance."[3] Egalitarianism's larger cultural roots also can be traced back to Christianity. Protestant Christianity, in particular, assumes that society consists of discrete individuals, which has led thinkers to distinguish between the person as a moral agent, the "primary role shared by all equally," and a person's secondary social role, such as his or her religion, nationality, or gender.[4] The intensification of this idea in the Protestant notion of the equality of believers played a central role in the philosophy of America's founders. All these ideas converge into a worldview that refuses to divide humans hierarchically into different kinds of beings.

Despite the long roots of the egalitarian ideal, egalitarianism only truly penetrated American society forty years ago, with the civil rights revolution of the 1960s. The logical trajectory of the civil rights revolution also produced, some claim, egalitarianism's other characteristics, moral relativism and devotion to personal autonomy. But we should be careful not to conflate these ideas, and, as a consequence, obscure the genuine ethical power of the idea of equality that is at the core of egalitarianism. In theory, there is no necessary connection between the pursuit of equality, on the one hand, and moral relativism or devotion to personal autonomy, on the other. One can easily conceive of a heteronomous system, a system in which the source of authority is divine legislation structured around a set of concrete obligations, in which equality, parity of treatment, and even the metaphysical uniformity of man are, nevertheless, regarded as basic principles and values. Moreover, the current acceptance of morally diverse ways of life is more properly understood as an outgrowth of liberal notions of tolerance, and not as an outgrowth of the ideal of equality.

According to the classical liberal formulation, tolerance is the willingness to live with ideas or practices that are regarded as erroneous and even reprehensible.[5] Liberal tolerance grew out of the religious wars that marked pre-Enlightenment Western civilization. In the wake of religious strife and bloody and ineffective coercion, liberal thinkers advocated tolerance of erroneous ideas and practices in order to maintain social peace and to enhance diversity of opinion. Religious toleration and later toleration of minorities such as Jews, Catholics, African Americans, homosexuals, and so on, call for restraint in response to various beliefs or practices, not because they are acceptable, but because we value personal autonomy (Mill) or view religious coercion as counterproductive (Locke), or because we value civil peace between the diverse groups within the nation. By definition, classical liberal tolerance is the opposite of moral relativism. The demand for tolerance, strictly speaking, only arises once an activity is judged morally wrong. Tolerance regulates how society responds to such activities.

Tolerance has developed in American society, however, in a way that resembles moral indifference, the easy acceptance of heterogeneous moral values and ways of life. In America, where the liberal distinction between public and private realms is sharp, toleration and respect for privacy have become equated. Most moral issues have been relegated to the private domain, while the public domain aspires to be, for the most part, morally neutral. Certain beliefs or practices are deemed private and almost by definition to be tolerated. This results in what might be called a "principled indifference—one has no right to intervene in private matters or even to judge them."[6] Private matters are now enshrined as substantive constitutional values and extended dramatically in recent years to cover abortion and, most recently, private, consensual gay activity.

The age we live in is also determinedly multicultural. Multiculturalism, the so-called "politics of recognition," has brought with it a demand for a new and different form of tolerance: pluralism. This, in turn, has created a culture of public acceptance of morally diverse ways of life.[7] The emergence of multiculturalism as a new political ideal in Western societies is, in part, a reaction against Enlightenment ideals. It is a reaction against the relegation of group particularity to the sphere of private life. As Charles Taylor tells it, its roots can be traced to the idea of authenticity.[8] The contemporary ideal of authenticity translates into a demand for public recognition of the individual as a member of a particular group to which his or her identity is tied. In other words, one can no longer be a Jew at home and a citizen (the same as everyone else) in public if one wishes to be "authentic." Different identities not only should be disregarded as a basis for disqualification from various entitlement rights—for example, gay identity may not form the basis for denial of rights to vote, public housing, and so on Instead, different identities should be given public recognition through public affirmation of the worth of identity groups and of the value of different lifestyles.

I have argued that egalitarianism and an attitude of indifference to morally diverse ways of life grow out of different political and philosophic assumptions. Egalitarianism is rooted in political and philosophic assumptions about human equality, while the acceptance of morally diverse ways of life is rooted in the postmodern transformation of the concept of tolerance. This does not make the task of formulating Orthodox Jewish responses to the present legal and social culture, taken in its entirety, easier. But it allows us to refocus attention on the ethical and pragmatic issues we face in a more cogent and systematic fashion. We face two distinct questions. First, does the *halakhah* have the capacity for greater openness to equality as an ethical ideal and to norms of mutuality and respect between persons, especially Jews and non-Jews? In other words, what is the appropriate balance between the particularist and universalist dimensions of Judaism? Second, what degree of tolerance should be extended to groups that pursue ways of life antithetical to halakhic norms? Before turning to these questions, allow me to comment briefly on the ethical and pragmatic dimensions of egalitarianism, as they affect the Jewish community.

II

How should religious Jews assess the values that characterize the egalitarian age? Halakhic responses to new social conditions too often are viewed as necessary accommodations to inescapable parts of life, or deserving attention primarily because they affect the security of the Jewish community. In this volume, however, we approach the issue in the spirit of free inquiry by asking whether aspects of egalitarianism have independent ethical value deserving our commitment, if possible, or reflect values latent in the *halakhah* which should be given further expression and development in this new age. This approach particularly befits a new stage in Jewish history, in which observant Jews are no longer merely responding to their social and political environment but, rather, here and especially in Israel, actively creating it. American Jews live in a uniquely tolerant society that grants orthodox Jews the power to assume leadership positions, a privilege that carries with it the responsibility not to react simply as a beleaguered minority. Jews in Israel are reconstituted as a political society. As the majority people in power, Jews are singularly responsible for shaping the ethos of that society.

The ethical appeal of egalitarianism need not be belabored. One may concede that in principle the *halakhah* does not contemplate an egalitarian political society, and, indeed, poses considerable obstacles to its achievement in Jewish political society. Yet, a return to a caste society that discriminated against minority groups or women in the public sphere would be deeply morally disturbing to all of us. Many of us are equally troubled by halakhic norms that discriminate against non-Jews in the private sphere of Judaism, that restrict norms of mutuality and social solidarity, and that perpetuate an attitude of disdain. Apart from abstract questions of principle, the privileged situation of American Jews gives rise to an additional ethical dilemma. Do Jews, who have benefited so dramatically from the spirit of egalitarianism, have an ethical obligation to reciprocate by supporting the struggle of other groups to achieve the civic equality that defines membership in our shared nation? Indeed, is reciprocity an ethical factor that ideally should affect how non-Jews are treated under Jewish law itself? Positing an unlimited obligation of Jews to reciprocate by supporting equal treatment of all identity groups in society, however, is equally ethically problematic. It would deny the political community to which we belong the moral perspectives of our tradition.

Concededly, American Jews also have a practical interest in fostering religious toleration and must examine carefully how egalitarianism and religious rights of free exercise are interconnected. There are those who argue that gay and other identity group rights are rooted in the principle of religious toleration.[9] Such arguments raise the question whether we should refrain from voicing any objection to same-sex marriage, for example, in order to cast a protective net around religious toleration. Judicial equation of identity group rights with the idea of freedom of conscience, which is the core principle of religious toleration, is unlikely.[10] Yet, there remains the practical question whether affirmation of group identity rights fosters a culture that is anti-assimilationist, more liable to decrease intermarriage, and particularly receptive to the free exercise claims of religious groups. Logic alone suggests that the more equality is instantiated in society generally, the more religious rights of Jews will be protected. Orthodox Jews have thrived in the new multicultural environment. It is far easier to be a religious Jew than at any other time in American history and far easier to pursue Jewish communal needs in the public realm. There are, to be sure, costs to such expanded religious opportunities. First, we must share public space with other groups whose values and lifestyles may be antithetical to halakhic norms. Second, the more equality is instantiated in society, the more it threatens to become a comprehensive principle. Not only does the instantiation of equality in society as a comprehensive norm increase intellectual tensions for observant Jews, it also poses the specter of governmental imposition of equality as a norm in the private realm of Jewish society.

From the perspective of ethics and practical politics, norms of equality and reciprocity clearly deserve our more active support. Accordingly, we reach the question whether it is possible to forge a bridge between *halakhah* and the egalitarian idea. Although that bridge may be subject to limitations, there is a growing sense that equality and reciprocity are values latent in the *halakhah* that require further development. Specifically, we should examine more carefully whether various minority views, such as that of Menahem ha-Me'iri, have been underutilized. Second, we should investigate whether halakhic principles that have a more universalist dimension, such as creation *be-tzelem* and *darkhei shalom*, might be elaborated so as to become more powerful means of fostering norms of equality and mutuality.

III

This threefold inquiry—assessment of the ethical value of equality, practical evaluation of the needs of our community, and the creative examination of halakhic precedents and principles—bears on the second question I have been asked to address for this volume: How do we distinguish "ordinary halakhic processes responding to new stimuli" from calls for direct revision of Torah? In other words, at what point does reliance on subjective ethical intuitions, on pragmatic factors, and on creative reinterpretations become an illegitimate attempt to change *halakhah* in order to conform Torah to contemporary ideology?

All legal systems face a version of this question. The Constitution, for example, is written, enacted law and can be changed only through amendment, not judicial interpretation. At what point does judicial discretion to interpret the United States Constitution become an illegitimate and unauthorized attempt to rewrite the Constitution in light of present ideology? The religious dimension of *halakhah*, however, introduces a far more anxious quality to the discussion. Torah, unlike the Constitution, is, after all, a transcendental and not a human document. The transcendental nature of Torah can paralyze decision making for fear that the Torah will be distorted. At the same time, the religious dimension of *halakhah* provides more leeways of judicial discretion than exist within other legal systems. Judges have the power to deviate from the law in order to effectuate the spirit of Torah.[11] This authority implies that greater trust is accorded the judge within the halakhic system than is true in other legal systems, where judicial discretion is viewed as in need of constraint. Such expanded authority is dependent on the community's perception of the judge as "the embodiment of Torah." Given this perspective, halakhic authority to innovate could be formulated, in broad terms, as dependent on two factors: first, the use of legal arguments that are recognizably within the authoritative tradition of *halakhah* and, second, their articulation by authorities who are recognized as Torah personalities—individuals with knowledge and, as Rashi put it, "purity of intent."[12] The first part of the test has analogues in secular jurisprudence.[13] The second is unique.[14]

This broad formulation, however, begs the critical issues we face today. Contemporary halakhic activity is set within an increasingly polarized community. On the one hand, halakhic authorities with the communal support to rule boldly are often perceived as insulated from knowledge of and exposure to new social conditions. Moreover, with few exceptions, they function within communities that do not reflect the worldview of modern orthodoxy, which places emphasis on openness to outside culture and universal aspects of *halakhah*. There also is a pervasive sense that halakhic decisors are generally reluctant to rule as boldly as was the case in the past.[15] On the other hand, orthodoxy is also concerned with articulating a response to increasing calls for direct revision of Torah in order to accommodate new ideologies. Such calls tend to proceed from the assumption that historical evidence of halakhic change in the past in itself provides authority for changing at will halakhic norms that are incompatible with the spirit of a new age. In light of both sets of current concerns, it is important to attempt to articulate more clearly the difference between relying on ethical concerns or more open-ended halakhic values in applying *halakhah* to new social conditions and illegitimate revision of *halakhah*. The halakhic corpus, needless to say, does not provide us with an explicit test to discern the difference between legitimate legal application and illegitimate legal change. American constitutional law and theory have been far more self-consciously deliberative in attempting to define the distinction between legitimate interpretation and application and illegitimate change and I shall draw on that literature in my own attempt to clarify this distinction.

A pivotal question bearing on this distinction concerns the role of morality or ethics in shaping halakhic norms. Although the relationship of law and morality is a problem in any legal system, the problem is exacerbated within a religious legal system. On the one hand, the *halakhah*, as the reflection of divine law, is thought to provide the definition of morality. Therefore, independent moral perceptions must be measured and judged in light of the *halakhah*. The danger of redirecting *halakhah* in light of present ethical sensibilities is felt to be all the more acute when ethical perceptions are stimulated by living in a society not governed exclusively by the value-system and ethos of the *halakhah*. On the other hand, the religious impulse to equate *halakhah* with morality itself leads to the question whether a norm that seems unjust is a result of incomplete or insufficient halakhic development or interpretation. New interpretations stimulated by living in a new age, in this view, do not redirect the halakhic process; rather, they uncover the *halakhah* as it was ideally intended to develop.

The question whether there is an ethic independent of *halakhah* has been discussed at length. Rabbi Lichtenstein, in his seminal article on that topic, makes the critical intervention that the classical depiction of *halakhah* as self-sufficient is inadequate. The *halakhah* contains gaps—areas in which it does not speak with specificity. Judges have no choice but to fill gaps in such cases and must resort to independent judgment, a judgment that should be informed by ethical thinking.[16] The idea that *halakhah* has gaps or is, to some degree, incomplete, is itself controversial. It challenges one traditional picture of *halakhah* as a comprehensive and complete set of legal norms rooted in divine command.[17] Far more controversial is the role of ethical perceptions in cases where no clear halakhic gap exists. Is there an ethic independent of *halakhah* by which the *halakhah* itself is interpreted?

The question whether halakhic norms are subject to interpretation in light of ethical values and intuitions is only one aspect of a much larger set of questions concerning the role of extra-halakhic considerations, not derivable from concrete halakhic norms, in applying *halakhah*. Extra-legal considerations may be rooted in moral or philosophical thinking, in the ethical thrust of *aggadot*, in political or economic realia, or in actual practices of the Jewish community. The very description of these considerations as "extra-halakhic" derives from a conception of *halakhah* as consisting solely of concrete legal norms. This understanding of *halakhah* conforms to the classical positivist definition of law as autonomous from all other disciplines, including moral, economic, philosophic, or political thought, and confined to the rules recognized as authoritative within a particular legal system.[18] It also is associated with the classical understanding of law as proceeding according to standards of legal reasoning that are objective on the order of mathematics, a mode of legal reasoning called formalism. Formalism asserts that the application of law takes place through a distinctive form of legal reasoning that has an axiomatic-deductive structure like geometry. Demonstrably correct, rather than merely plausible or reasonable answers to legal questions can be found by reasoning solely from authoritative rules. "Decisions follow deductively from the rules; the judge, as person," contributes little to the outcome.[19]

Pursuant to both understandings of law, judges apply the rules to new situations. They do not exercise discretion, except in cases where there is a gap in the rules themselves. Ethical considerations are not concrete and specific. They are debatable and, therefore, are not part of the system of legal rules. The geonic interdiction against deriving halakhic norms from the *aggadah* reflects this viewpoint.[20] The *aggadah* is too vague and subjective to constitute part of the legal corpus. Taken together, law's autonomy and formalism allow us to describe any legal "change" that occurs over time as one contemplated by the lawgiver and not as the product of judicial subjectivity. Rather, law has its own internal logic implanted in it and, therefore, when it seems to change, it does so in response to the promptings of its inner nature, like a caterpillar turning into a moth. According to this view, any perceived halakhic "change" was contemplated and foreseen by the divine lawgiver, who implanted the concrete norms and methods of legal reasoning into the *halakhah*.

Positivism, formalism, and law's autonomy from morality are descriptive theories increasingly challenged in current schools of legal thought. One objection to these theories is that they do not give adequate weight to the creative aspects inhering in the act of judicial interpretation. Another objection is that they give an inadequate account of the authoritative sources of law by confining these sources to concrete rules. Depictions of law and the process of legal interpretation different from the classical models now claim attention. The impetus for rethinking models of law in American jurisprudence was also a conflict between law and morality revolving around issues of equality. Modern models of law arose from a general effort to rethink how the Supreme Court could have avoided upholding slavery and all its later infections during the Dred Scott era and from a specific effort to secure the legitimacy of the Supreme Court's decision in *Brown v. Board of Education*.[21] In that opinion, the Court held segregation unconstitutional, without overruling prior precedent reaching the opposite result. The moral goodness of *Brown* is nearly universally acknowledged but the legal basis of *Brown*, given prior authoritative sources, is difficult to discern.

Modern challenges to positivism can be distilled into three. According to the legal realists, judges do not apply law through deductive methods. They make and change the law, unconsciously or deliberately, however much they may adhere to the rhetoric of the constraining force of precedent or of the formal application of norms. Judicial interpretation reflects the judge's ideological concerns and biases formed by the judge's life history. This may endanger the autonomy, integrity, and even legitimacy of law, but it is unavoidable reality.[22] According to natural law theory, a counter-tradition in Anglo-American law, the concept of law necessarily includes a moral element. A rule is not truly law unless it satisfies a moral test of acceptability.[23] In other versions, law is not the judicial decision, but law as it ought to be.[24] In this view, the judicial task has no gap-filling or law-making aspect but consists solely of discovering the law as it really was. Both schools of thought account for *Brown*. But neither gives an account of law as autonomous, as its own special discipline, nor an account of the difference between legal interpretation and legal change and, therefore, neither is viewed as a serious challenge to the classical positivist model.

What is now deemed "the third theory of law"[25] attempts to bridge the gap between positivism and naturalism by linking law to morality while still preserving law's autonomy. Its most forceful articulator is Ronald Dworkin.[26] Dworkin does not offer a universal definition of the concept of law. To know what the law is, Dworkin asserts, it is necessary to start with that which is recognized as law in a particular legal culture. In the Anglo-American legal system, the norms and opinions that positivists regard as exhaustive of law are not all that is internal to the law. Law does not consist solely of concrete norms or rules. Law also consists of values and principles, which are implanted in the legal system at its base. These values and principles, which are the internal aims and ends of the law, have gravitational weight in decision making that cannot be predicted in advance. They guide the judge in reading an authoritative text or prior opinion, in deciding how much weight to give prior opinions, or in deciding whether a rule or norm is applicable to the case at hand.[27] Legal interpretation is a purposive activity, in which judges must consider the point of the practice—the legal system's aim and ends—while applying authoritative rules. All the sources of a legal system, including its rules, values, and principles, must be made coherent and brought out in their best moral light. This purposive activity is not the ordinary stuff of judging, which is often mechanical. It is, however, called into play in "hard cases," such as *Brown*, where prior legal norms must be applied to changed societal conditions. Together, rules and principles, however, are sufficient to cover even hard cases. Law does not, in this theory, have gaps and judges do not make law in the gaps. Nor do judges "exercise discretion except in the weak sense of bringing to bear their judgment in interpreting the law."[28] Thus, Dworkin defends the formalist position that the law determines the outcome of cases. Judges discover the right legal answer by coordinating the rules and principles.

One of Dworkin's principal aims is to describe how legal continuity coexists with legal creativity. Hercules, Dworkin's model judge, is not a legal reformer. He is, however, a path-breaking interpreter, creative, and unconventional. Hercules must decide for himself what the practice requires and must not think about what other members of the legal community believe the practice requires or what future members might think of his work. Dworkin's model of interpretation is entirely backward looking—at the authoritative sources requiring interpretation—and not outward-looking at other judges. Nor is it forward-looking. The conscious decision to depart from prior norms in order to meet present or future needs of society is not a legitimate act of interpretation. Thus, he analogizes legal interpretation to the writing of a chain novel that the judge inherits and then must continue by writing the next chapter.[29] How that chapter is received, in turn, is of no concern to the judge. Ultimately, time will bear out whether Hercules correctly perceived the point of the practice. An interpretation viewed radical in its day may appear far less so over time.[30] The historical situatedness of the judge enhances legal creativity but legal creativity does not constitute deliberate reform or conscious legal change, given the backward-looking nature of interpretation and its confinement to authoritative sources internal to the law.

Turning now to the halakhic system, I want to briefly address the following questions: Is the application of *halakhah* to new societal conditions best described in terms of the classical positivist model of law, as the objective application of concrete rules, or can it be conceived as a purposive activity, in which the range of possible applications of a legal norm are determined in light of its overall aims and ends? Are values and principles also internal to the halakhic system and thus properly viewed as authoritative sources of the law? Is the determination of the law's aims and ends legitimately influenced by the judge's historical situatedness and, if so, how does one distinguish between legitimate interpretation and illegitimate revision of halakhic norms to conform them to values prevalent in current society?

These issues are well illustrated by halakhic approaches to the question whether religious behavior should be coerced indirectly through "religious" legislation in a societal age characterized by secularism and freedom. Halakhists have offered radically different opinions on this matter, reflecting different views of the aims of halakhic norms and different assessments of the progress of civilization. Thus, one may hold that religious coercion is a halakhic ideal and that religious legislation is mandatory. Or, one may take the position that coercion is an ideal applicable only when it has the capacity to bring about internal assent, possible in a religious but not in a secular age.[31] Or, one may take the position that religious coercion is not the ideal of *halakhah*; rather, coercion is antithetical to the general thrust of *halakhah* to limit punishment, and therefore the range of its application in an age of freedom may properly be restricted.[32] Judgments of this kind involve not only an evaluation of the thrust of *halakhah* itself but also an ethical evaluation of the positive or negative features of historical development. One may view the freedom ushered in by modernity as negative, a reflection of "God's hiddenness" that separates the Jew from Torah observance,[33] or as positive, leading to a more ideal state of religious observance.[34]

Thus, defining the range of application of a preexisting halakhic norm in new societal conditions calls into play evaluative judgments about the purpose of the halakhic norm within the overall system of *halakhah* as well as its fit with the conditions of a new age. This evaluative judgment takes place in time. The "historical formation of an authentic Jewish consciousness" should be frankly acknowledged.[35] Subjective ethical intuitions accessible at a particular historical time shape how the *posek* interprets and weighs authoritative sources as well as how he assesses the purpose of halakhic norms.

It may be argued that it is solely the inner logic of halakhic norms and the *posek*'s grasp of and identification with the "halakhic worldview" that determines how characteristics of an age are evaluated, whether positively or negatively. But there is clearly an interrelationship between halakhic values and societal change because the *posek*'s own historical situatedness affects the way he will perceive the thrust of halakhic norms and values in the first place. Thus, there is no pre-interpretive meaningful distinction between so-called foreign values and values internal to the halakhic system. One cannot know whether the value is foreign or internal until one engages in the act of interpretation itself. Voluntarism in matters of religion is a hallmark of modern liberal thought, yet some halakhists have discerned precisely this value within *halakhah*. The apprehension that religious coercion is a concession, and not an ideal, reflects an insight about halakhic norms and values accessible to a *posek* only at a particular point of historical or moral development in general society.

Consider increased efforts today to equalize the rights of women with that of men with respect to Jewish divorce. These efforts are attributable, in part, to the historical situatedness of halakhic authorities in an age of equality. It is not necessarily that "foreign values" have penetrated halakhic thought but, rather, that the historical situation allows us to see more vividly that the trajectory of Jewish divorce law from the biblical to the modern period is largely one of increasing halakhic efforts to ameliorate the status of women and equalize their rights with those of men. Developments in general society, such as enhanced equality between the sexes, may become a catalyst for halakhic innovation because a *posek*'s historical situatedness leads to the insight that the *halakhah*'s own values as yet have been imperfectly realized.

The claim that interpretation and application of halakhic norms in new societal conditions may be described as a purposive activity, requiring coordination of concrete norms with an evaluative assessment of their ideal aim—one necessarily influenced by the *posek*'s historical situatedness—should be distinguished from the argument that *halakhah* is revisable at will in order to conform it to new ideas appearing in general society that seem ethically compelling. The distinction between the two, as by now should be clear, is that between (re)interpretation—a backward-looking reassessment of all the authoritative sources of law in light of the law's internal aims and purposes—and conscious revision in the sense of an intentional act of departure from the norms and aims of the law. (The distinction might also be formulated as that between creativity and human conceit.) Yet, increasingly, arguments circulate about "the need for change to be introduced into Jewish law through a true understanding of its historical development."[36] Calls for conscious reform of halakhic norms based on historical evidence of legal change in the past have two defects. First, they turn historical arguments into normative ones. Second, they tend to adopt a viewpoint of the distinction between interpretation and reform that is not internal to law.

"Calls for direct revision" of *halakhah* seem to proceed from the assumption that the descriptive fact of past legal change provides legal authority in the present and future to change halakhic norms at will. But, as in all legal systems, "no normative conclusions can be drawn from the historical fact of legal change."[37] Appeals to adopt a new norm or rule of law must be based on arguments that fall within the class of arguments recognized as legitimate bases for legal action within the legal system. The historical fact of legal change in the past is not a recognized legal argument for current judicial "change" of the law within the halakhic, or any other, legal system.

Second, calls for direct reform often ascribe prior legal "change" to conscious reform, rather than creative legal interpretation, either because they assume that concrete norms are exhaustive of the sources of law or because they adopt an external analysis of judicial opinions. Judicial opinions can be assessed from two different perspectives. In an external analysis, judicial opinions are assessed from the perspective of an outside observer of the system—for example, an historian or legal realist. In an internal analysis of law, such as that of Dworkin, legal interpretation is assessed from the perspective of one who is acting inside the legal system, and who accepts and is committed to the legal system's modes of reasoning, norms, principles, and their elaboration—for example, a judge who possesses an internal sense of being bound by the law.[38] The internal sense of being bound by the law is not the equivalent of "being subject or subservient to the law."[39] To be bound by the law connotes a stance of internal commitment to the law as an ongoing normative project and, thus, to its elaboration based on authoritative considerations. By definition, from the internal viewpoint of law, legal "change" is understood as an internal dynamic. It is the process of internal development, which follows from a new insight into prior precedents made possible by new societal conditions, or from an expanded sense of the sources of law or of what sort of arguments are acceptable modes of legal reasoning, rather than a deliberate change, the result of consciously allowing external considerations to alter what would otherwise be the natural trajectory of the law.

Historians tend to adopt an external viewpoint of the law and therefore historical studies often describe legal development as conscious legal change. Pursuant to the external point of view of the historian, for example, the *halakhah* has undergone vast transformation. But where historians retrospectively see change, judges and legal theorists such as Dworkin see continuity through creative interpretation. Viewed synchronically, at a given moment in time, a novel judicial reading is perceived as implicit in the earlier rule. From the perspective of the particular moment in time, no conscious revision necessarily takes place. When viewed historically and diachronically, as legal interpretation accumulates, the law appears to have undergone radical change. But, absent a judge's own admissions, it is only the external, retrospective view that permits ascribing revision, rather than continuation, to an interpretation that seems unpredictable or forced.

To concretize this point, allow me to offer two examples, one culled from American law and the other from the halakhic corpus. The difference between the internal and external viewpoint is vividly exemplified in analyses of the Supreme Court's affirmation of the constitutionality of Roosevelt's New Deal legislation. These decisions, like *Brown*, posed a legitimacy crisis for those who saw them as directly responsive to Roosevelt's threat to alter the composition of the Court to secure a majority and, in effect, a constitutional amendment paving the way for the modern welfare state. Thus, for legal realists, the "switch in time that saved nine" merely affirmed their intuition that law is a mask for political ideology.

The New Deal cases generated an interesting debate among historians. Political historians tend to view the New Deal cases as capitulations to outside forces. Legal historians, by contrast, tend to point to precedents in constitutional cases decided before the court-packing threat that support the court's later cases, even if incipiently. They also point to changes in how the Court understood the curriculum and philosophy of constitutional interpretation, which also were inaugurated before the court-packing threat. In short, while political historians often look outside the system of law to explain the court's decisions, thus placing the emphasis on the free choice of the judge who is shaped by political ideology or political pressures, legal historians tend to look inside the law, at values, principles, and accepted modes of legal reasoning, which are internal to the legal system as it develops, to explain new interpretations.

The internal view of legal interpretation is well illustrated by the bold and novel opinion of the Me'iri, whose transformation of the talmudic rules that discriminate against non-Jews is most pertinent to the subject of equality and reciprocity that we address in this volume. The Me'iri, alone among medieval commentators, eliminated many of the discriminatory rules through comprehensive re-interpretation of the letter of the law. He held that the discriminatory rules are aimed at the pagans of talmudic time. Me'iri concluded that the Gentiles of his day, the *ummot ha-gedurot*, do not satisfy the implicit condition precedent of the talmudic rules because they are possessed of religion. The Me'iri's insight, to be sure, also may have been shaped by various philosophical assumptions about the role of religion in securing a lawful social order and ethical considerations such as reciprocity. Gentiles in a lawful society do not mistreat Jews; hence, Jews owe parity of treatment in turn.

From the internal perspective of law, the Me'iri proceeds along creative, yet conventional, paths of legal interpretation. He defines the range of application of a preexisting halakhic norm in order to apply it to a new historical age, discerning in the norm a condition precedent no longer applicable. Such halakhic narrowing of the range of application of a preexisting norm is not a form of disguised halakhic "change." Narrowing the range of application of prior legal norms is a common judicial technique in legal systems. It is properly classified as the process of applying and distinguishing precedents, and not as judicial "change" of the law. As the legal philosopher Joseph Raz points out, "distinguishing differs from the general power to modify rules and make new ones."[40] Distinguishing means restricting the application of the original rule by adding a new condition to it. With the new condition added to it, the rule no longer applies to the situation at hand. But the restricted rule is simply a possible alternative formulation of the original rule, in which a hidden additional factor that the prior ruling failed to make explicit is discerned. From the internal point of view of law, such narrowing is classic interpretation, not direct revision or conscious change. Additionally, where the historian may describe various philosophic and ethical motivations about the role of religion or reciprocity as factors extraneous to the legal system, a legal theorist such as Dworkin, who adopts an internal perspective of law, will ask whether these factors are more appropriately classified as values and principles internal to the law.

Thus far, I have argued that the application of halakhic norms to new conditions is a purposive activity, in which the purpose of the halakhic norm under scrutiny must be evaluated in order to discern its range of application in new societal conditions. The question I wish to consider now is whether more open-ended, general principles and values play a role in shaping halakhic interpretation. The *halakhah* contains several open-ended and general principles, some rooted in Scripture, that direct attention to ethical and pragmatic considerations. In addition to creation *be-tzelem* and *darkhei shalom*, principles such as *tikkun olam*, *hillul* and *kiddush ha-Shem*, and so on, appear throughout halakhic literature. The role of these principles within the halakhic system is unclear. Are such halakhic "principles" solely explanations of specific, concrete, and particular norms (that is, essentially *ta'amei ha-mitzvot*)? If so, these principles must be regarded as merely explanatory, external to the legal system, and thus having no special legal weight. Alternatively, does the *halakhah* view these principles as articulations of the *halakhah*'s overall internal aims and ends? If so, these principles have, to borrow Dworkin's term, "gravitational weight," in decision making. They may guide the *posek* in choosing between diverse opinions, in determining how much weight to give a minority opinion, or in determining whether a specific halakhic norm is applicable in a new situation and time. Although their weight cannot be predicted in advance, these principles, if viewed as internal to the legal system, properly enter into the formulation of *pesak*.

Even more critically, given the concerns of this volume, are principles such as creation *be-tzelem* also capable of generating new norms of behavior in light of social change, through a process that Gerald Blidstein has called "dynamic" elaboration?[41] In his study of the principle *kevod ha-beriyyot,* Blidstein suggests that, in the medieval period, this principle served to generate several new norms.[42] Blidstein advocates the dynamic elaboration of principles such as *darkhei shalom* and creation *be-tzelem*, as well, in order to meet the challenge of forging norms of equality and mutuality in a societal age in which equality is a basic expectation.[43] This argument is not free from difficulty, however. Blidstein's own study of *kevod ha-beriyyot* reveals that the range of halakhic application of this principle was severely circumscribed because of the principle's subjective, "aggadic," character and its radical potential to supplant other halakhic norms. The question whether halakhic principles such as *darkhei shalom* and especially creation *be-tzelem* can be seen as halakhic counterparts to modern concepts of reciprocity and equality is addressed in the next section.

IV

Other presentations in this volume discuss various rabbinic opinions that may serve as legal precedents for forging new norms of mutuality between Jews and non-Jews. An emerging consensus from these discussions is that the distinction between Jews and non-Jews need not be seen as an ontological division but, rather, one that is rooted in the question what makes a person and a society ethical and just. In contributing to this discussion, I concentrate on the question whether equality and reciprocity may be seen as internal halakhic values, values that may have gravitational weight in choosing between diverse opinions, in weighing minority opinions, or in determining the range of application of a specific halakhic norm in new societal conditions. A comprehensive analysis is not possible here. Rather, I briefly address whether there are halakhic counterparts to modern political and philosophic arguments for equality.

The biblical idea of man's creation *be-tzelem* is often viewed as the closest analogue to the modern ideal of equality. Indeed, Western civilization's gradual development of the egalitarian idea and of equality as a basic human right may be viewed as the slow working out of this biblical concept. This is nowhere more apparent than in the citation in America's Declaration of Independence that "all men are created equal," and in Lincoln's subsequent evocation of that phrase in the Gettysburg Address. American legal commentators concede that there is a distinctive "theological foundation for America's commitment to equality."[44] This is not surprising. Not only was America from its inception a deeply religious society that self-consciously modeled itself on the Hebrew Bible, the political philosophy of America's founders is rooted in Protestant Christianity. But the course of the Western development of equality as an ideal also underscores the difficulty of vesting creation *be-tzelem* with similar weight within the halakhic tradition. The working out of equality in the liberal tradition is a direct result of the translation of biblical themes through Christianity into political thought—a process that bypasses the rabbinic tradition. Within the rabbinic tradition, by contrast, creation *be-tzelem* occupies a relatively negligible role.

From the perspective of the rabbinic tradition, the creation of humans in God's image implies that humanity has special worth distinguishing it from other creatures. Creation in the image may even embody an ethical ideal of social harmony between the diverse members of humankind, one that the prophets envision as the goal of the end of days. But, even in the biblical portrayal, humanity is not intended to be a universal human order, "one fellowship and societie," as Locke wrote.[45] Rather, creation in the image is the beginning of the unfolding in biblical and certainly rabbinic thought of a drama of hierarchy, distinction, and difference that moves from humanity to Noahide (civilized) society; to the political community of resident strangers and Jews; to the congregation of Israel charged with becoming "a holy nation of priests"; and, then, to the community of fellows, which at least in theory, excludes rebellious Jewish sinners. Within the rabbinic tradition, different classes of people are treated differently with regard to basic legal rights and obligations of social solidarity. The rabbinic tradition thus offers an alternative model of how associational life should be structured in a pluralistic society. Communal and religious bonds, social proximity, political and material dependence, beliefs, and conduct determine the level of social solidarity and reciprocity (equality under the law) owed to society's diverse members. This system is at odds with the notion of creation *be-tzelem* as mandating "equal respect for all persons," in a manner that is relevant to the modern ideal of equality.[46]

Few halakhic norms are derived from or justified by reference to creation *be-tzelem*. As a halakhic category, man's creation *be-tzelem* is invoked to justify the intrinsic equal value of human life,[47] the duty to procreate,[48] and the respect owed to the human body, even to the corpse of a killer. All these invocations of creation *be-tzelem* are limited to physical matters. True, for Ben Azzai, creation *be-tzelem* is the cardinal principle of the Torah (whereas Rabbi Akiva invokes a genuinely egalitarian principle, "love thy neighbor as thyself," one limited, however, to Jewish society). The Mishnah in Sanhedrin, in discussing creation *be-tzelem*, emphasizes humanity's diversity and each individual's uniqueness.[49] God created each human in His likeness, yet no two people are the same. The Mishnah's comment is meant to underscore God's unique creative capacities, rather than to serve as a positive valuation of pluralism. Moreover, Ben Azzai's statement and that of the Mishnah, and later philosophical speculation about the precise nature of the similitude between man and God, provide no guidance as to the kind of respect Jews owe to humanity on account of creation *be-tzelem*. These statements hardly illuminate whether the principle of man's creation *be-tzelem* is capable of supplying the crucial equality of people that entitles them to be treated equally under general or Jewish law.

More disturbing is the persistent strain of rabbinic thought that further limits the ambit of creation *be-tzelem* by seeking to restrict its application to Jews. There is the view of Rabbi Shimon bar Yohai, which gave rise to the tosafists' question: "Are the gentiles called man (*adam*)?"[50] The tosafists seem to reject bar Yohai's opinion and Rabbenu Tam suggests that Scripture uses the term *adam* in different ways, some of which do include Gentiles. But the Zohar and kabbalistic literature (although not halakhic sources) take up the view of bar Yohai in pursuing an ontological division between non-Jews and

Jews. This problem resurfaces in the contemporary application of *be-tzelem* as a halakhic category in connection with the question whether autopsies done for the advancement of medicine are permissible. In contrast to Rabbi Uziel, who equates all humans in the matter of respect for the dead,[51] Rabbi Kook rules that such autopsies may be conducted only on non-Jews. He comments: "The prohibition of desecrating a corpse is derived from the *tzelem Elohim* in man, which is unique to Israel in its greater sharpness as a result of the sanctity demanded by the Torah."[52] The messianic and idealistic tendencies of Rabbi Kook's rulings have been addressed by Michael Nehorai, who points to the significance of the concept of the *segulah* of the Jewish people in his thought.[53] In this ruling, Rabbi Kook notes the unique sanctity of the body of Jews who are charged with ritual commandments such as *kashruth* that fashion the body's sanctity.

Yet, Rabbi Kook does not, strictly speaking, limit the concept of *be-tzelem* to Jews. Instead, he writes that Jews are, as it were, "more fully *be-tzelem*" than non-Jews as a result of the sanctity bestowed by the Torah's ritual commandments. Although unpromising at first blush, Rabbi Kook's opinion may provide a new avenue for further development of the principle of creation *be-tzelem* in a manner consonant with the modern ideal of equality. Rabbi Kook treats creation *be-tzelem* as a comparative concept, a matter of degree, and not as an ontological division between Jews and others. Jews are more fully *be-tzelem* than non-Jews because they perform more commandments. In this view, the concept of *be-tzelem* is a statement about the potential of humans to perfect themselves through observance of Torah law. It is a theory about human potentiality to become full moral and legal subjects.

The conceptual link between man's creation *be-tzelem* and equality is as follows: All humans are born equal in their capacity to become full moral and legal subjects and perfect themselves. When humans realize their potential sufficiently, they are entitled to parity of treatment under Jewish law. But when has this potential been sufficiently realized? Rabbi Kook implies that only full observance of Torah suffices. In this view, non-Jews are entitled to parity of treatment under Jewish law only upon conversion. But other stopping points might be posited. The Me'iri ruled, for example, that juridical equality is owed to the non-Jews of his time, because they are members of nations under the rule of religious law. According to the Me'iri, societies bound by religious law occupy an intermediate category between idolaters of old and Jews. Such societies have critically progressed toward perfection. Their final perfection, he writes, is conversion.[54] Yet, those within the intermediate category are entitled to juridical equality. The critical question, then, is what makes a person or a society ethical or just, so as to merit juridical equality under Jewish law: observance of the entirety of Torah, observance of Noahide commandments, or, as David Berger argues in this volume, the empirically observed creation of a just and decent society committed to the rule of law.

To summarize, creation *be-tzelem* can be viewed as a concept that rejects the idea of inherently biological, racial, or even ontological divisions between humanity. But resort to creation *be-tzelem* as a source for positive halakhic valuation of equality under the law remains problematic. It is difficult to tell whether this universalist concept has been underelaborated until now because of lack of historical opportunity or because of a more general rabbinic concern to confine the ambit of theological and open-ended legal principles, especially those that are largely set within the fluid aggadic realm and that have the potential to undermine Jewish distinctiveness. Like the principle *kevod ha-beriyyot*, creation *be-tzelem*, if "dynamically elaborated," has the capacity to reduce significantly the set of halakhic norms that preserve Jewish particularity. Nonetheless, creation *be-tzelem* could be viewed as a theory of potentiality, emphasizing the capacity of humans to become full moral and legal subjects so as to trigger rights of equal treatment under Jewish and a fortiori general law. This theory is fully compatible with various halakhic approaches detailed in other contributions to this volume, which emphasize that the ethical level of a society is a relevant factor in determining the scope of Jewish obligations to its members.

Is legal equality regarded as a halakhic value in other contexts? Some theorists argue that the rule of law requires the enactment of non-discriminatory laws and the non-arbitrary execution of these laws. (Pursuant to this view, the equal protection clause merely reinforces the rule of law by providing an alternative way of testing whether, when the state acts to distribute benefits and burdens, they are distributed so as not to discriminate against or in favor of a particular group.) This perspective has halakhic parallels. The principle of *dina de-malkhuta dina* only applies to laws that bind all of the sovereign's citizens in an equal fashion. Equality is a pre-condition that has to be satisfied before non-Jewish legal activity will be deemed "law"—*dina*. This halakhic pre-condition is, to use Lon Fuller's term, a "procedural rule of legality."[55] Procedural rules of legality do not tell us about the justness of any individual substantive norm. Rather, they describe the basic characteristics that any law must possess in order to be deemed a legitimate law.[56] Pursuant to the *halakhah*, taxes imposed in a discriminatory fashion on Jews as a class or on particular persons within that class are not legitimate laws of the sovereign.[57] The sovereign is permitted to differentiate between citizens and aliens but not between citizens.[58] Thus, no class of citizens may be excluded by the sovereign from the proper generality of the law in distributing burdens or benefits.

Another argument advanced for equality is political. This argument has been stated in both negative terms—it is better to treat people as equals than run the risk of hatred between groups within the population—and positive terms—equality under the law fosters bonds of affection and loyalty among citizens of the nation. Obligations of social solidarity to non-Jews living in proximity to Jews traditionally were imposed to promote social peace (*darkhei shalom*).[59] It is customary to view *darkhei shalom* as a negative prudential principle, motivated by the need to fend off Gentile hatred. It is more appropriate today, however, to interpret the principle of *darkhei shalom* as equally based on a positive, ethical concept of reciprocity, emphasizing norms of mutuality, moral symmetry, and gratitude. Various Jewish sources stress reciprocity as an ethical ideal. The Bible appeals to one form of reciprocity as a value when setting forth the proper treatment of the *ger toshav*—"for you, too, were strangers in the land of Egypt." Hillel's famous statement, "Do not do to others what they did to you; what is hateful to you do not do to others," is a succinct expression of the value of reciprocity and certainly a basis for Jewish support of the struggle of other groups in American society to achieve the equal treatment granted to Jews. The more positive dimension of reciprocity, moral symmetry, seems to underlie the Me'iri's ruling that the discriminatory juridical rules of the *halakhah* apply only to members of non-Jewish societies that are unconstrained by religious law. Societies that have reached a sufficiently developed ethical level, evidenced by their decent treatment of Jews, deserve reciprocity under Jewish law.

That the ethical level of society is a factor in determining Jewish obligations toward its members thus seems fully compatible with a variety of halakhic principles. One may add the basic halakhic principle obligating Jews to adhere to ethical standards of behavior instantiated in general society, even when not specifically mandated by Jewish law. Thus, the talmudic rule: "There is nothing permitted to an Israelite yet forbidden to a gentile."[60] The underlying logic of this rule also finds expression in various applications of *dina de-malkhuta dina* to incorporate just and equitable rules promulgated by other legal systems, which prohibit conduct that Jewish law permits.[61]

V

The question must be raised, however, whether the instinct shared by many of us that we are living in a civilized and just society, a critical factor in determining Jewish obligations toward its members, ought to be tempered, given societal tolerance and even support of sexual practices that contravene universal halakhic standards of behavior. Thus, David Berger addresses the question whether the Me'iri's assessment of the progress of civilization is applicable to secular societies lacking belief in a cosmic God, and constrained not by religious law but, rather, by the rule of law. A similar question is posed by the emergence of societies that reject Noahide precepts regarding sexual norms. Rabbinic sources distinguish between societies in which homosexual conduct is prevalent and those that formalize it through marriage, with the latter viewed as a mark of societal decay.[62] This distinction is replicated in current American public debate. Although the Supreme Court recently extended constitutional protection to private, gay activity and several states have legalized same-sex marriage, the formalizing of gay lifestyle through marriage still is viewed as a highly contested social issue in the United States.

From a halakhic perspective, then, there is a crucial difference between the prevalence of homosexual activities within society, which may properly be the subject of Jewish tolerance, and official recognition of same-sex marriage. Thus, the pursuit of equal civil rights for gays in the workplace or the political sphere presents little difficulty. There is no more reason to countenance discrimination in the distribution of governmental burdens or benefits against gay individuals than against individuals who violate other halakhic norms, including sexual norms such as adultery. The parameter of tolerance in the Jewish tradition is a large topic.[63] The justification for tolerance most compatible with the Jewish sources is respect for persons. Tolerance is a virtue that exists in the sphere of interpersonal relations, as much as in the political sphere.[64] Tolerating the sinner but not the sin rests on the notion that being judgmental toward persons is not always a virtue, because we should sometimes respond to persons not through their actions, but through the reasons for their actions. The individual sinner can be tolerated because the fault for the sin lies in inferior education or upbringing, intellectual seduction, or other forces, including desire, that shape the actual self. The model, moreover, has been relied on to justify continued social relations not only with Jews, whom there is heightened incentive to retain within the collectivity of Israel, but also with non-Jews, even pagan idolaters.

Is this model of tolerance appropriate where a group, whose very identity is defined by its association with halakhically forbidden sexual activity, seeks public recognition and affirmation of that identity through heightened protection of equal citizenship rights? There are valid reasons to oppose public affirmation of gay rights such as same-sex marriage, chief among them the preservation of a neutral public space in which contested forms of sexuality are not unduly displayed. The realm of the public, the *pharhessia*, is a concept that has significant halakhic ramifications. Because it is the sphere of communicative action, public space matters. It may be questioned, however, whether the concept of *pharhessia* has relevance to non-Jewish space or in conditions of modernity. Moreover, there is a genuine issue whether the *halakhah* recognizes a status and, therefore, gay identity altogether, for just as acts do not translate into identities, identities do not translate into acts. Nonetheless, because the message sent is so powerful from an educational standpoint, "making peace" with official state affirmation of gay identity, such as formalizing same-sex marriage, remains a thorny issue for modern orthodoxy.

VI

The procedural aspect of formulating responses in an egalitarian age deserves comment. There is concern, even yearning, today for a spiritually and intellectually satisfying articulation of a halakhic principle, a theory that would affirm the value of equality and yet set forth the limits of that equality, in light of halakhic norms both forbidding intermarriage or homosexual acts and maintaining divisions between men and women. Hence, the increased attraction of the Me'iri's views, which rest on a comprehensive principle. Of course, recourse to casuistic reasoning, ad hoc solutions, localized decision making, and even silence remains a possibility. Increasingly, such muddling through "seems inadequate—inadequate educationally and inadequate socially."[65] This is especially the case for Jews living in Israel, where Jews are responsible for shaping the very ethos of society. Yet, common sense suggests that, given a social phenomenon of such complexity as the one we discuss in this volume, no such principled response will be forthcoming soon.

I wish to raise the question whether "muddling through" as a form of response to societal change might still have virtue. Another name for "muddling through" is pragmatism, the anti-theory of choice of judges from Oliver Wendell Holmes to Richard Posner.[66] Pragmatists, in contrast to theorists such as Dworkin who see the task of judicial interpretation as one of making all the prior sources of the legal system coherent and viewed in their best moral light, assert that law is not necessarily coherent or utopian. It is inconsistent and reflects diverse aims often in tension with one another. Accordingly, rather than pursue a grand theory or principle, judges should make small decisions that work, using all the legal resources available, including legal fictions, casuistic reasoning, and creative analogies, to problem-solve on a local basis. Pragmatists are optimists and they believe the sources of the law are adequate to the task. In its least radical versions, it is the description of the common law method employed by its best practitioners, such as Justice Cardozo, and the chief characteristic of complex legal systems.[67]

Casuistic reasoning, also the chief characteristic of the *halakhah*, is capable of achieving satisfying results. Thus, sensitive issues of religion and state in Israel have been addressed through casuistic reasoning, such as analogizing participation of non-Jews in governmental functions, which raise issues of *serarah*, to participation in a business partnership. A sensible result was achieved, although no statement of principle about civic equality issued. Muddling through may even have its advantages. First, when one examines new social phenomena or is faced with a hard case and tempted to strike out in a bold direction, it is often difficult to avoid slippery-slope arguments about the dangers of a bold course or to assess them dispassionately. Second, it is easier to incorporate moral or pragmatic concerns in case-by-case reasoning. Third, ad hoc or local solutions preserve inconsistency, and therefore a continuing dialectical tension between two polar concerns, such as between universalism and particularism. Finally, gradualism, slow development, through arguments from analogy and careful distinguishing of one situation from another, is a virtue because it combines flexibility with stability. By contrast, attempting to articulate a principle or position may solve one problem in a satisfying fashion and yet create a new set of intellectual, spiritual, or practical problems. It may even lead us to the very disturbing conclusion that no reconciliation is possible.

NOTES

1. Ernest Gellner, *Culture, Identity, and Politics* (London: Cambridge University Press, 1987), 91. Gellner offers a penetrating analysis of the social roots of egalitarianism. Ibid., 91–110.

2. See Kenneth J. Karst, "The Bonds of American Nationhood," *Cardozo Law Review* 21 (2000), 1141–62, which summarizes his seminal work on this topic.

3. Gellner, *Culture, Identity, and Politics*, 110.

4. Larry Seidentop, "Liberalism: The Christian Connection," *Times Literary Supplement*, Mar. 24–30, 1989, 308.

5. See generally David Heyd, ed., *Toleration: An Elusive Virtue* (Princeton: Princeton University Press, 1996).

6. Adam B. Seligman, "The Problem of Religious Toleration," Berlin, January 1998 (unpublished manuscript, on file with author).

7. I examine multiculturalism and its effects on nationalism and liberalism in Suzanne Last Stone, "Comment: Cultural Pluralism, Nationalism, and Universal Rights," *Cardozo Law Review* 21 (2000), 1211–24.

8. Charles Taylor, "The Politics of Recognition," in Amy Guttman, ed., *Multiculturalism: Examining the Politics of Recognition* (Princeton: Princeton University Press, 1994), 25, 28–37.

9. According to the legal philosopher David Richards, there is a conceptual link between the rights of gays, blacks, and women, on the one hand, and religious freedom, on the other. Discriminatory practices based on religion, race, gender, or homophobia create a state of "moral slavery"—"the unjust degradation" of what a person reasonably assumes to be central to his or her public and private identity. Moral slavery is the deprivation of the moral right to personality—to express oneself not only privately but also publicly. Richards argues that the moral right to personality can be equated with conscience, which is the core right protected by the free exercise of religion clause of the United States Constitution. See David A. J. Richards, *Identity and the Case for Gay Rights* (Chicago: University of Chicago Press, 1999).

10. Protection of conscience from governmental coercion rests on the inviolability of private beliefs. Richards' equation of the *public* display of personality with freedom of conscience is problematic because any social organization limits the identities individuals can assume in public. Thus, even clearly religious forms of public display,

such as the wearing of skullcaps in public or holiday displays, are subject to governmental regulation.

11. *Sanhedrin* 46a ("I heard that the *bet din* punishes not according to the Torah.").

12. Rashi, *Hagigah* 3b, s.v. "*aseh*."

13. On constitutional adjudication as a normative practice defined by the use of arguments that come from within the legal tradition and are recognizable to those within the legal community, see Phillip Bobbitt, *Constitutional Interpretation* (1991); Dennis Patterson, *Law and Truth* (1996); Owen Fiss, "Objectivity and Interpretation," *Stanford Law Review* 34 (1982), 739–58. These theories, which seek to account for law's autonomy, draw on the epistemology of the later Wittgenstein.

14. I address the similarities and differences between secular and halakhic conceptions of interpretation and authority in greater detail in Suzanne Last Stone, "In Pursuit of the Countertext: The Turn to the Jewish Legal Model in Contemporary American Legal Theory," *Harvard Law Review* 106 (1993), 813–96, and Suzanne Last Stone, "Book Review: Rational Rabbis," *Iyyun: The Jerusalem Philosophical Quarterly* 49 (January 2000), 97–104.

15. See Daniel Sperber, "Paralysis in Contemporary Halakha?" *Tradition* 36:3 (2002), 1–13.

16. See Aharon Lichtenstein, "Does Jewish Tradition Recognize an Ethic Independent of Halakha?" in Marvin Fox, ed., *Modern Jewish Ethics* 62 (1975).

17. See, e.g., Rabbi Abraham Yeshayahu Karelitz, Sefer Hazon Ish: Hoshen Mishpat 16:1, at 464 (1965). The Hazon Ish takes issue with the admission by the Shakh that Jewish law may have gaps and lack an explicit rule to cover a specific situation. The Hazon Ish writes: "The language of the Shakh is hard to understand, because one cannot make a distinction between explicit rules and those that are not explicit. No rules are not explicit, for everything is explicit in our Torah."

18. See, e.g., H. L. A. Hart, *The Concept of Law* (1961), 77–96.

19. George P. Fletcher, *Basic Concepts of Legal Thought* (Oxford: Oxford University Press, 1996), 47.

20. Saadia Gaon, *Otzar Ha-Geonim*, *Berakhot*, ed. B. Levin (Jerusalem), 91; Rabbi Hai Gaon, *Otzar Ha-Geonim*, *Hagigah* 14a.

21. 347 U.S. 483 (1954).

22. See, e.g., Jerome Frank, *Law and the Modern Mind* (New York: Brentano's, 1930); Karl Llewellyn, "Some Realism about Realism: Responding to Dean Pound," *Harvard Law Review* 44 (1931), 1222.

23. For an account of natural law theories, see Martin P. Golding, *Philosophy of Law* (Englewood Cliffs, NJ: Prentice-Hall, 1975), 30–33, 46–51.

24. Richard Fallon distills this view from I William Blackstone, Commentaries. See Richard H. Fallon, Jr., "Reflections on Dworkin and the Two Faces of Law," *Notre Dame Law Review* 67 (1992), 553–85.

25. See John Mackie, "The Third Theory of Law," *Philosophy and Public Affairs* 7 (1977), 3.

26. Dworkin's theory was first articulated in "The Model of Rules," *University of Chicago Law Review* 35 (1967), 14, and "Hard Cases," *Harvard Law Review* 88 (1975), 1057. The theory is developed further in several books, including *Taking Rights Seriously* (Cambridge: Harvard University Press, 1977) and *Law's Empire* (Cambridge: Cambridge University Press, 1986).

27. For Dworkin, principles are not only teleological, pointing to a result that ought to be reached, but also reflect dimensions of ideal or political morality embedded in the law. They provide guidance only. Unlike rules, they do not dictate the outcome of problems to which they apply.

28. Fletcher, *Basic Concepts*, 54.

29. See Dworkin, *Law's Empire*, 229.

30. This is both the strength and chief weakness of Dworkin's model. The individualist and heroic quality of Hercules, which Fallon terms "irreducibly protestant" (Fallon, "Reflections on Dworkin," 560), could lead to sectarianism if Hercules does not read the social text adequately; that is, if Hercules departs too far from that which the community of interpreters regards as an acceptable interpretation. As Fallon points out, Dworkin places little emphasis on "system-maintaining social forces, including social pressure to conform," in contrast to Hart. Others, such as Stanley Fish, although critical of Dworkin on other grounds, claim that there is little risk of straying too far from communally acceptable interpretations because interpreters are always embedded in a practice that will constrain their interpretations to that which is possible and therefore acceptable within the practice. Stanley Fish, *Doing What Comes Naturally: Change, Rhetoric, and the Practice of Theory in Literary and Legal Studies* (Durham: Duke University Press, 1989).

31. Rabbi Shaul Yisraeli, *HaTorah ve-HaMedinah* 9–10 (1958–59). The line of thought derives from Or Same'ah, *Hilkhot Gerushin* 2,20; *Hilkhot Mamrim* 4,3. Gerald Blidstein notes that the Or Same'ah's remarks are more limited. Their expansion indicates "ideological need." Gerald J. Blidstein, "Halakhah and Democracy," *Tradition* 32:1 (1997), 36 n. 19.

32. Rabbi Nahum Rabinovitch, *Darkah shel Torah*, cited in Blidstein, "Halakhah and Democracy," 35 n. 9.

33. Rabbi Avraham Yeshayahu Karelitz (Hazon Ish), Commentary on Yoreh De'ah, 13:16.

34. On Rabbi Abraham Isaac Ha-Kohen Kook's view of freedom as progressive, leading to increased opportunity for spirituality, see Tamar Ross, "Between Metaphysical and Liberal Pluralism," *AJS Review* 21 (1996), 1.

35. Blidstein, "Halakhah and Democracy," 8.

36. Izhak Englard, "Research in Jewish Law," in Bernard Jackson, ed., *Modern Research in Jewish Law* (Leiden: Brill, 1980) citing Boaz Cohen, "Towards a Philosophy of Jewish Law," in *Law and Tradition in Judaism* (New York: Ktav, 1959), 26.

37. Englard, "Research in Jewish Law," 108.

38. This is Dworkin's contribution.

39. Fletcher, *Basic Concepts*, 55.

40. Joseph Raz, *The Authority of Law* (Oxford: Oxford University Press, 1979), 183–89.

41. See Blidstein, "Halakhah and Democracy," 29, who argues that norms such as *darkhei shalom, kiddush ha-Shem*, and *hillul ha-Shem*, which I term principles, have a dynamic quality, expanding and contracting "according to social realities and expectations." They "seem to respond to, and assimilate, the expectations and standards of their surroundings when these cohere with basic Jewish ethics." Ibid.

42. See Gerald J. Blidstein, *K'vod Habriyyot*: Studies in the Development of Halakhah (Heb.), *Shenaton Ha-Mishpat Ha-Ivri* 9–10 (1982–1983).

43. Blidstein, "Halakhah and Democracy," 29, 33.

44. George P. Fletcher, "In God's Image: The Religious Imperative of Equality under Law," *Columbia Law Review* 99 (1999), 1608. Fletcher argues that the principle of equality is best grounded in a holistic view of human dignity, and draws on the biblical ideal of creation in God's image as well as on Kant.

45. John Locke, "The Second Treatise of Civil Government," in Peter Laslett, ed., *Locke's Two Treatises of Government* (Cambridge: Cambridge University Press, 1967), 401.

46. I address the rabbinic "ethical vision of social life" and its contemporary challenges at greater length in Suzanne Last Stone, "The Jewish Tradition and Civil Society," in Will Kymlicka and Simone Chambers, eds., *Alternative Conceptions of Civil Society* (Princeton: Princeton University Press, 2000), 208.

47. Genesis 9:6.

48. Tosefta, *Yevamot* 8:6.

49. Mishnah, *Sanhedrin* 8:4.

50. Tosafot, *Bava Kamma* 38a, s.v. "*ela*."

51. Piskei Uziel, *Orah Hayyim*, 178–79. See also Rabbi Eliezer Waldenberg, *Tzitz Eliezer* 4:14.

52. Rabbi Abraham Isaac Ha-Kohen Kook, *Da'at Kohen*, no. 199, 383.

53. Michael Z. Nehorai, "Halakhah, Metahalakhah, and the Redemption of Israel: Reflections on the Rabbinic Rulings of Rav Kook," in D. Shatz and L. Rosen, eds., *Rabbi Abraham Isaac Kook and Jewish Spirituality* (New York: New York University Press, 1995).

54. Rabbi Menahem Ha-Me'iri, *Sanhedrin* 59a.

55. Lon Fuller, *The Morality of Law* (New Haven: Yale University Press, 1964).

56. For further discussion of how rabbinic elaboration of both the Noahide commandment of *dinin* and of *dina de-malkhuta dina* may reflect rabbinic views on the procedural rules of legality that must be satisfied to generate legitimate law, see Suzanne Last Stone, "Sinaitic and Noahide Law: Legal Pluralism in Jewish Law," *Cardozo Law Review* 12 (1991), 1157.

57. This principle of equality is formulated by ibn Migash and codified by Maimonides. See generally Shmuel Shiloh, *Dina de-Malkhuta Dina* (Heb.) (Jerusalem: Magnes Press, 1974).

58. Shmuel Shiloh, "Equity as a Bridge between Jewish and Secular Law," *Cardozo Law Review* 12 (1991), 737.

59. "We support the heathen poor along with the poor of Israel, visit the heathen sick along with the sick of Israel, and bury their dead along with the dead of Israel in the interest of peace." *Gittin* 61a.

60. *Sanhedrin* 59a.

61. See Shiloh, "Equity as a Bridge," supra, for a fuller discussion.

62. See Rashi, *Hullin* 92a.

63. See Suzanne Last Stone, "Tolerance versus Pluralism in Judaism," *Journal of Human Rights* 2,1 (March 2003), 105–17; Moshe Sokol, ed., *Tolerance, Dissent, and Democracy* (Northvale: Jason Aronson Inc., 2002); Aviezer Ravitzky, "The Question of Tolerance in the Jewish Tradition," in Yaakov Elman and Jeffrey S. Gurock, eds., *Hazon Nahum: Studies in Jewish Law, Thought, and History* (New York: Yeshiva University Press, 1997), 359–91.

64. For an analysis of tolerance from this perspective, see Heyd, *Toleration*, 10–17.

65. Blidstein, "Halakhah and Democracy," 33.

66. On old and new versions of pragmatism in law, see Richard A. Posner, *Overcoming Law* (Cambridge: Harvard University Press,. 1995), 2–21, 387–405.

67. Pragmatism is actually both a weak form of legal realism and an outgrowth of a jurisprudential shift associated with Justice Holmes in which law came to be seen as a science and judges as legal scientists, policy makers, or problem solvers. For them, legal sources—cases—may be distinct vehicles for problem solving, but the law itself is not an autonomous discipline consisting of reasoning through the authoritative cases and precedents for the right answer to a legal question; rather, the law is just an aspect of the larger discipline of general social science, of making law more progressive and responsive to contemporary social needs. Judges are therefore not primarily interpreters who harmonize prior rules with present opinions. They are, like legislators, forward-looking policy makers who ask what is reasonable in order to govern this society now. But judges still need to use the cases and authoritative sources to accomplish this end. Judges cannot simply change the rules and doctrines whenever such a change would improve the world. Although deeply anti-formalist and anti-positivist, in theory, pragmatists use the concrete rules of the legal system in a way that is unthreatening to positivist and formalist conceptions of law.

4

Jews, Gentiles, and the Modern Egalitarian Ethos: Some Tentative Thoughts

David Berger

The deep and systemic tension between contemporary egalitarianism and many authoritative Jewish texts about gentiles takes varying forms. Most Orthodox Jews remain untroubled by some aspects of this tension, understanding that Judaism's affirmation of chosenness and hierarchy can inspire and ennoble without denigrating others. In other instances, affirmations of metaphysical differences between Jews and gentiles can take a form that makes many of us uncomfortable, but we have the legitimate option of regarding them as non-authoritative. Finally and most disturbing, there are positions affirmed by standard halakhic sources from the Talmud to the *Shulhan Arukh* that apparently stand in stark contrast to values taken for granted in the modern West and taught in other sections of the Torah itself.

Let me begin with a few brief observations about the first two categories and proceed to somewhat more extended ruminations about the third.

Critics ranging from medieval Christians to Mordecai Kaplan have directed withering fire at the doctrine of the chosenness of Israel. Nonetheless, if we examine an overarching pattern in the earliest chapters of the Torah, we discover, I believe, that this choice emerges in a universalist context. The famous statement in the Mishnah (*Sanhedrin* 4:5) that Adam was created singly so that no one would be able to say "My father is greater than yours" underscores the universality of the original divine intent. While we can never know the purpose of creation, one plausible objective in light of the narrative in Genesis is the opportunity to actualize the values of justice and lovingkindness through the behavior of creatures who subordinate themselves to the will of God. If God created the world for his glory, that glory is expressed through human recognition of divine authority as a vehicle for forging just relationships with others. Tragically, however, repeated divine efforts to achieve this objective on a universal level fail.

Not only do Adam and Eve not subordinate themselves to God; they aspire to "be like God by knowing good and evil." Later, the generation of the flood precipitates the destruction of the world by actions that *Hazal* understand as violations of the canons of proper behavior toward others. "Their final fate was sealed because of robbery"[1]—a point whose essential message remains intact even if we assign a broader meaning to *hamas*. But God does not give up, and once again he attempts to create a world without divisions among people. And again he "fails"—and precisely because of another effort, this time on the part of "the generation of division," to ascend to a level where they can challenge God.

It is only at this point that the Creator, forced as it were by his recognition of the failings of human nature, introduces division in mankind and chooses one family to bear the torch of the original, ultimately universal, objective of creation. The choice of Abraham rests precisely on qualities that counteract those earlier failings. In contrast to the hubris of earlier generations, Abraham declares himself dust and ashes, and in contrast to the unethical behavior of the generation of the flood, he "will instruct his children . . . to do what is just and right." The tension between Abraham's two famous confrontations with ethically problematic divine behavior underscores precisely these two characteristics. Faced with a direct divine command, he utterly submits; told of a divine plan affecting others, he issues a challenge based on his perception of a violation of what is just and right, though it is on that very occasion that he underscores his standing as dust and ashes.[2]

Though the choice of Abraham and his descendants represents a short-term narrowing of God's focus, it seems highly improbable that it represents a permanent abandonment of the great aim of creation implied in all that went before. Rather, it is God's way of taking a longer, slower, surer path to the achievement of his universal objective. The messianic dream in its broadest and most inclusive version is implicit at the moment of creation—this, I think, is the meaning of the rabbinic vision of the preexisting soul of the Messiah—as well as at the election of the father of Israel, who is also the father of a multitude of nations.[3]

Notwithstanding this universal goal, the election of Israel, formalized at Sinai, unquestionably establishes deep differences between Jews and non-Jews. Israel becomes a kingdom of priests and a holy nation with all that such hierarchical language implies; the set of obligations and beliefs embodied in the Torah elevate the recipients of the revelation even as they are warned that it was not their own righteousness that entitled them to this privilege; the status of Jews and gentiles with respect to ritual, to purity and impurity, and to the establishment and dissolution of marital ties is marked by sharp distinctions. On the whole, I do not think that this complex of differences, especially if understood in the way that I have presented it, strikes contemporary Orthodox Jews as troubling. Quite the contrary. The sanctity of Israel, with all the responsibilities that it imposes, is a badge of honor. We are inclined to see the radical leveling of difference and the relentless relativization of values in extreme expressions of multiculturalist ideology as proper objects of criticism rather than ideals worthy of emulation.[4]

The manner in which some of the differences in ritual statutes are formulated can nonetheless jar our sensibilities. Thus, there is—or should be—nothing troubling about the position that the ritual status, or non-status, of gentiles excludes them from performing valid ritual slaughter even if they are under constant observation. But anyone attuned to an egalitarian ethic will be deeply shaken by Ravad's extraordinary outburst in response to Maimonides' admittedly surprising ruling that a gentile's slaughter, while not rendering the animal fit for consumption, can remove it, if only on the level of biblical purity law, from the status of *nevelah*: "This is one of his ideas, and none of them is less worthwhile than this one. For gentiles are like animals; they neither impart impurity nor become impure. A people compared to a donkey. The nations are like a drop in a bucket (Isaiah 40:15). Let the wind carry all of them away, and anyone who regards them as anything has gathered a handful of wind."[5]

This is no ordinary disagreement even by the standards of Ravad's tempestuous personality, and we are eminently justified in seeing it through the prism of the Jewish experience in medieval Europe. I do not advocate mechanical historicizing of such statements, nor do I believe that positions influenced by a rabbi's experience should automatically be discounted. Nonetheless, not only do I see no religious obligation to read the formulation of this stricture in a historical vacuum; the change in context is precisely what gives us the right to denounce a contemporary Jew who would use this language while retaining our reverence for the great medieval talmudist.

Sometimes the relationship between sharp language and the essential position is more intimate, and it appears more difficult to separate the two. One can assert, for example, that Jewish law does not recognize some gentile family relationships or that sexual relations between a Jewish woman and a non-Jewish man do not have certain legal consequences without resort to demeaning categories. In these instances, however, the Talmud's assertion of the former position and Rabbenu Tam's affirmation of the latter are explicitly grounded in the biblical verse that "their issue is the issue of horses."[6] Nonetheless, it is beyond question that neither the Talmud nor Rabbenu Tam held the generalized position that gentiles are not to be considered human; the extreme language here was generated by the biblical verse, and its application is limited to the immediate contexts.

Rabbenu Tam's reaction to the well-known Talmudic assertion that Jews are called *adam* while gentiles are not demonstrates his readiness to assign untrammeled "adamhood" to non-Jews. *Tosafot* notes an apparently contradictory Talmudic statement, based on a verse containing the word *ha-adam*, that a gentile who studies Torah is like a high priest. Though other solutions are possible—and attested—Rabbenu Tam famously provided what appears to be a purely technical distinction between *adam* and *ha-adam*, leaving gentiles in the latter category without hesitation or limitation.[7] With specific reference to medieval Ashkenazic texts, Jacob Katz has emphasized the importance of local context in limiting the scope of halakhic statements. In his study, the emphasis was on "liberal" statements that were not generalized beyond their original application, but the point is no less valid with respect to "intolerant" statements. It is not apologetics but simple common sense and the consistent application of scholarly method that preclude the assertion that Rabbenu Tam—or the Talmud—equated gentiles and horses.

Even the phrase "a people compared to a donkey," alluded to by Ravad and used by the Talmud in discussions of gentile slaves, does not intend such a simplistic, generalized equation. The Talmud (*Ketubbot* 111a) asserts that even a gentile maidservant in the Land of Israel is guaranteed a place in the world to come. How do we know this? The remarkable answer is that we derive it from the "fact" that gentiles are called "a people compared to a donkey" combined with Isaiah's declaration that God gives life to "the people" living in the holy land. What makes this derivation all the more striking is that the term "people" (*'am*) in the rabbinic phrase is a play on words based on an expression in Genesis where the relevant word is "with" (*'im*). Thus, intellectual dexterity of the most flexible sort is mobilized to grant these so-called donkeys eternal bliss.

We move now from difference in ritual standing and sanctity—intrinsically untroubling though sometimes described in disturbing language—to affirmations of essentialist distinctions of the most profound sort. Precisely because Adam was created singly, anyone arguing for a metaphysical chasm between the Jewish and gentile soul must overcome a daunting obstacle. "Beloved is man because he was created in the image; special love is accorded him because he was created in the image of God. . . . Beloved are Israel because they are called children of God; special love is accorded them because they are called children of God" (*Avot* 3:14). Israel's privilege is monumental, but it does not penetrate to the core, defining element providing human beings with their unique dignity.

The Talmudic assertion that serves as justification for a far-reaching position standing in considerable tension with this mishnah is the ascription of a largely undefined taint to non-Jews. The serpent, understood to have had sexual relations with Eve, injected her with filth. This filth was removed from those who stood at Sinai—including indirectly future converts to Judaism—but not from gentiles. In one of the passages in which this assertion appears, the retention of this impurity explains the presumably unhealthy sexual proclivities evident among non-Jews.[8] Granting full allowance to this rabbinic position, I think it is fair to say that it describes a taint, not a qualitative difference in the soul itself.

The views of medieval and early modern Jews on this matter span a substantial spectrum. While most if not all Jews affirmed that the chosen people had certain moral qualities or inclinations absent or less pronounced among gentiles, I do not believe that either philosophically oriented Sephardim or Ashkenazic talmudists thought in terms of radically different souls for Jews and gentiles. Medieval philosophers addressed the nature of the human soul and its component parts in numerous contexts without proposing such profound distinctions, and I am inclined to regard this as more than an ordinary argument from silence. Jews have superior characteristics, but they are made of essentially the same spiritual ingredients.[9]

There is, however, a different strain in the tradition. It is very well known that Judah Halevi ascribed a special divine element to the Jewish people accounting most notably for the restriction of prophecy to Jews. This element was latent even in Terah, though it abandoned the Jews, at least in its manifest form, during the exile. Converts purify their soul through the pursuit of Jewish practices, but in the first generation they remain excluded from prophecy.[10] A perusal of this skeletal and perhaps tendentious summary makes it clear, I think, that even Halevi speaks of a distinction that does not cut to the very core. The divine element can somehow be attained within two generations through spiritual effort, and it can be submerged during conditions of adversity. Halevi's converts are not excluded from the drawbacks of the gentile soul because they stood at Sinai; at the same time, the purification resulting from observance of the Torah does not appear to be directed to the uprooting of a deep-seated, metaphysical filth.

Maharal provides a somewhat stronger contrast. Jews, including converts, possess a soul that is more separated from the body than that of gentiles and hence less susceptible to its influence. In addition, it is better prepared for spirituality, so that Jews are more resistant to passions and more receptive to Torah.[11] These and other differences affirmed by Maharal are surely profound, but even they do not amount to the existential chasm that appears in some kabbalistic texts and reaches a crescendo in certain forms of hasidic thought, most notably the *Tanya*. All people, we are told, have a soul formed from the husks (*qelippah*), but the Jewish soul is from *qelippat nogah*, which contains good. The gentile soul, on the other hand, is from the other three *qelippot*, "which contain no good at all" (*she-ein bahem tov kelal*). In addition, Jews have a divine soul (*nefesh elokit*), "a part of God above," which is entirely absent in gentiles.[12] While "no good" may well mean only "no accessible good," we find here a stark contrast on the deepest existential level.

I see no honest way to mitigate the force of this position significantly, but someone more conversant with hasidic thought may. An unqualified affirmation that there is no good in gentiles flies in the face of a mountain of contrary evidence: the creation of all human beings in the image of God, the ability of gentiles to become *gerei toshav*, their capacity to become *hasidei ummot ha-olam* and attain a portion in the world to come, their potential, even if only metaphorically, to be like high priests. Whatever the approach of the *Ba'al ha-Tanya* may have been to these texts, we are in any event not dealing with binding doctrine. A believing Jew is free to reject the positions of Halevi, of the Maharal, and of the *Ba'al ha-Tanya* on this matter and embrace the position that whatever advantages the chosenness of Israel confers, they do not extend to a radical difference in the essential makeup of the Jewish soul.

And so we arrive at the third and most daunting category, where we do confront binding doctrine, or binding law. The list of discriminatory provisions in Jewish civil and criminal law (some of which do not apply to a *ger toshav*) need not be assembled through painstaking original research. The task has been performed for us by apostates from Nicholas Donin to Johannes Pfefferkorn and beyond, by their Christian disciples in medieval and early modern times, by more recent missionaries, by the rabbinic contributors to the Baruch Goldstein memorial volume, and by modern anti-Semites, both Jewish and gentile. These provisions include *inter alia* the exemption from returning money obtained through an error made by a gentile, the exemption from returning his or her lost object (and, according to the Rambam, even a prohibition against doing so), discrimination regarding liability for damage to property, the existence of a death penalty for killing a Jew but not for killing a gentile, the imposition of a death penalty for violation of any of the Noahide laws, and the injunction to avoid saving the life of a gentile even on a weekday.

It is an understatement to assert that such laws violate the contemporary egalitarian ethic. While the Torah contains other provisions that appear ethically problematic, they apply in limited or exceptional situations: Amalek, the seven nations, Midian, *mamzerut*, *iggun*. Ultimately, we recognize that the will of God does not always yield to our understanding. In this case, however, we face regulations built into the everyday functioning of Jewish law in absolutely normal situations that sharply contradict the moral instincts of many religious Jews. This is the only area of *halakhah* where I have been told by more than a handful of serious Orthodox Jews over the years that they really do not care what rabbinic authorities may say. They know what is right and wrong and are certain that a true understanding of the Torah would have to accord with so primal an instinct. We often point—with absolute justice—to the ethical teachings of the Torah as one of the arguments for believing in its divine origin. From this perspective, a set of laws so deeply in tension with our ethical sense can constitute a challenge to faith itself.[13]

In extremis, believing Jews are obligated to believe come what may. But the suppression of doubt in a matter like this may well interfere with our ability to understand the true intent of the Torah, whose meaning is routinely uncovered through a process of questioning, of adducing contradictions, of expressing perplexity. This particular perplexity cuts much deeper than most, but perhaps that means that we should confront it all the more seriously rather than declare it too dangerous to touch.

It is for this reason that I welcomed the controversial publication of R. Yehiel Weinberg's letters expressing his distress over some of these texts.[14] That very distress is Torah—*ve-lilmod anu tzerikhim*. R. Weinberg has taught us that we are permitted to agonize over these questions, that we are not defying God's will in doing so, that this is not, as a *talmid hakham* told me about a related matter, *periqat 'ol*.

My personal perplexity about these matters was initially awakened as a teenager when years of reading the Hertz *humash* suddenly collided with the *Entziqlopedia Talmudit* article on *Ben Noah*. (I still regret the eclipse of the Hertz *humash*, which, for all its drawbacks, introduced a generation of Jews to a humane and uplifting vision of Judaism.) To a significant degree, my mind was set at ease during my second year at Yeshiva College, when I studied in the *shiur* of R. Ahron Soloveichik. Time after time, both in his celebrated *hashkafah shiurim* and in the course of standard analyses of *gemara*, R. Soloveichik reflected profound sensitivity to moral issues of the sort that concerned me.

Forty years later, I would not want the recollected impressions of a youngster to serve as definitive statements of R. Ahron's views. Nonetheless, my antennas with respect to these issues were very sensitive, and this is what I think I remember. He described slavery as a concession to human frailty analogous to the *eshet yefat toar*. He made the point that *lo taguru mi-penei ish* does not apply to the realm of Noahide law, indicating, I believe, that the absence of this requirement to apply the full force of the law come what may meant that prosecution and sentencing are open to the discretion of the court. He argued that one reason why we stop the recitation of the divine attributes after *ve-naqqeh*, refraining from listing the attributes of vengeance, goes beyond the obvious point that we do not want to remind God of those attributes. After all, he indicated, this self-interested reason may not be sufficient to overcome the stricture against ending a biblical quotation in the middle of a verse. Rather, we remind ourselves that the principle of *imitatio Dei* is restricted to the attributes of mercy. *Mah hu rahum, af attah rahum*. Not *mah hu qanna, af attah qanna*. Only God can apply the attributes of vengeance properly.

With respect to another moral issue unrelated to our concerns, he made an amusing but deeply serious observation about a passage in *Bava Metzi'a*. The *gemara* asserts that the financially strapped borrower tends to trust the more successful lender because he is impressed by the verse, "The integrity of the upright guides them (Proverbs 11: 3)." The latter, on the other hand, does not trust the former because of the second half of that verse, which asserts that "the deviousness of the treacherous leads them to ruin" (*Bava Metzi'a* 35a). "Do you think," exclaimed Rabbi Soloveichik, "that the *gemara* is a Republican?!" The passage, he said, reports the erroneous assumptions of the parties; it does not endorse those assumptions. A theological-moral judgment determined the interpretation of the text.

Finally, and most important of all for our purposes, Rabbi Soloveichik addressed the understanding of *kiddush ha-Shem* as a reason for returning a lost object to a gentile. He insisted with uncompromising vigor that this is not merely a pragmatic concern with the displeasure of gentiles. There are many things we do in conformity with Torah law that gentiles do not like. Do we, then, abrogate the *halakhah* in all those instances? The question answers itself. Rather, the category of *kiddush ha-Shem* is activated precisely when the deep values of the Torah really demand a particular behavior. Evidence for this position, he said, is in Shimon ben Shetah's indignant response when his students suggested that he exercise his legal prerogative to keep the precious stone found on an animal purchased from a gentile. He did not say, "I prefer to bring about a *kiddush ha-Shem* by returning it." He did not even say, "How can you imagine that I would choose wealth in preference to a *kiddush ha-Shem*?" Rather, he introduced this point by exclaiming, "Do you think Shimon ben Shetah is a barbarian?!"(*Yerushalmi Bava Metzi'a* 2:5 [8c]). As in the case of the Ramban's discussion of *naval bi-reshut ha-Torah* and the Rambam's description of the proper treatment of a gentile slave, the Torah can require an action that the *halakhah* does not.[15]

I shall return to this critically important matter later on, but first we need to examine the approaches of earlier Jews who were not unaffected by the ethical concerns raised by some of these laws. Every *bar bei-rav de-had yoma* conversant with this issue is familiar with the fact that ha-Meiri must play a significant role in this discussion, and I shall discuss his views presently. First, however, we must set forth the outlines of the complicated relationship between treatment of gentiles in general and treatment of idolaters in particular. I have already alluded to the fact that many of the discriminatory laws do not apply to a *ger toshav*, who formally accepts the seven Noahide laws that include the abjuring of *avodah zarah*. One is obligated to save the life of such a gentile and to support him. On principle, then—and this is a matter of the first importance—gentiles do command a level of treatment much closer to genuine equality in Jewish civil and criminal law once they assume the obligations that the Torah requires of them.

The use of this category, however, is problematic for at least two reasons. First, even if the procedure for accepting a *ger toshav* were operative when the Jubilee is not, hardly any gentiles could be expected to appear before a rabbinic court to formalize their status, and, in all candor, any such expectation on our part would not be reasonable. Second, even if we were to dispense with a formal declaration, the most upright Christians would run afoul of the problem of *avodah zarah*. It is well known that long before ha-Meiri, Jews in Christian countries began to struggle with the question of Christian *avodah zarah* for reasons that had nothing to do with theology or tolerance and everything to do with the need to make a living in *galut Edom*. I have recently written an assessment of Jacob Katz's *Exclusiveness and Tolerance*[16] and will not traverse in detail the territory covered in that work. It is, however, essential to recognize that despite widespread misunderstanding, Ashkenazic Jews almost certainly never asserted that classical Christianity was not *avodah zarah*—even for gentiles. A crucial *tosafot*[17] does recognize that Christianity differs from paganism since its adherents intend to worship the Creator of heaven and earth; nonetheless, because Jesus of Nazareth is included in their conception of God, technical *avodah zarah* remains, all the more so when they mention him explicitly.

If, then, we apply all the discriminatory laws to anyone who has not fulfilled the formal requirements for becoming a *ger toshav*, we face an acutely uncomfortable moral situation. That Orthodox Jews benefit from the modern egalitarian ethic is too obvious to require demonstration. Beyond this, we participate, though perhaps less often than we should, in the moral discourse of the broader society, describing Jewish values as a model for the world. Orthodox Jews, to take the most relevant issue, have taken positions on abortion, assisted suicide, and the termination of life support in which we regularly speak of the sanctity of life as a supreme Jewish value. What do we say if a knowledgeable non-Jew proceeds to ask how it is that—leaving aside medical professionals and considerations of *eivah*—we are forbidden to save the life of a gentile, even a decent gentile living in a decent society? Do we respond that all this upright, endangered gentile would have had to do is formally (or, if we are feeling generous, informally) accept the Noahide covenant, which includes abjuring both Christianity and secularism? Would we be embarrassed to say this only because of *eivah*? Do we believe that this position sits comfortably with the moral tenor of the written and oral Torah as a whole? To make an already sharp formulation sharper, what would we say if the gentile in question risked his life to save Jews during the Holocaust and did so, as many of the rescuers in fact did, precisely out of Christian convictions?

Let us return now to the era of *Tosafot*. With the Paris disputation of 1240, a new form of pressure was brought to bear regarding the moral issues of direct concern to us here. Nicholas Donin leveled more than one accusation against the Talmud, but its discriminatory approach toward gentiles was a significant component of his indictment. Some of his examples, most notably, "Kill the best of the gentiles" presented as a standard injunction of Jewish law, could honestly be countered as the hostile distortions that they were. But others were accurate depictions of real *halakhot*. R. Yehiel of Paris responded by pointing to a series of positive Talmudic statements about attitudes toward gentiles (e.g., *Gittin* 61a), and we would do well to remember that those passages are also real. He went on to assert that many of the discriminatory laws apply only to pagans of old, perhaps only to the seven nations of ancient Canaan, not to contemporary Christians. To demonstrate this, he pointed to the undeniable fact that Northern European Jews, who were willing to die for their faith, engaged in business dealings with Christians that contravened many of the Talmudic prohibitions against pursuing such activities with idolaters.

Not all of R. Yehiel's assertions were sincere, but I think that Katz was correct in asserting that "the situation created by the controversy may have advanced the thought of the [Jewish] disputants." In the case of the Church, the disputation was a move away from toleration, but with respect to the Jews, "the same event assisted, or even compelled [them] to take a further step toward the ideal of religious tolerance."[18] Writing about a later polemic in which the post-Meiri Jewish author was very likely sincere in distinguishing Christians from the gentiles of the Talmud, I put the point as follows: "In the fourteenth century, Iberian Jews were faced with a massive paradox that they could not exploit. Hostile, intolerant Christians attacked Jews for being hostile and intolerant. It is not a pleasant sight to watch [the author's] attempt to reevaluate Talmudic material while conceding by his silence—and sometimes by more than silence—the kindness and benevolence of late medieval Christian society. And this paradox may be eclipsed by an even greater one. The pressures of the new Christian attack may well have been instrumental in broadening and deepening a sincere Jewish interpretation of sacred texts in a direction that created a genuinely more positive attitude toward the religion of the oppressor."[19]

As Jews faced these *halakhot* in polemical and non-polemical contexts, some of them began to ask whether the larger will of God made larger demands than those of the formal law. The Bible, as I have already implied, says things about non-Jews that do not sit well with the assumption that discriminatory laws represent an ideal. God's mercy, as the Rambam himself notes in a related context (*Hilkhot Melakhim* 10:12), is upon all his creatures. Moab is destroyed for disrespectful treatment of the bones of the king of Edom (Amos 2:1). Jonah is sent to warn the inhabitants of Nineveh so that disaster may be averted. R. Moses of Coucy, who participated in the Paris disputation, required rectitude in dealing with gentiles to a degree that went beyond the letter of the law, appealing to the verse, "The remnant of Israel shall do no injustice and shall not speak what is false" (Zephaniah 3:13).[20] There is something disconcerting about using such language to describe supererogatory behavior, implying that the Torah itself may permit injustice and falsehood. As in R. Ahron Soloveichik's understanding of *kiddush ha-Shem*, R. Moses' rhetoric strongly implies that the *demands* of God, not merely his preferences, go beyond the letter of the law.

Why then does the letter fall short of the ultimate will of the Lawgiver? Arguably, God wanted to give a people that He knew would be persecuted and beleaguered some leeway to respond to their oppressors in less than ideal fashion when circumstances genuinely demanded this. Perhaps He needed to reinforce a sense of special standing so that a positive Jewish self-image would be sufficiently strong to withstand the deflation of exile, subordination, and suffering.[21] Perhaps He wanted to provide us with the test of developing our moral character in the absence of rigid commands.[22] Perhaps some of these considerations played a role, perhaps none, perhaps all of them and many more. In the final analysis, we cannot know. But the assumption that we are in fact called upon to transcend the parameters of these laws is rooted in authorities of impeccable credentials.

This approach, however, is insufficient to allay some of the most insistent doubts since a number of the *halakhot* at issue, from returning a lost object to saving a life, appear to *prohibit* behavior that our instincts consider meritorious and even morally required. R. Yehiel's approach addressed this difficulty by narrowing the focus of these laws to ancient pagans, but his assertion was made under pressure, so that its sincerity, as I have already noted, is in question. We turn, then, to ha-Meiri. Like R. Yehiel, he does not ask that we go beyond the letter; rather, he redefines the letter. Unlike R. Yehiel, his sincerity is not—or should not be—in question. Our insight into his position has been markedly enhanced by the recent studies of Moshe Halbertal, but a clear sense of this position can complicate as well as clarify the task of translating his attractive but highly problematic views into guideposts for contemporary *halakhah* and *hashkafah*.

Let me begin by devoting a single paragraph to a summary of these views. Contemporary Muslims and even Christians are not idolaters. In dealing with them, we need not be concerned with laws that are grounded in a fear of facilitating idolatry, so that we may do business with Christians on their holidays and even sell them items that might be used in their houses of worship. As to discrimination in civil and criminal law, distinctions between Jews and adherents of Christianity and Islam are virtually wiped out. The reason for this is that these distinctions were intended to apply to pagans who behave in an uncivilized fashion. But worshippers of the one cosmic Deity, even if they affirm some erroneous conceptions about Him, are impelled by their faith to establish moral societies. Such believers enjoy all the protections extended to Jews.

Even before Halbertal's study, I had understood the overall difference between ha-Meiri's discussion of laws regarding idolatry and his treatment of discriminatory legislation. I had, however, regarded the distinction between civilized and uncivilized societies as the key to the abolition of civil and criminal discrimination and did not see why ha-Meiri occasionally blurred the issue by mentioning *avodah zarah* in this connection. For me, then, the key contribution of Halbertal's analysis is his demonstration, based largely on philosophical sources, that ha-Meiri's work must be seen within a framework that linked religion with an ordered, ethical society. Worshippers of a multiplicity of deities are effectively people without religion; worshippers of a cosmic Deity, who fear His intervention and cannot hide from Him, are "people of religion" (*ba'alei dat*), or, in ha-Meiri's still more famous phrase, "nations bound by the ways of religions."[23]

To help us decide how to respond to this position, we must take the analysis a bit further. The most disconcerting element of ha-Meiri's stance is his apparent view that Christian worship is not *avodah zarah* at all. Since no other medieval halakhist ever said this, and it seems almost impossible to defend, I resisted this understanding for many years. In a recent treatment of the laws of *avodah zarah*, Rabbi Yehudah Herzl Henkin[24] affirmed that ha-Meiri would certainly not have said that one who actually bows to an icon of Jesus has not committed *avodah zarah*. When I first read that assertion, I answered amen despite the fact that the concrete evidence seemed very weak. In the oral version of my paper on Jacob Katz delivered in the Spring of 2000, I was still saying that I could not overcome my instinct that ha-Meiri would not go so far as to deny that such an act is *avodah zarah*. Nonetheless, after much soul-searching, I have come to believe that I was probably wrong.

My own view is that Christianity is non-pagan *avodah zarah* in a monotheistic mode, and I used to attribute this view to ha-Meiri. When I initially read Rabbi Henkin's analysis, I was very pleased to see that he understood ha-Meiri precisely in this manner and appeared to consider the position eminently defensible. But even such *avodah zarah*—what a critic of mine in a private message described as *avodah zarah* light—remains forbidden to both Jews and gentiles. I cannot see how to reconcile the view that Christianity is *avodah zarah* even in a limited, technical sense with ha-Meiri's rulings with respect to the laws relating to Christian ritual, for example, that one can do business with Christians on their holidays because what they do in their houses of worship is not *avodah zarah*, and that one who is not a *ba'al nefesh* can sell them objects that may be used in their religious services because the remnants of idolatry survive only in a few faraway places.[25] Unlike *tosafot*, ha-Meiri unambiguously means such assertions as a fundamental assessment of Christian practice.

One can turn in desperation to *shinuyei dehikei*. Perhaps ha-Meiri believed that the relevant prohibitions, which are for the most part *mi-derabbanan*, were intended to apply only to the standard, pagan form of *avodah zarah*. In other words, it is permissible to consummate a business deal that may well cause a gentile to engage in technical *avodah zarah* as long as it is not of the pagan variety. This is remotely possible, but one searches in vain in *Bet ha-Behirah* to *Massekhet Avodah Zarah* for any hint of such a distinction.[26] And then there is Rabbi J. David Bleich's suggestion that ha-Meiri believed that his Christian contemporaries were adherents of a heresy that was arguably not *avodah zarah*, while Catholicism survived somewhere on the remote periphery.[27] I am now more sympathetic to the motivation that impelled Rabbi Bleich to put forth this desperate suggestion, but as a historical proposition it is virtually impossible to defend.

We inevitably arrive, then, at the seductive temptation to solve this problem by suggesting that ha-Meiri regarded Christian worship as *avodah zarah* for Jews but not for Christians. But this distinction, as I have already noted, rests on an almost certainly erroneous understanding of a *tosafot*, and I know of no medieval authority who made such an assertion. To make matters worse, a remarkable passage in ha-Meiri underscored by Katz maintains that the rabbinic category of "heretic" (*min*) applies to a Jew who has lost faith in Judaism but has not embraced another religion. Once he joins one of the other genuine religions, clearly including Christianity, he becomes a man of religion and enjoys all the protections granted to such a man.[28] Since these protections apparently flow from adherence to non-idolatrous faiths, it seems to follow that even a Jew who engages in Christian worship does not commit *avodah zarah*. The mind boggles at such an assertion. To the best of my knowledge, no halakhist of stature before or after ha-Meiri ever said such a thing.[29] I do not believe that any later *poskim*, even those twentieth-century authorities who said that we should rule in accordance with ha-Meiri, meant to endorse this understanding of his position. But I am afraid that I no longer resist the conclusion that this is what he maintained. If this is so—and I still hope I can be convinced that it is not—then the decision to "*pasken* like the Meiri" is greatly complicated. Authorities like Rabbi Jehiel Weinberg affirmed their support of ha-Meiri's position[30] despite the fact that doing so violates the usual rules of *psak*. There is little doubt that they did so because their moral sense told them that his position yields results that accord most closely with the deepest values of the Torah. It is eminently clear by now that for whatever my opinion is worth, this is my instinct as well. But such a ruling, if described simply as the view of ha-Meiri, may now collide with another value that goes to the core of Judaism—safeguarding our resistance to *avodah zarah*.

In *The Rebbe, the Messiah and the Scandal of Orthodox Indifference*, I have suggested that leaving aside Maimonides' atypical case of "the root form of *avodah zarah*" (*Hilkhot Avodah Zarah* 1:1), a serviceable definition of this cardinal sin is "the formal recognition or worship as God of an entity that is in fact not God." As I understand the *tosafot* about associating God with something else, even worshipping the Creator with the understanding that one of his aspects is fully manifested in Jesus of Nazareth crosses the line, and worshipping Jesus himself with this understanding surely does.[31] If ha-Meiri thought otherwise, his view contradicts a universal Jewish consensus and imperils resistance to Christianity.

Indeed, in our own orphaned generation, it imperils even more than that. Neither ha-Meiri nor any other *rishon* could have imagined that a generation would arise in which Torah observant Jews would assert that a recently deceased human being was literally nothing but God, that he was consequently omniscient, omnipotent, unbounded, incapable of sin, a "man-God," that when you speak to him you speak to God, that it is permissible to invoke his aid and even bow to him with this understanding, and that his apparent death was illusory because an entity without limits cannot die. It is surely inconceivable that any *rishon* could have imagined that rabbinic authorities would treat Jews who affirm this set of beliefs as rabbis in good standing, support the institutions in which they teach, and see them as acceptable religious functionaries in every respect. The awareness that *avodah zarah* can exist in a monotheistic mode has never been more important.[32]

If, then, the humane consequences of ha-Meiri's position could be achieved only by compromising the definition of *avodah zarah*, I would—with a very heavy heart—reject them. But I do not think that this is necessary. In ha-Meiri's own mind, civilized behavior was linked with belief in a cosmic Deity, and for him such a belief may have been a sufficient condition to eliminate *avodah zarah*. But the logic of his position that this belief generates a civilized society is quite independent of the theological-halakhic judgment regarding *avodah zarah*. Moreover, his argument in the sphere of discriminatory law often appears rooted in the existence of a civilized society in and of itself.

What is arguably the crucial prooftext for ha-Meiri's position is the Talmudic statement that in certain areas—the immediate context is freedom of liability for damage caused by a Jew's animal—God has permitted gentile property to the Jews. Why? Because he saw that the nations did not observe the seven laws that he had imposed upon them (*Bava Kamma* 38a). Here is ha-Meiri's comment:

> [The reason for this is] that because they do not care about the property of others they are punished so that they should not habituate themselves to cause damage. In light of what is stated in the *gemara* this applies only to the nations that are not bound by the ways of religions and laws, as it says in the *gemara*, "He saw that the Noahides did not observe the seven commandments that they had accepted, and so he permitted their property" so long as justice condemns them to this. Thus, as long as they observe the seven commandments, their law with respect to us is the same as our law with respect to them, and we do not favor ourselves. This, then, is the case *a fortiori* [*ve-'attah ein tzarikh lomar she-ken*] with regard to the nations that are bound by the ways of religions and laws.

The key argument here is, I think, that they are punished for not caring about the property of others. Since ha-Meiri does not consider Christianity *avodah zarah*, he has no difficulty in coordinating this argument with the Talmudic assertion about the seven commandments, even though they include a prohibition against *avodah zarah*. Nevertheless, the essential logic of ha-Meiri's contention can clearly stand or fall on the existence of a just legal system irrespective of theology. Once such a system is in place, discrimination is manifestly unjust.

Before we proceed, it is worth noting the superficially incomprehensible term "a fortiori," whose implication was noticed by Halbertal.[33] The formula is perfectly understandable once we have absorbed the truly stunning extent of ha-Meiri's egalitarian radicalism. In a number of instances, he extends a more advantageous legal status to the nations bound by the ways of religions than the Talmud does to the individual *ger toshav*. Thus, their lives should be saved even at the cost of desecrating the Sabbath, and a Jew who kills such a person is apparently subject to the same penalty as one who kills a Jew. An individual who accepts the Noahide laws is deserving of many forms of protection not granted to a pagan, but a member of an entire society of civilized people is elevated to full equality.

In sum, ha-Meiri's essential position can be encapsulated in three basic propositions:

1. Discriminatory laws do not apply to decent societies.
2. Such societies exist only where there is a belief in a single cosmic Deity.
3. Such a belief places its adherents (whether Jews or gentiles) outside the category of worshippers of *avodah zarah* even if they make errors as far reaching as those of Christians in their understanding of that God.

While to the best of my knowledge no other Jewish authority of any standing ever endorsed proposition 3 (and I would like to believe that I am wrong about ha-Meiri as well), the position that many of these laws do not apply to Christians, let alone Muslims, was affirmed by mainstream authorities. The best known passage making such an assertion is in R. Moses Rivkes's *Be'er ha-Golah* to *Hoshen Mishpat* 425:5, which points to Christian belief in creation, the exodus, and the revelation at Sinai, notes the remark originating in *tosafot* that the intention of Christians is to the Creator of heaven and earth, and makes the point that Jews live under Christian protection.

Jacob Katz asserts flatly that this passage affirms the position that Christians—I assume he means gentile Christians—do not worship *avodah zarah*. While this is possible, it is not necessarily the case. The very *tosafot* alluded to in *Be'er ha-Golah* makes clear that even though a Christian who says "God" intends to refer to the Creator of heaven and earth, the name "Jesus" is the name of an *elohim aherim*, and, properly understood, the analysis there almost certainly assumes that if a Jew caused a Christian to worship Jesus, he would violate the prohibition against causing someone to sin. The sin in question, is, of course, *avodah zarah*.

Nonetheless, the tosafists do recognize that this "intention to the Creator" sets Christianity apart from paganism. It is *avodah zarah*, but of a very special sort. To repeat my earlier formulation, it is non-pagan *avodah zarah* in a monotheistic mode. Thus, although a proper understanding of *tosafot* does not establish a two-tier system defining *avodah zarah* differently for Jews and gentiles, it does draw a deep distinction between Christianity and standard expressions of *avodah zarah*. Moreover, with respect to the larger, crucial question of whether or not "*avodah zarah* light" is a coherent category in Judaism, even the erroneous understanding that the tosafists exempted Christians from the prohibition against *shittuf* has great relevance. Authorities who attributed this view to *tosafot* held the position that a theology called Christianity exists in which an act that would be unambiguous *avodah zarah* if performed by a Jew is permissible if performed by a gentile. Clearly their instinct did not rebel against the principle that there can be a form of *avodah zarah* that is less serious than the norm. If we look at the criteria for the application of discriminatory legislation through a theological lens, this distinction may well be enough to exempt Christians from such discrimination. I am strongly inclined to think that this is precisely the position of the *Be'er ha-Golah*, though he would surely not have gone as far as ha-Meiri in the scope of the exemption.

In contemporary times, however, a question arises that was not addressed by these earlier solutions. What of decent secular societies and decent secular individuals who live in them? Here we confront ha-Meiri's second proposition as well as the formulation in *Be'er ha-Golah*, which propose an inextricable link between moral behavior and belief in a single cosmic God. But if the ethical argument in proposition one is self-sufficient, then empirical evidence of a just, enforced, largely obeyed legal system should be sufficient to trigger exemption from discriminatory laws without regard to religious underpinnings. By removing such underpinnings, we eliminate the divine dimension, but in a Christian environment, we also eliminate *avodah zarah*. It is at least slightly strange to say, "We will treat you equally provided that you do not abandon your (admittedly exceptional) *avodah zarah* for secularism."

In a single sentence in the middle of a lengthy footnote, Halbertal makes a remark that bears on this issue. Rabbi Meir ben Shimon of Narbonne had proposed a contrast between *benei dat* and philosophers who deny divine providence and consequently allow themselves all sorts of immoral behavior. Ha-Meiri, says Halbertal, draws the same contrast between *ba'alei dat* and early idolatrous nations, substituting the latter for R. Meir's philosophers. The reason for this change is that "in [ha-Meiri's] opinion the philosopher recognizes that the masses require religion, while he himself is restrained by ethical requirements out of internal reasons rather than religiously generated fear."[34] This assertion, unsupported by any specific citation, is probably based on ha-Meiri's affinity to the medieval philosophers who held precisely this position. However, since Halbertal demonstrated in an earlier chapter that ha-Meiri espoused considerably more moderate, traditional views on related matters than a philosopher like Samuel ibn Tibbon, the assumption that he considered philosophers at least equivalent to *ba'alei dat* cannot be regarded as certain. He explicitly connects moral behavior with belief in a God who exercises providence, and his contrast with ancient idolaters rather than philosophers is necessitated by the Talmudic contexts that he addresses. Having said this, I am nonetheless inclined to think that Halbertal is probably correct; if so, then ha-Meiri himself actually maintained the view that I would like to tease out of his expressed position.

The view that gentile behavior rather than theology determines how Jews should treat them is at least implicit in a relatively recent English essay by R. Ahron Soloveichik. He argues that love of other Jews must be blind, but love of gentiles, which he sees as an obligation expressed in the Rabbinic principle called "love of people" (*ahavat ha-beriyyot*),[35] is grounded in the intellect and varies with the degree to which gentiles lead moral lives and treat Jews decently. This position is spelled out more rigorously in his novellae to *Sefer ha-Madda*. Here he maintains that the discriminatory laws against non-Jews result only from their status as evildoers (their *shem rasha*). Non-Jews who behave righteously by following the six Noahide laws other than the prohibition against *avodah zarah* are not considered evil as long as their theological error was inherited, as the Talmud suggests about pagans in the diaspora, from their parents and is thus considered inadvertent or even a result of compulsion. It is worth quoting more fully R. Jacob Emden's application of this talmudic dictum in a responsum to which R. Soloveichik alludes. "The Sages," says the responsum, "declared, 'The gentiles outside the Land of Israel are not worshippers of *avodah zarah;* rather, they follow the customs of their ancestors.' Therefore their blood is precious in our eyes and would remain so even if we were ruling over them so that they were conquered under our control in our own land. After all, the Sages said—even with respect to full fledged idolaters—that one does not lower them into a pit. How much more is this so in the diaspora where we take refuge under their protection; we are, then, obligated to protect them with all our ability and save them from death and from any loss or damage to the point where even guarding their money should be a labor of love."[36]

Finally, Rabbi Soloveichik's invocation of ha-Meiri[37] in the course of his analysis clearly implies that he regards the latter's distinction between ancient idolaters and his Christian contemporaries as normative.[38]

We return, then, to ha-Meiri. Regardless of whether or not he himself envisioned such a possibility, his analysis allows for the conclusion that an empirically observed social and legal system that follows norms of decent conduct is sufficient to propel a society into the category of civilized nations even if it is not technically bound by the ways of religions. I am acutely aware that such a conclusion requires at least two bold steps.

First, there is the decision to rule in accordance with ha-Meiri's basic position that nations bound by the ways of religions are exempted from discriminatory laws. This does not require that we go as far as ha-Meiri himself did by applying this principle even to some matters of ritual law[39] or denying that Christianity is *avodah zarah* at all. I have already noted that this step was taken by both Rabbis Weinberg and Soloveichik—and they were not alone. Rabbi Isaac Herzog indicated that one could legitimately rely upon ha-Meiri's view.[40] The elder Rav Kook wrote explicitly that "the correct position (*ha-iqqar*) is that of ha-Meiri that all nations bound by decent practices between man and his fellow man are considered as *gerim toshavim* with respect to all obligations involving human beings," and a similar approach was affirmed by Rabbi Samson Raphael Hirsch, Rabbi David Zvi Hoffmann, and Rabbi Hayyim David Halevi.[41] The distinguished decisor R. Eliezer Waldenberg pointed to ha-Meiri's position, denied the plausibility of the notion that he had constructed an entire approach out of fear of censorship and the desire for peace, and concluded that his position can serve us as "a paradigmatic source (*makor beit av*) as we come to consider these problems regarding the nations in our age."[42] Finally, Rabbi Yosef Eliyahu Henkin wrote a remarkable essay asserting that Noahides are not commanded regarding *shittuf*, referring with approval to a strongly positive passage about non-Jews in *Tiferet Yisrael* (*Avot* 3:14),[43] wondering whether even those contemporary non-Jews who bow to images really worship them, insisting that the vast majority of today's gentiles are *gerei toshav*, a category that he says does not require a formal declaration before a court for most purposes, and arguing that both the judicial procedures and the punishments characterizing Noahide law are discretionary.[44] Beyond the fundamental endorsement of ha-Meiri's position, the link between civilized status and theism would have to be severed. The motivation for these steps would lie, as I have already noted, in the *posek*'s belief that they best reflect the moral teachings of the Torah and hence the true will of God.

In certain circles, it has become fashionable to speak with disdain of ha-Meiri as a halakhic authority, sometimes, I am afraid, precisely in the context of his views about non-Jews. This assessment was not shared by the author of the *Shittah Mequbbezet*. In one of his responsa, R. Bezalel Ashkenazi vigorously dismissed a legal opinion because it disagreed with "the pillars of halakhic decision-making (*ammudei ha-hora'ah*): the Rif, the Rambam, the Ramah, the Rosh, and the Meiri."[45] We need not apologize for accepting the judgment of Rabbis Hirsch, Hoffmann, Kook, Herzog, Halevi, Weinberg, Waldenberg, Henkin, and Soloveichik as the basis for endorsing the position of an authority included in such august company by a man who, to paraphrase the famous remark of Samuel, knew the pathways of the *rishonim* like those of his hometown.

The most intractable obligation to exercise intolerance remains the requirement to root out *avodah zarah* from the Land of Israel. As I understand ha-Meiri himself, he would permit even crucifixes worshipped by Jews to remain in their undisturbed churches in the heart of Jerusalem because Christian worship is simply not *avodah zarah*. For all my admitted desire to find grounds for tolerating Christianity in Israel, I am not willing to accept the position that such crucifixes are free of the taint of *avodah zarah*.[46] Rabbi Yehudah Herzl Henkin[47] suggests that our inability to uproot such *avodah zarah* at this time may well represent a providential act designed to postpone a potentially wrenching confrontation to the messianic age, when all the world will willingly abandon all forms of foreign worship.

May I dare, in the spirit of ha-Meiri and *Be'er ha-Golah*, to broach the possibility that the biblical requirement to eliminate *avodah zarah* from Israel applies only to the forms of *avodah zarah* that prevailed in antiquity? The Torah regularly connects the uprooting of paganism to the abominable acts associated with it. In our time, we find ourselves allied with Christians in a struggle against precisely the forms of immorality that ancient paganism fostered. Even Traditionalist Orthodox groups that avoid any formal dialogue with Christian churches engage in cooperative pursuits in the interest of protecting "family values" in legislation and public policy. Perhaps, just perhaps, the uprooting of *such avodah zarah* in pre-messianic times is not required by the Torah. There is no practical halakhic consequence to this suggestion since everyone agrees that the need to maintain harmonious, secure relations with the nations of the world rules out any effort to enforce a ban on *avodah zarah* in Israel. Nevertheless, the matter is of great relevance in the realm of *hashkafah*, and I can console myself that the suggestion is no more radical than the actual position of ha-Meiri. Still, I am well aware that no *posek* has ever said that any form of technical *avodah zarah* may theoretically be allowed in Israel, and I raise the matter only in the context of *derosh ve-qabbel sekhar* (though many readers will surely have serious doubts about the last two words).

I have left this last paragraph as I presented it to the Orthodox Forum so that I can express my full measure of satisfaction upon discovering that the final sentence is incorrect. After reading the typescript, Avie Walfish pointed me to a footnote that I had missed in Rabbi Herzog's article dealing with the standing of non-Jews in a sovereign Jewish state. "Only full-fledged idolaters (*ovdei avodah zarah gemurim*)," suggests Rabbi Herzog, "pursue a form of worship bound up with licentiousness and sorcery and all forms of impurity, and it is only about them that the Torah said, '[They shall not remain in your land] lest they cause you to sin against Me' (Exod. 23.33)."[48]

Finally, just the briefest of observations about the issue of non-Jews' eligibility for a portion in the world to come. It is very well known that the Rambam, based on a passage in *Mishnat Rabbi Eliezer*, requires observance of the seven Noahide commandments out of a belief that they were revealed by God. It is reasonably well known that he sets forth a more lenient criterion in a letter (whose authenticity, to be sure, has not gone unchallenged) to R. Hasdai ha-Levi of Alexandria, where he asserts that what matters is the intention of the heart, so that a gentile who has achieved knowledge of God and developed good character traits will enter the world to come.[49] Since it obviously cannot be taken for granted that a non-Jew who meets these criteria will automatically observe the prohibition against *ever min ha-hai* in all its details, it appears to follow that a Noahide may not have to receive a perfect score in observing his commandments to be eligible for eternal life.

On this point, there is an extraordinarily important and little known observation in the responsum of R. Jacob Emden to which I have already alluded:

> If [Noahides] violate their commandments they are punished, and ultimately they achieve restoration (*yesh lahem tikkun*) after they have received their punishment; they have a dwelling place and portion in the world to come in accordance with what is appropriate for them. The Sages have said, "The pious of the nations of the world have a portion in the world to come." They did not say, "The sinners of the nations of the world are judged for untold generations." Such an eternal punishment would apply only to those who sin with a transgression of the body,[50] as is the case with respect to Jews as well, but other sinners, Jews and gentiles, are not punished forever but, rather, achieve a restored state.[51]

Since, as we have seen earlier, R. Emden is explicitly discussing gentiles who engage in what would be culpable *avodah zarah* if not for the fact that they are following their ancestors' customs, it is clear that such behavior does not exclude them from the category of those who ultimately achieve a portion in the world to come. All this is apparently so despite the fact that R. Emden, in response to an inquiry from Mendelssohn, famously defended the Rambam's view that the salvation of non-Jews depends upon their acknowledgment of the source of the Noahide covenant in divine revelation.

In his classic commentary to the Mishnah, R. Israel Lifshitz unequivocally affirms that Christians have a portion in the world to come. With specific reference to Johannes Reuchlin, he argues that it is unimaginable that God would not reward a man who struggled successfully to defend the Talmud and was consequently driven to an embittered death by anti-Semites. Elsewhere in the commentary, he insists that even gentiles who are less than fully righteous (*beinonim*) have a portion in the world to come, since the Mishnah specifies that Balaam, who is, of course, an exemplar of extraordinary evil, is denied such a portion.[52]

For the Rambam himself, the criterion of knowledge of God is, for philosophical reasons, indispensable for ultimate salvation. Only one who has reached a minimum level of the proper apprehension of God can connect to the spiritual realm to the degree necessary for immortality.[53] Thus, it is unlikely that the Rambam would have affirmed that one with a conception of

God as erroneous as that of Christianity could attain eternal life. However, I think it is fair to say that a large majority of Jews, including major rabbinic authorities, did not and do not share the technical, almost mechanical understanding of immortality characteristic of medieval philosophers. And so we can once again allow ourselves to ask whether a Christian who has perfected his moral traits—a Holocaust rescuer, to return to the most powerful example—might not enter the world to come. How can we not hope that the answer is yes?

Let me conclude by addressing a question that lurks beneath the surface of this entire discussion. If we choose to follow a minority position, or even carve out a new variant of that position, because we feel a powerful moral imperative to do so, are we not running the risk of suggesting that the majority of great Jewish authorities through the ages suffered from a severe moral failing? For two complementary reasons, I do not believe that this is the case. First, people who lived in a society that attempted—with considerable success—to degrade and humiliate them would have understandably felt little motivation to qualify and reinterpret explicit directives in the Talmud. When a Holocaust survivor says something sharply pejorative about all *goyim*, I react very differently than I do when an American-born Jew below the age of fifty says the same thing. There is nothing remarkable in the *rishonim*'s acceptance of discriminatory laws; what is remarkable is ha-Meiri's striking reassessment.

Second, there is the fundamental point that *halakhah* is ultimately rooted in the word of God. With varying degrees of success, we all set aside moral qualms with respect to absolutely unambiguous divine directives that appear problematic to us. In the context of authentic Judaism, submission to the divine will is paramount, and suppression of some humane instincts in the face of clear-cut *halakhah* may be necessary. To ascribe moral failings to the rabbinic authorities of an oppressed people for failure to reinterpret the straightforward meaning of sacred texts discriminating against their persecutors is inappropriate, unfair, insensitive, and incorrect. But this does not mean that we must suppress our own moral instincts when we honestly see them as consistent with, even generated by, the values and teachings of the Torah writ large. We have *'al mi lismokh*, and our religiously informed ethical instincts have a role to play as we examine text and tradition to reach a conception of our relationship to non-Jews that will honor the universal mission assigned to the children of Abraham.[54]

NOTES

1. Rashi's famous comment on Genesis 6:13, paraphrasing R. Yohanan's observation in *Sanhedrin* 105a.

2. I refer, of course, to the contrast between Genesis 22 and Genesis 18:23–33.

3. I compressed the essential argument of the last four paragraphs into one in my contribution to a symposium entitled "What Do American Jews Believe?" in *Commentary* 102:2 (August, 1996): 20. In the discussion of this paper at the Orthodox Forum, Rabbis Norman Lamm and Shalom Carmy noted Buber's similar analysis, and Rabbi Carmy pointed me to R. Ovadiah Seforno's introduction to his commentary on the Torah, where he summarizes the unfolding of the divine plan in Genesis as one of repeated efforts to perfect the human species as a whole ultimately culminating in the need to choose a single *hasid* among the entire species to fulfill the divine plan. See his introduction in *Torat Hayyim* (Jerusalem, 1986), p. 23.

4. When values close to the heart of the contemporary liberal ethos clash with unfettered moral relativism, limits are sometimes rediscovered. Thus, clitoridectomy is often seen as beyond the pale of even an expansive respect for cultural difference.

5. *Hilkhot Avot ha-Tum'ah* 2:10 (omitted for obvious reasons in some printings).

6. Ezek. 23:20. See *Yevamot* 98a; *Tosafot Ketubbot* 3b, s.v. *lidrosh*. Evidence that the Talmud itself did not apply the principle that "their issue is the issue of horses" to sexual relations with a non-Jew was provided by Rivam in his refutation (ibid.) of Rabbenu Tam's position.

7. See *Tosafot Yevamot* 61a, s.v. *ve-ein*. For the wide spectrum of interpretations suggested through the ages regarding this talmudic passage, see Avi Sagi, *Yahadut: Bein Dat le-Musar* (Tel Aviv, 1998), pp. 163–181. Michael Breitstein, in a paper that he submitted to me in a course at Yeshiva University's Bernard Revel Graduate School, called my attention to the remarkable discussion in Rabbi Israel Lipschutz, *Tiferet Yisrael* to *Avot* 3:14 (*Boaz* #1), which argues that Jews are like Adam because their understanding was given to them directly by God; the other nations, unlike Adam, achieved their moral and intellectual insights through their own efforts. Consequently, the appellation "Adam" is "not such a term of praise" for the Jews.

8. *Avodah Zarah* 22b.

9. For a sustained argument that the Rambam denied an essentialist distinction between Jews and non-Jews, see Menachem Kellner, *Maimonides on Judaism and the Jewish People* (Albany, 1991). He has since reinforced this argument in a series of articles and plans a greatly expanded Hebrew version of the book. See the references in his "Maimonides on the Nature of Ritual Purity and Impurity," *Daat Jubilee Volume* (2003): II, n. 5.

10. For a brief discussion of Halevi's ethnocentric position in its cultural context, see my remarks in Gerald Blidstein, David Berger, Sid Z. Leiman, and Aharon Lichtenstein, *Judaism's Encounter with Other Cultures: Rejection or Integration?*, ed. by Jacob J. Schacter, pp. 77–79, and the references in notes 31 and 32.

11. For a succinct summary, see Aharon Kleinberger, *Ha-Mahashavah ha-Pedagogit shel ha-Maharal Mi-Prag* (Jerusalem, 1962), pp. 37–42.

12. *Tanya* 1:1, end. See Adin Steinsaltz, *Be'ur Tanya*, vol. 1 (Jerusalem, 1989), pp. 62–64.

13. On the general question of ethics and law in Judaism, see R. Aharon Lichtenstein's celebrated essay, "Does Jewish Tradition Recognize an Ethic Independent of Halakhah?" in *Modern Jewish Ethics: Theory and Practice* (1972), pp. 62–88, reprinted in M. Kellner, ed., *Contemporary Jewish Ethics* (New York, 1978), pp. 102–123. See too Sagi, *Yahadut: Bein Dat le-Musar* (above, n. 7). Eugene Korn's

"*Tselem Elokim* and the Dialectic of Jewish Morality," *Tradition* 31:2 (Winter, 1997): 5–30 directly addresses issues central to the concerns of this paper, as does R. Yoel Schwartz, *Am Segullah: Yalqut be-Inyenei Ma'alat Am Yisrael ve-Nizhiyyuto*, chapter 3, pp. 43–62. I am grateful to Rabbi Yona Reiss for bringing Rabbi Schwartz's book to my attention.

14. Marc B. Shapiro, "Scholars and Friends: Rabbi Jehiel Jacob Weinberg and Professor Samuel Atlas," *The Torah u-Madda Journal* 7 (1997): 105–121. Note too Gerald Blidstein's report that although Rabbi Joseph B. Soloveitchik did not hesitate to rule that as a practical matter one is obligated to save the life of a non-Jew on the Sabbath, he acknowledged his moral unease with the theoretical prohibition. See *Gilyon* (Heshvan 5754 [1993]): 25, cited in Shapiro, *Between the Yeshiva World and Modern Orthodoxy: The Life and Works of Rabbi Jehiel Jacob Weinberg, 1884–1966* (London and Portland, Oregon, 1999), pp. 182–183, n. 47.

15. This final sentence along with the specific formulations of the alternative questions that R. Shimon ben Shetah might have asked are mine, not Rabbi Soloveichik's. I think, however, that they capture the thrust of his presentation. His views on some of the key issues were later committed to writing in *Sefer Parah Matteh Aharon: Hiddushim al ha-Rambam Sefer Madda* (1997), pp. 138–153. I thank Rabbis Jeremy Wieder and Meir Soloveichik for urging me to read that passage, to which I shall allude further in the course of this discussion. For a vigorous expression of the position that the *kiddush ha-Shem* engendered by returning a lost object to a non-Jew emerges not out of a deception as to what the Torah requires but out of its deepest values, see Schwartz, *Am Segullah*, p. 55. Indeed, he writes, the return of such an object is a full-fledged obligation rooted in the requirement of walking in the ways of God (pp. 60–61). For a defense of the absence of such an obligation, see Michael Broyde and Michael Hecht, "The Gentile and Returning Lost Property According to Jewish Law: A Theory of Reciprocity," *Jewish Law Annual* 13 (2000): 31–45.

16. "Jacob Katz on Jews and Christians in the Middle Ages," in Jay M. Harris, ed., *The Pride of Jacob: Essays on Jacob Katz and His Work* (Cambridge, Mass., 2002), pp. 41–63.

17. *Sanhedrin* 63b, s.v. *asur*. I have discussed the various interpretations of this *tosafot* in Appendix III of *The Rebbe, the Messiah and the Scandal of Orthodox Indifference* (London and Portland, Oregon, 2001), pp. 175–177.

18. *Exclusiveness and Tolerance* (London, 1961), p. 113.

19. "Christians, Gentiles, and the Talmud: A Fourteenth-Century Jewish Response to the Attack on Rabbinic Judaism," in *Religionsgespräche im Mittelalter*, ed. by Bernard Lewis and Friedrich Niewöhner (Wiesbaden, 1992), p. 130.

20. See Katz's discussion in *Exclusiveness and Tolerance*, p. 104. See too Judah Galinsky's Yeshiva University Master's thesis, *R. Moshe mi-Coucy ke-Hasid, Darshan u-Pulmesan: Hebbetim me-Olamo ha-Mahshavti u-Pe'iluto ha-Tzibburit* (New York, 1993).

21. I have addressed some aspects of the complex question of self-image and image of the other in the medieval Jewish-Christian relationship in "'Al Tadmitam ve-Goralam shel ha-Goyim be-Sifrut ha-Pulmus ha-Ashkenazit," in *Yehudim mul ha-Zelav*, ed. by Yom Tov Assis et al. (Jerusalem, 2000), pp. 74–91. The article also analyzes views of the eschatological fate of gentile nations, a much-debated issue in recent scholarship that I have not considered here.

22. See Walter Wurzburger, *Ethics of Responsibility: Pluralistic Approaches to Covenantal Ethics* (Philadelphia, 1994), and Yitzchak Blau, "The Implications of a Jewish Virtue Ethic," *The Torah u-Madda Journal* 9 (2000): 19–41. Cf. Schwartz's remarks in *Am Segullah*, pp. 58–60.

23. Halbertal argued this position first in "R. Menahem ha-Meiri: Bein Torah le-Hokhmah," *Tarbiz* 63 (1994): 63–118 and again in his *Bein Torah le-Hokhmah: Rabbi Menahem ha-Meiri u-Ba'alei ha-Halakhah ha-Maimunim bi-Provence* (Jerusalem, 2000). An English translation of much of the relevant chapter appeared in the online *Edah Journal* 1 (2000). This understanding of ha-Meiri's view of the relationship between the theological and ethical realms also appears, perhaps independently, perhaps in consequence of Halbertal's *Tarbiz* article, in a 1995 responsum by R. Yehudah Herzl Henkin, *Shu"t Benei Banim* 3 (1997): 121.

24. Ibid.

25. A. Sofer, ed., *Beit ha-Behirah le-Massekhet Avodah Zarah* (Jerusalem, 1964), pp. 4, 9, 32, 189. See Halbertal, *Bein Torah le-Hokhmah*, pp. 84–86.

26. I re-read the relevant material with the wistful hope that ha-Meiri might make consistent use of the term *avodat elilim* rather than *avodah zarah* in passages where he denies the persistence of such practices. Disappointingly, the two terms appear to be used interchangeably.

27. "Divine Unity in Maimonides, the Tosafists and Meiri," in Lenn Evan Goodman, ed., *Neoplatonism and Jewish Thought* (Albany, NY, 1992), pp. 237–253.

28. A. Sofer, ed., *Bet ha-Behirah le-Massekhet Horayot ve-Eduyot* (Jerusalem, 1958), p. 275. See Katz, *Exclusiveness and Tolerance*, pp. 123–124 and Halbertal, *Bein Torah le-Hokhmah*, pp. 101–102.

29. This is not to say that no other Jews ever expressed such views. See Ishmael Hanina ben Mordekhai ha-Rofe, *Sheva Haqirot* (Husiatyn, 1903), pp. 2ff. *Ha-Shahar* 2, pp. 17–19, whose comments were made under Christian interrogation in sixteenth-century Italy. Compare the similar, uncoerced argument of Solomon Modena, another sixteenth-century Italian Jew, published and discussed in David Ruderman, "A Jewish Apologetic Treatise from Sixteenth-Century Bologna," *Hebrew Union College Annual* 50 (1979): 253–276. I elaborated very slightly on these sources in *The Rebbe*, pp. 160–161, n. 2.

30. Shapiro, "Scholars and Friends," p. 118. See too Shapiro's *Between the Yeshiva World and Modern Orthodoxy*, p. 183.

31. See Appendix II ("The Parameters of *Avodah Zarah*") and Appendix III ("The *Tosafot* on Association [*Shittuf*])," in *The Rebbe*, pp. 159–177.

32. Some measure of consolation can be derived from the fact that one reason for the failure to exclude such believers from Orthodox Judaism is the conviction that these views are held by less than a handful of marginal, even unbalanced individuals. This conviction results from behavior not very different from that of Galileo's famous visitor—a steadfast refusal to look at manifest evidence, in this instance evidence that the theology in question is affirmed and disseminated by prominent rabbis serving in the central institutions of Chabad-Lubavitch and has penetrated deeply into the lay community. I am afraid, however, that even when observers reluctantly conclude that they are not dealing with a figment of my imagination, the effective legitimation of the believers remains intact.

33. *Bein Torah le-Hokhmah*, p. 87, n. 13.

34. *Bein Torah le-Hokhmah*, p. 101, n. 35.

35. R. Soloveichik (*Logic of the Heart, Logic of the Mind*, 1992, p. 70) cites R. Hayyim Vital's affirmation of an obligation to love even gentiles, as does Schwartz, *Am Segullah*, p. 62. Yitzchak Blau has provided a list of five additional authorities who maintain this position; see Blau, "The Implications of a Jewish Virtue Ethic," p. 27.

36. *Sefer She'elat Yavetz* (Lemberg, 1884), responsum 41, p. 36b, column 1. For a discussion of some of the relevant issues and sources, see R. Ovadiah Yosef's responsum encouraging Jews to pray for the recovery of sick gentiles: *She'elot u-Teshuvot Yehavveh Da'at* (Jerusalem, 1976/7), vol. 6, #60.

37. Pp. 139, 151.

38. Rabbi Soloveichik (p. 140) goes further by inferring the position that he advocates from *Tosafot Hullin* 13b, s.v. *nokhrim*. (Because of a typographical error, his first reference to the *tosafot* cites *Hullin* 10 rather than 13.) In this instance, his deduction seems to go beyond the evidence.

39. I did not address these examples in my discussion because discrimination in ritual law is not my major concern. For details of ha-Meiri's almost incredible (and to some observers who believe these passages are forgeries, fully incredible) application of his category to matters of *yihus* and preparing food on holidays, see Halbertal's discussion, pp. 92–96.

40. See R. Yitzhak Eizik ha-Levi Herzog, *Tehuqah le-Yisrael al pi ha-Torah*, vol. 3, (Jerusalem, 1989), p. 278. See too Itamar Warhaftig, "Rabbi Herzog's Approach to Modernity," in Moshe Sokol, ed., *Engaging Modernity: Rabbinic Leaders and the Challenge of the Twentieth Century* (Northvale, NJ, and Jerusalem, 1997), pp. 288–289. (Warhaftig's translation does not properly reproduce the clause "Gam le-aharei she-anu meqabbelim et divrei ha-Meiri ha-yedu'im al ha-ummot ha-gedurot be-darkhei ha-datot," so that the reader is puzzled by his assertion that R. Herzog relies on ha-Meiri's position.) In addition to R. Ahron Soloveichik's discussion in the works cited in notes 15 and 35, see his "Be-Inyan Bikkur Holim u-Refuah," *Beit Yitczhak* 22 (1990): 218–248, which was brought to my attention by Jeffrey Hochberg.

41. Rabbi Avraham Yitzhak ha-Kohen Kook, *Iggerot Ra'yah*, vol. 1 (Jerusalem, 1961), p. 99; I am grateful to Rabbi Dov Linzer and Prof. Marc Shapiro for calling my attention to this passage. Prof. Shapiro also alerted me to the comments by Rabbis Hirsch, Hoffmann, and Halevi. See Rabbi Samson Raphael Hirsch, *Judaism Eternal*, vol. 2 (London, 1956), pp. 167ff.; Rabbi David Zvi Hoffmann, *Der Shulchan-Aruch und die Rabbinen ueber das Verhaeltnis der Juden zu Andersglauebigen* (Berlin, 1894); and Rabbi Hayyim David Halevi, *Aseh Lekha Rav*, vol. 9 (Tel Aviv, 1989), #32. See too vol. 8 (Tel Aviv, 1988), #68. (I had long been familiar with Hoffmann's position—see n. 4 of my article in the Katz volume [above, n. 16]—but had neglected to cite it in the initial version of this paper.) In the last three cases, the exclusion or near exclusion of Christianity from the category of *avodah zarah* goes beyond the point that I think the evidence warrants, but the substantive position of these authorities significantly augments the list of rabbinic figures who insisted upon equal treatment for ethical non-Jews. R. Hirsch does not explicitly cite ha-Meiri, but, in sweeping terms clearly intended to include Christians, he writes of our obligation to treat non-Jews who observe their commandments exactly as we would treat Jews.

42. Introductory letter to Hayyim David Halevi, *Bein Yisrael la-Ammim* (Jerusalem, 1954), pp. 16–17. Here again I am indebted to Marc Shapiro for the reference.

43. See above, n. 7 and the text below at n. 52.

44. He remarks—without specifying examples—that there are many proofs of this position in the Bible. When a twentieth-century authority proves a point about Jewish law directly from the Bible, it is clear that unusual concerns are at work. R. Henkin goes on to assert that a Talmudic term describing a harsh form of indirect execution (*kippah*) really refers to ordinary imprisonment; however, it comes with an option allowing the court—under unusual circumstances—to impose the more extreme measure described in the Talmud. Those who interpret the matter otherwise speak evil (*dovrim sarah*) of the Sages. Similarly, the law that a non-Jew can be convicted in a judicial process involving just one witness and one judge does not establish a norm or an ideal, merely a permissible procedure. The proper approach, says Rabbi Henkin, is that of the United States, where the judgment of many individuals (presumably jurors) is required to impose punishments. See Henkin, "Qetz ha-Yamin," *Ha-Darom* 10 (Elul, 5719): 5–9.

45. Yisrael Feldman, ed., *She'elot u-Teshuvot Rabbenu Bezalel Ashkenazi* (1955), #6, p. 22a, col. 1.

46. I doubt that we are helped very much even by the view that Christianity is permitted to gentiles. There are, after all, Jewish converts to Christianity in Israel, and they too kneel before Israeli crucifixes in Israeli churches.

47. Pp. 131–132.

48. "Zekhuyot ha-Mi'utim le-fi ha-Halakhah," *Tehumin* 2 (1981): 174, n. 9.

49. *Kovetz Teshuvot ha-Rambam ve-Iggerotav* II, pp. 23b–24a; Yitzhak Shailat, *Iggerot ha-Rambam* (Jerusalem, 1987), vol. 2, p. 681. Both Rabbi Soloveichik (*Parah Matteh Aharon*, p. 153) and Rabbi Schwartz (*Am Segullah*, p. 47) made reference to this letter. See Shailat's objections to its authenticity in his edition, pp. 673–676.

50. *Tosafot* understands the talmudic formulation defining *posh'ei ummot ha-olam begufan* as those who transgress "ba-averah" to refer to sexual sin. See *Rosh ha-Shanah* 17a.

51. *Sefer She'elat Yavetz*, responsum 41, p. 36b, column 1.

52. *Tiferet Yisrael to Avot* 3:14 (*Boaz* #1) and *Sanhedrin* 10:1 (*Yakhin* #2), brought to my attention by Michael Breitstein.

53. Cf. Arthur Hyman's argument that this is why the Rambam requires an understanding of the non-corporeal nature of God as a sine qua non for entry into the world to come; see "Maimonides' 'Thirteen Principles'," in Alexander Altmann, ed., *Jewish Medieval and Renaissance Studies* (Cambridge, Mass., 1967), pp. 141–142.

54. I complete the written version of this paper during a period of horrific crimes committed against the Jewish people—and the world at large—by the bearers of a monotheistic culture. On the one hand, these events make it difficult to avoid a reassessment of the relationship between monotheism and an ethical way of life, though we must keep in mind that the medieval Christians whom ha-Meiri declared to be bound by the ways of religion hardly represented an ideal society. On the other hand, the evident disregard for the most elementary rights of the Other that arouses our instinctive revulsion as we witness these terrible events should inspire us to ever greater sensitivity in our own understanding of the ethical obligations imposed by a faith whose ways are the ways of pleasantness and all of whose pathways are peace.

Finally, let me note with gratitude that R. Aharon Lichtenstein, while not addressing any specific argument in this article (and asserting in fact that he feels that "the uniqueness of *kedushat Yisrael* is somewhat diluted"), affirmed among other very kind comments that its "quest for the resolution of a difficult ethical and religious issue" constitutes "not an exercise in 'honest doubt' but rather a manifestation of *avodat Hashem*."

5

Jewish Law and American Public Policy: A Principled Jewish View and Some Practical Jewish Observations

Michael J. Broyde

MEA CULPA

I am not a political scientist, and I am not active in American political life, such that my observations about what is good or bad for Jews in America are worthy of publication or even discussion. In the synagogue where I worship, we have a rule that the rabbi is not allowed to speak about naked political matters from the pulpit, even Israeli matters, and that has struck most of the congregants, and the rabbi himself, as a wise idea, since these are exceedingly divisive matters whose truth is hard to prove, other than with hindsight—and then it is too late!

Having said all of this, the reader might ask why I was asked to present a paper on law and public policy—and why I agreed to do so.

The answer is that this paper is primarily focused on what Jewish law *requires of Jews* in matters of public policy. This is a matter that my scholarly skill can address. At the end of the paper, I cannot help but do that which I know I lack the credentials to undertake: I apply the principles that I develop to the public arena, as I perceive it. That final step is the one most vulnerable to criticism and for that, I apologize.

MONOTHEISM AND FUNDAMENTALS OF JEWISH LAW

Jewish law presupposes that there is just one God, and that such a Deity is the sole God in the heavens and the earth, unmatched and omniscient. Jewish law expects that all people—Jews and Gentiles—will accept this one God as THE GOD and worship God appropriately, Jews according to Jewish law, and everyone else according to Noahide law. (Noahide law is that area of Jewish law that discusses what Jewish law thinks Gentiles should be doing, and is, in the eyes of Jewish law, as binding as Jewish law itself).[1] To the extent that one can speak about a single Jewish contribution to religious civilization, it is this exact notion of monotheism; this single value permeates every facet of rabbinic thought. Inversely, Judaism's profound distaste for polytheism or paganism, either by Jews or Gentiles, is profound and pervasive.

A word on paganism—a distasteful word to the modern American mind—is needed. Jewish law is rigorously monotheistic and has a considerable amount of religious contempt for faiths that deny the unity of God. These faiths are referred to in this article as pagan or polytheistic.[2] Conversely, the Jewish tradition has a great deal of respect for the inherent validity of monotheistic faiths other than Judaism. The Jewish tradition does *not* maintain that all must acknowledge the "Jewish" God; rather, it recognizes that monotheism need not be accompanied by recognition of the special role of the Jewish people.[3] Maimonides' opening formulation of the Jewish view of messianic times is revealing. He writes:

> One should not think that in messianic times that the normal practices of the world will change or that the laws of nature will change. Rather, the world will be as it always is. The words of the prophet Isaiah "and the wolf will dwell with the lamb, and the leopard shall lie down with the goat" are metaphors meaning that the Jews will live peacefully among the gentile nations of the world.[4]

Even in messianic times, the Jewish tradition avers *that there will and should be* Gentiles—people who are not members of the Jewish faith. *The existence of those who are not Jewish is part of the Jewish ideal, which requires that all worship the single God, although not exclusively through the Jewish prism of worship.* The Talmud insists that in messianic times conversion into Judaism will not be allowed; Jews and Gentiles will peacefully co-exist.[5] Jewish law is not the ideal legal code for all—only for Jews. For example, consider the remarks of Rabbi Judah Loewe of Prague concerning the Jewish law prohibition of crossbreeding in animals. He states:

> There are those who are aghast of the interbreeding of two species. *Certainly, this is contrary to Jewish law which God gave the Jews, which prohibits interspecies mixing.* Nonetheless, Adam (the First Person) did this. Indeed, the world was created with many species that are prohibited to be eaten. Inter-species breeding was not prohibited because of prohibited sexuality or immorality. . . . Rather, it is because Jews should not combine the various species together, as this is the way of Jewish law. As we already noted, the ways of the Jewish law

> and the [proper] ways of the world are distinct. . . . *Even those forms of creativity which Jewish law prohibits for Jews, are not definitionally bad. Some are simply prohibited to Jews.*[6]

What flows most clearly from this is that there is nothing intrinsically wrong with crossbreeding, even if it violates Jewish law; indeed, Rabbi Loewe nearly states that such conduct by Gentiles is good. Jewish law is not a general ethical category governing the conduct of all; its scope and application is limited to Jews, not merely jurisdictionally, but even theologically.

JEWISH LAW AND PAGANISM

An interesting trend can be found in modern American culture; once freedom of religion was genuinely granted to all Americans (about 50 years ago),[7] pagan and polytheistic religions began to multiply—they asked to be a part of the public religious dialogue in American culture. It is almost as if the talmudic observation that the hunger for paganism was dead[8] had been proven wrong in America. No less a public religious figure than Rev. Pat Robertson, founder of the Christian Coalition, recently decried this phenomenon, and has even indicated that he will oppose faith-based government funding unless something can be done to eliminate the "deviant" religions from the right to receive government funding. Robertson states:

> Our laws do not let government engage in content discrimination of speech. The same government grants given to Catholics, Protestants and Jews must also be given to the Hare Krishnas, the Church of Scientology or Sun Myung Moon's Unification Church—no matter that some may use brainwashing techniques or that the founder of one claims to be the messiah and another that he was Buddha reincarnated. Under the proposed faith-based initiative, all must receive taxpayer funds if they provide "effective" service to the poor. In my mind, this creates an intolerable situation.[9]

Although Rev. Robertson does not explicitly explain why this is "an intolerable situation," what he undoubtedly means is that any religion whose founder claims to be the messiah or Buddha reincarnated ought not be allowed to be part of any government program. It is better to have no government programs than to have programs that support any and all religions. These religions, Robertson feels, ought to be not supported.

This paper will address whether the across-the-board support for all religions—including pagan faiths—creates an intolerable political situation for Jews who adhere to Jewish law. How should we respond to attempts to deny pagans the right to worship freely? This article will explore how Jewish law and Orthodox Jewish society should respond to requests for religious freedom by members of secular society to the secular government, when we know that many will use their newly minted Freedom of Religion to engage in pagan rituals and practices that are categorically and absolutely forbidden to all (Jew or Gentile) according to Jewish law. It will then address a related question: What should Jewish public policy be when addressing other matters that violate Jewish law or that encourage the violation of Jewish or Noahide law?

Consider, for example, a stark case of conflicting values. In 1989, the city of Hialeah, Florida, passed an ordinance that suppresses the right of a group of pagans to engage in their animal sacrifice, rites which are central to their religious belief and ritual conduct. The members of the suppressed religious faith sued, alleging a violation of their First Amendment right to freedom of religion. This case is more complex as a matter of American law than it might appear, as the Supreme Court had recently ruled in *Employment Division v. Smith*[10] that neutral governmental rules can be applied against religious activity—thus, for example, a law that prohibits medically unnecessary surgical procedures for children could ban ritual circumcision.[11] Should a Jewish institute for public affairs support Hialeah's law because it does, in fact, suppress paganism (as Jewish law wants) or should it support the right of the pagans to worship freely, as freedom of worship is a valuable principle that we ought to defend even if the people who are now using this principle conduct their lives in violation of Jewish law (Noahide law) principles, since they are pagan polytheists worshiping many gods?

The theme of this paper is that these decisions are in the eyes of Jewish law, broadly speaking, political decisions, and not strictly ones of Jewish law. They are not governed by a tight calculus of always requiring that one seek from the secular government a policy that maximizes observance either of Jewish law or of Noahide law. If one can persuasively argue this approach with regard to paganism, then I believe that this argument extends *mutatis mutandis* to every other violation of the Jewish law, each of which is less serious than the utter rejection of monotheism.

Jewish Law Is Not Internally Religiously Pluralistic

Before one proceeds to analyze an exact response to polytheism in Jewish law, one must realize that the unvarnished Jewish law (stripped of any nuances and complexities) is neither very pluralistic in its core values nor deeply tolerant of rooted and structured dissent from principles of Jewish law. The simple quotation from Maimonides directly lays out the pristine Jewish law as he understood it. Maimonides states:

> Heretics and apostates, those who worship idols yet are Jewish, or they sin in other ways to flaunt their sinfulness, even eating not kosher or wearing mixed

wool and linen garments, are heretics. Heretics—which are those who deny torah and prophecy among the Jews—it is a good deed (*mitzvah*) to kill them. If one can kill them in public, with a sword, do that; otherwise, interact with them in stealth, until you can kill them. For example, if one sees one of them fall into a pit, and the ladder is in the pit, quickly grab the ladder from the pit and tell them "I am running to take my child down from the roof and then I will return it" [and then do not return it] or other such actions.[12]

One can find many medieval Jewish law commentators who argue with the details of this exposition of the Jewish law. One can note that most medieval commentators prohibit actually killing even an intentional first-generation heretic. However, merely permitting indirect murder or even simply noting that one should not save such people from death and we wish they were dead[13] is illustrative of the fact that there is very little substantive textual support in Jewish law for the "live and let live" classical religious pluralism adopted by American law.[14]

One is hard-pressed to find—internal to Jewish law—much that is positive to be said about the values of letting people worship whichever gods they see fit. The structured response of one group of commentators is that such people ought to be killed in public as a display of what happens to those who rebel, and a "more liberal" view is that we should merely arrange for the indirect death of these people, without actually killing them! Yet a "more liberal" view posits that one should merely not save such people and let them die. None are very "pluralistic" in their orientation. Jewish law has the same theoretical view towards Gentiles and central violations of Noahide law; violations are punished, by execution and sometimes by other means, and systemic rebellion is punished by death.[15]

Thus, those who seek to advocate tolerance and pluralism as a political agenda by the Jewish community will not find it in the classical rabbinic sources themselves when they deal with flagrant and open sinners. Where then does this approach come from? The answer, I suspect, is in the logic of practical calculus captured well by the rabbinic phrase *yatza sekharo be-hefsado*[16]—the gain accrued through any given action can sometimes be lost through the price paid. Whenever the Jewish community sets out to advance a political or religious agenda, it should not only look at the gain from advance, but also the losses it must sustain to accomplish this advance, and whether—no matter how hard it tries—it will lose anyway, and thus ought not even try.

Elsewhere I have developed a model for reciprocal economic rights according to Jewish law, which is a more principled exposition of this notion. That article posits that:

in the area of financial rights, duties and obligations, Jewish law frequently excluded Gentiles from the full benefits of Jewish law because Jewish law did not

> consider them to be bound by the obligations of Jewish law. Thus, for example, Jewish law did not compel the return of the lost property of a Gentile, since he was not legally obligated to return lost property belonging to others. Exclusion was based on a failure of reciprocity—the privileges of Jewish law were given only to those who were fully obligated in and thus accepting of Jewish law, in this case, the laws of lost property. . . .
>
> Thus, one can now fully comprehend the importance of personal status and reciprocity plays in the law of lost property. The unmodified talmudic rule for property of a person who does not consider himself bound by Jewish law is that one is under no obligation to return the lost property of such a person, since that person—honest as he might be—does not consider himself reciprocally legally obligated to return such property. Jewish law ruled that one may—but need not—return his property, just as he may—but need not—return your property. On the other hand, in the case of a person who considers himself bound by Jewish law to return lost property, one is obligated to return the property of such a person precisely because the person feels legally obligated to do the same. Indeed, the same rule is true for the lost property of a person who is legally bound according to secular law to return lost property to others. Jewish law would require that his property be returned, as he would do the same to a Jew.[17]

In this approach, Jewish law codified reciprocity as the manner of measuring the gain and loss. Indeed, a case can be made that this type of balancing is substantively principled in that it extends Jewish law rights to people who grant Jews secular rights. However, it is clear that this calculus is not grounded in a moral theory of political rights such as Dworkin or Rawls would consider consistent with liberal conceptions of political justice. A case could be made that the principles demonstrated in that article can form a basis for political pluralism in the Jewish tradition grounded in more than mere politics of survival.

If the proper Jewish response to a request for civil rights for pagan rites is to engage in a political calculus of reciprocity—rather than to automatically support restrictions that diminish paganism—the same political calculus is needed for every component of basic morality. The decision by the Jewish community to support the expansion or contraction of civil or political rights in secular law is not a Jewish law discussion and it never has been. Why this is so is explained in the next section.

THERE IS NO OBLIGATION TO PREVENT SECULAR SOCIETY FROM SINNING

In an earlier article of mine, presented at an earlier Orthodox Forum of Yeshiva University, entitled "Jewish Law and the Obligation to Enforce Secular Law,"[18] I there reviewed the relevant technical Jewish law and concluded that *classical Jewish law does not compel a Jew to persuade or entice a people generally to observe the law* and that Jewish law sees no technical obligation in most situations—even as it is morally laudatory—to insure that Noahides obey their laws.

Why is there no obligation to monitor secular law and values to insure that they are consistent with Jewish law? The answer (as explained in the above quoted article) is that most decisors of Jewish law rule that—other than in situations where one is the "but for" causation of a person sinning—Jews are not responsible, in a formal, technical, Jewish law sense, for the content of secular law or for its enforcement. (This is even more so true for the general tone of secular society.)

Even though there is no technical Jewish obligation to inform uninterested Gentiles of the Noahide law, and no obligation upon Jews to enforce Noahide law, there are no less than five reasons why the Jewish community might, nonetheless, choose to participate in the articulation of values and law in Gentile community. They are:

A. Heightened Ethical Duties to All People Created in God's Image

Jewish law recognizes that it is morally laudatory to inspire people to observe Noahide law. Ethics of the Fathers (Perkai Avot) states: "Rabbi Akiva used to say, Humanity is precious since people were created in God's image."[19] And Rabbi Lipman Heller comments: "Rabbi Akiva is speaking about the value of all people. . . . He wished to benefit all people including Noahides. . . . Rabbi Akiva seeks to elevate all inhabitants of the world."[20] Rabbi Judah the Pious observes: "When one sees a Noahide sinning, if one can correct him, one should, since God sent Jonah to Nineveh to return them to his path."[21]

Thus, there are many theological reasons why it might be good to teach Noahide laws generally, and indeed, a claim can be made that Jewish law obligates a truthful response to an honest query from a person concerning his obligation under the Noahide code.[22]

B. Corruption in Society Affects Us All

Jews are part of the general society, and what ails a general society will come to ail Jews, too. Rabbi Moses Schick states:

> [I]t appears that any situation that involves judging violators, even if they are Noahides, is a Jewish person's concern, for others will learn from any wrong done in public and will follow suit and, in the least, the sight of evil is harmful to the soul. Thus, it is our concern. In any case, it is inconceivable that any person living among the residents of a given city be beyond the jurisdiction of the [Jewish] court.[23]

Rabbi J. David Bleich puts it a little differently. He states:

> Despite the absence of a specific *obligation* to influence non-Jews to abide by the provisions of the Noahide Code, the attempt to do so is entirely legitimate. Apart from our universal concern, fear lest "the world become corrupt," as Maimonides

> puts it, it is also very much a matter of Jewish concern and self-interest. Disintegration of the moral fabric of society affects everyone. Particularly in our age we cannot insulate ourselves against the pervasive cultural forces which mold human conduct. Jews have every interest in promoting a positive moral climate.[24]

Corruption of values affects all, and one needs to work to insure values in society—our society in which we fully participate.

C. Desecration of God's Name

By standing by silently when others sin, Jews sometimes appear to be supporting or condoning violations, which are themselves a desecration of God's name. It is possible that there could be situations where public institutional silence by Jewish groups as to the propriety of a particular activity by Government or other groups, particularly when other religious groups are protesting this activity as immoral, could lead to desecrations of God's name and thus a wrong. On the other hand, the more clearly known it is that governmental policy is non-religious in nature and that Jewish law imposes no obligation on Jews to protest, the less serious an issue this becomes.[25]

D. Fixing the World: Tikun Olam

The mandate of *tikun olam*, a Jewish obligation to make the world a better place, might provide some direction.[26] Volume VI of the Orthodox Forum series was directed towards this principle, and the many different essays shed some light on this concept.[27] However, fixing the world has never been treated as a mandatory Jewish law principle in the same way as any general *religious obligation*, or even as a rabbinic obligation. One can choose, in particular circumstances, not to fix the world now if the consequences of fixing are deleterious to one's long-term interest.

E. Being a Light unto the Nations: Ohr la-Goyim

There is the philosophical mandate to be a "light unto the nations of the world." As noted by medieval scholar Rabbi David Kimchi commenting on the words "light unto the nations" (Isaiah 42:6), "because of the influence of the Jews, the Gentiles will observe the seven commandments and follow the right path." While an elaboration on this concept is beyond the scope of this paper, and deserving one of its own, a brief review of the use of the term "light unto the nations" indicates that it is normally used to mean that the Jews should behave in an exemplary manner such that Gentiles will wish to imitate Jews, and not as a mandate to proselytize observance of Noahide law.[28]

Summation

There is a wealth of rabbinic sources that encourage one to be an active participant in the secular society which one resides in. However, this participation was never deemed, either formally nor informally, to be a *mitzvah* and was never formulated as any sort of a Jewish religious imperative.

CONCERNS IN THE OPPOSITE DIRECTION

The absence of a general obligation upon Jews to increase observance of the Noahide code by Gentiles, or to rebuke Gentiles when they violate Noahide law, or to separate Gentiles from sin, allows for a balancing of Jewish interests to occur; Jews need not participate in general society to the detriment of the Jewish community or individual Jews. This is even true given the presence of such concepts as the prohibition of generating hatred through rebuke,[29] which certainly allow one to be silent in the face of sin by both Jews and Gentiles. So too, the lack of obligation to rebuke an intentional sinner[30] diminishes the obligation mandating conduct to castigate sinners and remove sin. Even more so, the license to facilitate sin when the sin will happen no matter what a Jew does (and the sinner is a knowing and willing participant in a deliberate violation of Jewish or Noahide law) further reduces the force of the obligation.[31]

In sum, Jewish law does not mandate that Jews need to craft a policy towards secular law that always penalizes a violation of either Noahide or Jewish Law. Jewish history supports this understanding of obligation. One sees very little overt response—in the sense of active involvement—by the Jewish law community to the conduct of the Gentile community.

Of course, it would be ideal if we could always adopt a policy that increases fidelity to Noahide law by Gentiles, to Jewish law by Jews, and was also consistent with the Constitution of the United States. Sadly, we cannot—because these values are frequently mutually exclusive. Frequently, we are called upon to make hard choices about which values we want to put on the public agenda before other values. The possibility that there might be circumstances where the unfettered teaching of the Noahide code in the United States (where distinctions based on religious affiliation, content, or practice cannot be governmentally defended) could be deleterious to the observance of Jewish law by Jews is not to be dismissed.[32] The possibility that a clearly Jewish attempt to seek enforcement of Noahide laws could result in vast antagonism and backlash towards Jews and Judaism from those groups whose conduct is categorically prohibited by Noahide law cannot be ignored. The consequences of endorsing and supporting a governmental policy that denies civil rights and encourages economic discrimination against people who engage in pagan conduct which violates Noahide law, but which harms no one other than other willing participants, might be very drastic and deleterious to the Jewish community, which has benefited mightily from ironclad rules against religious discrimination, both on a private and a public level.

This view of the mandates of Jewish law is supported by the Orthodox Jewish response to the *Church of the Lukumi Babalu Aye*[33] (discussed as a hypothetical on page 112) dealing with pagan animal sacrifice. This case, in fact, was litigated, and many different Orthodox Jewish organizations briefed in the Supreme Court in support of pagans' right to worship.[34] Not a single Orthodox group briefed in favor of the City of Hialeah and the suppression of paganism. Why? Certainly not because the conduct in this matter is permitted by Jewish law or Noahide law. One can claim that the conduct of this group is a central breach of everything the Jewish tradition stands for—monotheism. Nevertheless, the institutional advocacy groups within the Orthodox community realize that freedom to worship ought to be protected as a matter of secular law, even when the way worship occurs is a fundamental violation of our most basic Jewish rules and values. Were pagans to spread their religious values, one could readily see an anthropological change in how religion would be viewed, just as Judaism was viewed dramatically differently two thousand years ago when surrounded by polytheistic pagans. Yet, the Orthodox Jewish community and its various institutions have all been diligent in supporting freedom of worship for all, because, in the totality of the picture, it is of benefit to Orthodox Judaism.[35]

Thus, the central question is simple to state when it comes to matters of civil rights: what policy will leave the Jewish community better off? Indeed, this is part of a very complicated general question about whether the Orthodox community ought to seek the expansion of civil rights generally and political pluralism specifically, so as to protect the economic and political interest of the Jewish community.

(My own view of what is needed is stated in the next section, but the answer I provide is centrally unimportant to this methodological discussion, because the details of my calculus may be wrong—I, of course, think not. However, precisely because there is no exact Jewish law mandate compelling one to support increased observance of Noahide law as a Jewish law obligation, one must weigh a political calculus of what to do.)

Legislative goals which do not necessarily seek to enforce Jewish law can be well supported from the positions taken by decisors of Jewish law on political questions. For example, in 1977 Rabbi Moses Feinstein—the dean of the Orthodox Rabbinate in America—was asked what statutory changes Orthodoxy should seek from the New York State government on the issue of time of death. He replied that Orthodoxy should seek a legislative mandate that allows each person (or family) to determine the time of death in accordance with their own religious or personal beliefs. He did not suggest that the proper governmental policy to seek is that New York State should be urged to adopt Jewish law in this area. The public policy advocated by Rabbi Feinstein in the context of time of death—one of Orthodoxy seeking to allow Jews to follow Jewish tradition, without forcing our standards on non-believers—was the preferred one. This was so notwithstanding the certainty that some people, given this new freedom, will adopt a standard for time of death which violates Jewish law by withdrawing care before a time permitted by Jewish law and thus committing murder—the only violation on par with polytheism. Rabbi Feinstein did not feel compelled to seek the enforcement of Jewish law by the secular state.[36] As Rabbi Chaim Dovid Zweibel of Agudath Israel of America puts it: "The principle of religious accommodation is one that has stood the American Orthodox Jewish community in good stead in a wide variety of secular legal contexts. . . . For what is really at issue here is . . . whether it is in the interest of the Torah observant community to combat secular laws that preclude individuals from following the guidance of their individual [Jewish law] decisors."[37]

Indeed, in the famous amicus brief filed by Agudath Israel of America in *Webster v. Reproductive Health Serv.*, 429 U.S. 490 (1989), Agudath Israel of America argued that secular abortion law ought never be allowed to become law if such a law would preclude individuals from following the guidance of their individual religious leaders and having an abortion when mandated (as Jewish law sometimes does) by their own religious beliefs. This, one assumes, includes pagan religious leaders as well, and would include abortions that are murder in the eyes of Jewish law.

The portion of the paper that I feel fully comfortable with is now over, and is worthy of summary. Jewish law imposes no religious obligation upon its adherents to seek to impose Jewish law as a personal religious value on individual members of society who do not wish to accept it. Thus, Jews who function according to Jewish law are not obligated to adopt political strategies that maximize adherence to Jewish or Noahide law by others, and may instead adopt alternative strategies with alternative goals.

PRACTICAL APPLICATIONS

This section is written with a more tentative voice. See the mea culpa introduction.

What is the political calculus that one must weigh? What policy is in the long-term best interest of the Jewish community? To me, the answer is increasing religious, social, and cultural freedom, even if it leads to violations of Jewish or Noahide law. Freedom is a better alternative for a Jewish society than one which suppresses people, as eventually we will be suppressed in such a society. Returning to our opening question in Reverend Robertson's mind—that it is better to fund no faith than to fund ones whose founder thinks himself to be the messiah—why should a religious faith that denies that the messiah has yet to come (Judaism) be treated any better, as a matter of principle, than one that thinks its founder is the messiah?

Thus, the decision by Jewish organizations to support, oppose, or remain neutral in a dispute where certain people desire to expand their civil rights or general legal rights is not determined solely by whether the group under discussion is one generally in compliance with Jewish law or morality or even whether this particular claim is grounded in Jewish law or ethics. It is in the best interests of Judaism to support the continued granting of basic civil rights to all, *while making clear our moral opposition to the underlying conduct of those who exercise their freedom in violation of basic ethical norms of Judaism*. We are providing no moral legitimization for an activity if we seek to prohibit firing a person from his or her job because of it, and we make no claim of general ethical application when we seek to legalize or even protect sinful conduct from suppression by the secular law.[38]

My political thesis can be summarized as follows: *Religious Judaism is providing no moral legitimization to an underlying activity when it seeks to prohibit firing a person from his job, or evicting him from his house, because of that (unethical) activity*. This ought to be the basic rule of civil rights. Like free speech, where we all understand that supporting the right of another to speak is not the same as agreeing with what the person says, supporting civil rights for people is not synonymous with morally approving of their actions. Thus, Orthodox Judaism should support the right of all individuals to be free from harassment and discrimination in their jobs and homes and to insure everyone's physical safety. *Judaism should seek to prevent or prohibit people from being fired from their jobs or evicted from their homes for reasons unrelated to their suitability for the job or as a tenant.*[39] Certainly, traditional Judaism should oppose, for example, a law that seeks to give homosexuals a *preferred place* in the legal or social spectrum. Thus, school curricula that teach the moral equivalency of homosexuality, governmental attempts to redefine marriage to include homosexual relations, and governmental attempts to prohibit religious organizations from declining to hire overt homosexuals should be opposed.[40] However, merely because we favor the decriminalization of what we religious insist is odious conduct and the granting of civil rights for those who engage in such conduct does not mean that, in the name of religious freedom, we need to support the placement of such conduct in a privileged position with society. Indeed, it is a nearly "risk free" fulfillment of the Jewish people's mandate to be a moral "light unto the nations of the world" and demonstrate our moral and religious disagreement with such conduct.[41] We must realize that the political freedoms granted to minority religious communities through laws which prohibit religious, racial, and sexual discrimination in commerce are quite vital to the economic survival of Judaism in America. These laws are not guaranteed by the Constitution, and are subject to simple repeal by Congress and the dictates of the majority. They have been passed through the support of a broad consensus of minority religious and political organizations. Should each of these groups conclude that they no longer support civil rights for the other groups due to philosophical or theological opposition to the underlying conduct, *all* of the groups risk losing the protection granted by law. In such a climate, one could easily imagine feminist groups supporting laws which discriminate against Judaism based on their understanding of our ritual practices.[42]

There are those who will reply by asserting that I am understating the countervailing factor: the cultural influence secular society has on religious Judaism. The advocacy of governmental non-intervention in "private" matters will, these people claim, lead to a society so morally and socially disfavored by classical Judaism that our political freedoms will be of no value in such a society as we will not be able to function.

That is a danger; however, it seems to this writer that historical precedent runs counter to the belief that such a danger is the most serious. While one can cite numerous examples of Jewish societies within the last thousand years that have been destroyed by cultural and religious intolerance (the Crusades, the expulsion from Spain, the many pogroms, the Holocaust), one is hard-pressed to cite a Jewish culture destroyed by pluralism. Indeed, the Golden Age of Jewish life in Spain six hundred years ago and the incredible religious accomplishments of the Jews of Babylonia more than thirteen hundred years ago can be attributed to the religious freedom found in those times—and each magnificent era ended as religious freedom was abolished in the area. In fact, the political, economic, and cultural resurgence of Religious Judaism in America since the 1960s can be directly attributed to precisely the pluralism in American society. The ability to work as a white-collar professional while keeping kosher, taking off for the Jewish holidays, and even wearing a *yarmulke* at work, is a result of tolerance by the secular society for cultural deviance. While Judaism does face certain challenges in a morally pluralistic society, these are challenges that we can (and will) overcome through heightened observance and additional outreach to the unaffiliated. Governmental persecution, massive societal anti-Semitism, or significant commercial discrimination against Jews are obstacles that pose much greater danger and are frequently beyond our ability to overcome.

The tenuous basis of our religious freedoms is continuously demonstrated. In 1990 the United States Supreme Court, in *Employment Division v. Smith*,[43] ruled that when a state passes a criminal law, it need not exempt from prosecution people who violate the law even if they harm no one and are motivated by a sincere religious belief. It was only through the efforts of a multi-denominational ecumenical coalition of very diverse religious groups that the detestable result the Supreme Court sought to make the law of the land was avoided through congressional legislation—*The Religious Freedom Restoration Act of 1993*, which was struck down as unconstitutional by the Supreme Court as it applies to the States in *Boerne v. Flores*.[44] The right to the free exercise of religion remains unclear in America, as legislation of general application (such as legislation that surgery may only be done by a licensed physician in an authorized hospital) can still be applied to destroy religious duties (such as the obligation to circumcise one's child)—and the right to free exercise of our Jewish faith is a right worth protecting.

CONCLUSION

The problem examined by the paper—the attack from both sides, and the uncertainty of the correct outcome—is brought home by recent events. In the first few months of 5764 (late 2003 and early 2004) we have witnessed two dramatic cultural events, neither of which is deeply favorable to the Jewish people. The first is the lurching move of this country to homosexual marriages as exemplified by the pronouncement of the Massachusetts Supreme Court,[45] and the second is the success of the recent movie *The Passion of the Christ*.[46] Each contains the outline of a serious problem in a community, and we do not really know whether we should find refuge among the supporters of gay marriage from the outrage of the *Passion*, or the reverse. Compounding this is the steadfast support of the fundamentalist Christian community of Israel, which has brought us into a deep political alliance for a blessed common cause. In truth, I am not sure what the proper outcome is, as the reality changes all the time. Thus, it is important to return to the theory, to establish whether Jewish law directs an outcome for us, no matter what the consequences, or are we authorized to use our own judgment to seek the best answer we can find.

This paper seeks to establish that no technical Jewish law obligation is present mandating that Jews seek to enforce Noahide law, and that even in cases where central values directly related to our Creator's revelation to us are at stake, we need advance an agenda focusing on what will be in the long-term best interest of the Jewish people. Jews need to look both ways before crossing the street, lest the society that we are part of rise up and oppress us. May we be blessed with wise leaders to counsel and direct the community properly.

NOTES

1. The universalistic law code governing those who are not Jewish (called the Noahide code) requires the observance of many commandments that are basic to the moral existence of people. The Talmud (Sanhedrin 56a) recounts seven categories of prohibition: idol worship, taking God's name in vain, murder, prohibited sexual activity, theft, eating flesh from a living animal, and the obligation to have a justice system or enforce laws. These seven commandments are generalities which contain within them many specifications—thus, for example, the single categorical prohibition of sexual impropriety includes both adultery and various forms of incest. As has

been noted elsewhere, these Noahide laws appear to encompass nearly 60 of the 613 biblical commandments traditionally enumerated as incumbent on Jews from the bible itself, which is nearly one-fourth of those biblical commandments generally applicable in post-temple times; see Aaron Lichtenstein, *The Seven Laws of Noah* (New York, 1986) at 90–91. A majority of the commandments found in Jewish law that are unrelated to ritual activity are also found in the Noahide code. The Noahide code was intended to be a practical legal code, and form a system that satisfied the social, legal, and religious needs of peoples outside the framework of Judaism. For more on this, see my "Jewish Law and the Obligation to Enforce Secular Law," in D. Shatz and C. Waxman, eds., *The Orthodox Forum Proceedings VI: Jewish Responsibilities to Society*, 103–143 (1997) and "Proselytizing and Jewish Law," in John Witte, Jr., and Richard C. Martin, eds., *Sharing the Book: Religious Perspectives on the Rights and Wrongs of Proselytism* (Maryknoll, NY, 1999), 45–60.

2. It is a complex matter of comparative theology to examine particular faiths and see where they fit. However, there is no doubt in this author's mind that many new age religions are polytheistic.

3. See generally, Maimonides, Law of Kings, Chapters 9 and 10. For a thorough discussion of these issues, see David Novak, *The Image of the Non-Jew in Judaism* (New York, 1983).

4. Maimonides, Law of Kings 12:1.

5. Yevamot 24b.

6. Judah Loewe of Prague (*Maharal me-Prague*), *Be'er Hagolah* at pages 38–39 (Jerusalem 5731).

7. Such that people could choose their mode of worship unafraid of consequences. To explain why this happened in America when it did is beyond the scope of this work. Profound freedom of religion—by which I mean a person suffers no legal or economic consequences of his religious beliefs or conduct—did not really exist until after World War II. For more on this, see John Witte, Jr., *Religion and the American Constitutional Experiment: Essential Rights and Liberties* (Westview, 2000), 117–149.

8. *Sanhedrin* 63a–b.

9. Pat Robertson, "Bush Faith-Based Plan Requires an Overhaul," *USA Today*, March 5, 2001, Page 15a.

10. 494 U.S. 872 (1990).

11. For exactly such an article, see Ross Povenmire, "Do Parents Have the Legal Authority to Consent to the Surgical Amputation of Normal, Healthy Tissue from Their Infant Children?: The Practice of Circumcision in the United States" 7 *Am. U.J. Gender Soc. Pol'y & L.* 87 (1999). See also 139 Cong. Rec. H2356, H2363 (daily ed. May 11, 1993) (Rep. Maloney) ("The Jewish practices of kosher slaughter and circumcision, for example, might be threatened [by *Smith*]").

12. Maimonides, Laws of Murder, 4:10. This is not the place to address in detail the exact view of Maimonides, which also might prohibit direct murder. The first word of this section is, in the uncensored text of Maimonides, the Hebrew word *min*, which could be translated as "troublemakers" and thus this provision of Jewish law could be understood as limited to pagan troublemakers and not merely all pagans. With this tool, one can resolve the apparent tension between this section of Maimonides' code and his categorical statement in Laws of Murder 1:11 prohibiting all extra-judicial

punishment, except in the case of a pursuer. This case, which permits extra-judicial killing, is thus limited to cases of people who are both sinful pagans and troublemakers. Mere sinful troublemakers are covered by the rules found in 1:11, and may not be killed. However, Maimonides in Laws of Murder 4:11 is quite clear that "Gentiles with whom we have no dispute and Jewish thieves one does not cause their death, but it is prohibited to rescue them if they are dying, such as when one sees such a person drowning in the sea one may not rescue him as it states 'do not stand by while your neighbor's blood is shed' and this is not your neighbor."

13. This is the view of the Rosh as cited in the *Kessef Mishneh* on Rotzeach 4:10. See also Tur, *Hoshen Mishpat* 222.

14. Even the Rambam's formulation for wayward children (*tinokot she-nishbu*) is not exculpatory in the classical sense of the word, as it is the possibility of repentance and change, combined with the status of these individuals as *annussim,* that generates the leniencies. The conduct of these individuals is still "off the charts."

15. For excellent works surveying issues concerning Noahide law generally, see R. J. David Bleich, "Mishpat Mavet be-Dinei Benei No'ah," *Sefer ha-Yovel li-Khavod Morenu ha-Gaon Rav Yoseph Dov Soloveitchik,* eds. S. Yisrachi, N. Lamm, and Y. Rafael, v. 1 (Jerusalem, 1984), 193–208; *idem*. "Hasgarat Poshe'a Yehudi shebarakh le-Erez Yisrael," *Or ha-Mizrah* 35 (5747):247–269; Nahum Rakover, "Jewish Law and the Noahide Obligation to Preserve Social Order," *Cardozo Law Review* 12 (1991):1073–1136; *idem*., "Hamishpat ke-Erekh Universali: Dinim bi-Bnei No'ah" 15–57 (Jerusalem, 5748); "Ben No'ah," *Entzklopedia Talmudit,* 3:348–362; Aaron Lichtenstein, *The Seven Laws of Noah* (New York, 1986). While undoubtedly the view of R. Menahem ben Meir ha-Meiri needs to be quantified, one is hard-pressed to accept that Meiri extends his view even to those who unquestionably violate central provisions of Noahide law. Rather, he is adopting a view of idol worship that excludes most Christians from that status. For more on this, see J. David Bleich, "Divine Unity in Maimonides, the Tosafists and Meiri," in *Neoplatonism and Jewish Thought*, Lenn E. Goodmann, ed. (1992), 237–254.

16. Avot 5:11–12.

17. See "The Gentile and Returning Lost Property According to Jewish Law: A Theory of Reciprocity," *Jewish Law Annual* XIII 31–45 (2000).

18. *The Orthodox Forum Proceedings VI: Jewish Responsibilities to Society*, D. Shatz and C. Waxman, eds. (1997), 103–143.

19. Avot, 3:14.

20. *Tosafot Yom Tov* on id.

21. *Sefer ha-Hasidim* §1124.

22. Support for this proposition can be found in Seforno, commenting on Exodus 19:6 which clearly indicates that Jews must answer such questions from Noahides. See generally comments of Maimonides, Ma'aseh ha-Karbanot 19:16 and Meiri Sanhedrin 59a.

23. Maharam Schick, *Hoshen Mishpat* 144. An example of this can also be found in the letter of R. Moshe Feinstein sent to the New York State governor favoring the implementation of the death penalty for certain crimes; Iggrot Moshe, *Hoshen Mishpat* 2:68.

24. Rabbi J. David Bleich, *Contemporary Halakhic Problems* ("Teaching Torah to Non-Jews") 2:339.

25. See Rabbi Yehuda Gershuni, *Kol Tzofech* (unnumbered pages in the back of the book, seven pages after numbering ends) (2nd ed. 5740) where he discusses the possibility of selective teaching of the Noahide laws.

26. See generally R. Nissim, *Derashot ha-Ran*, Number Eleven (which uses the term *tikun siddur ha-medini* to refer to Noahide activity). For a brief discussion of this issue, see Suzanne Last Stone, "Sinaitic and Noahide Law: Legal Pluralism in Jewish Law," *Cardozo L.R.* 12:1157 (1990). On the use of *tikun olam*, it is also important to examine the way that term is used by Maimonides, in Law of Kings 11:4 in the uncensored versions of his text (for example, see *Rambam Le'am*). This issue is quite crucial, as Maimonides' image of *tikun olam* seems to be directed at the reason for religions other than Judaism; see also *Responsa Kol Mevasser* 1:47 and *Hechail Yitzchak Hoshen Mishpat* 38.

27. *The Orthodox Forum Proceedings VI: Jewish Responsibilities to Society*, D. Shatz and C. Waxman, eds.

28. This is exemplified by the use of the phrase in Isaiah 60:3; for examples of that in rabbinic literature, see Bava Batra 75a; Midrash Rabbah Esther 7:11; Midrash Berashit 59:7; and Midrash Tehillim (Bubar) 36:6. For a sample of its use in the responsa literature, see *Tzitz Eliezer* 10:1(74); *Ya'avetz* 1:168; and particularly *Hatam Sofer* 6:84; see also *Responsa of Rosh* 4:40 which is also cited in *Tur Orah Hayyin* 59. None of these authorities uses the citation in a legal context to direct Jewish participation in Gentile activities—citations are homoletical (*Maharit Even ha-Ezer* 2:18 does appear to use it in a legal context concerning an inter-Jewish dispute; however upon further examination one sees that not to be so). This concept plays yet a more prominent note in cabalistic literature; see Sefer *Resesai Layla*, §57 *s.v. techlat* and *ve-zehu*. For a defense of this beacon-like (*i.e.*, Jews behave properly and this illuminates the world) understanding of the verse as the proper understanding of the literal meaning of the bible itself, see Harry Orlinsky, "A Light unto the Nations: A Problem in Biblical Theology," in Neuman and Zeitlin, *The Seventy-Fifth Anniversary Volume of the Jewish Quarterly Review* (1967), 409–428. For an indication as to why Radak might use both the phrase "observe the seven commandments" and the phrase "follow the right path," see *Iggrot Moshe, Yoreh Deah* 2:130 who indicates that the two are separate concepts.

29. *Evah* in Hebrew.

30. R. Shabtai Meir ha-Cohen (*Shakh*), *Yoreh Deah* 151:6 and R. Ezekiel Landau, *Dagul me-Revavah*, commenting on *Yoreh Deah* 151.

31. Thus, a Jew may sell items whose purpose is sinful when others are selling these items also. See my *The Pursuit of Justice: A Jewish Perspective on Practicing Law* (Yeshiva University Press, 1996) where this issue is repeatedly addressed and "Enabling a Jew to Sin: The Parameters," *Journal of Halacha and Contemporary Society* 19:5–36 (1990).

32. For example, the promulgation of an abortion law in the United States consistent only with the Noahide code would cause situations to arise where halacha's mandates could not be fulfilled.

33. *Church of the Lukumi Babalu Aye, Inc. v. City of Hialeah* 580 U.S. 520 (1993).

34. See amicus curiae brief of COLPA in *Church of Lukumi Babalu Aye, Inc. v. City of Hialeah*, United States Supreme Court (No. 91-948) (which states in note 1 that both the Orthodox Union and the Rabbinical Council agree with the legal position taken in this brief). No Orthodox Jewish organization filed an amicus brief against the Church.

35. Let me give another example. Recently there has been a great deal of discussion about government funding of religious schools, a concept that certainly is within the pale of both legal and social policy in the United States. However, such funding, were it to occur, would undoubtedly have to be blind to the substantive religious values these schools articulate. While a goodly number of the Jewish schools will remain (one hopes) true to authentic Jewish values, we can readily predict that many will advance visions of Judaism with which we do not agree. Among the parochial schools for Gentiles, one hopes that most will be Godly. Some of these schools will be centrally anti-Semitic even as they are Godly; others will undoubtedly support and foster pagan worship—and some of these pagans will be sympathetic to Jewish causes and others will not. But yet, the Orthodox Jewish community and its various institutes have all been diligent in supporting school vouchers, because, in the totality of the picture, it is of benefit to Judaism.

36. See Letter of Rabbi Feinstein dated 8 Shevat 5737 provided to this author by R. Chaim Dovid Zweibel of Agudath Israel.

37. See Rabbi Chaim Dovid Zweibel, "Determining the Time of Death: Legal Considerations," *Journal of Halacha and Contemporary Society*, 17:49 (1989).

38. However, I recognize that my answer to this question is based on my read of American political history and a prediction of the future as I see it—and I could be wrong in either or both of these determinations. One makes the best political judgment that one can. That is all that is expected of us.

39. New York State has precisely such a law. The "legal activities law" essentially prevents a person from discriminating against employees or job applicants based on their participation in legally permissible activities unrelated to employment outside of times and places of employment; see *New York Law Journal*, "Employment Law Update," September 3, 1992.

40. There historically have been statutory exemptions for religious organizations from anti-discrimination laws.

41. Now comes the difficulty: Do we, as Orthodox Jews, seek to grant equal civil rights to all or should we join hands with those groups that seek to deny political rights to those engaging in a consensual, but immoral, activity? It requires nearly an act of prophesy to determine which position is in our best long-term interest. Frankly, this writer is inclined to answer that we should err on the side of more political freedom, rather than less. The fact is that many of the non-Jewish groups that seek to curtail the political rights of those who deviate from the "Judeo-Christian" ethic have historically been the profound enemy of the Jewish community.

Thus we are confronted by a set of difficult choices:

1. We can politically join with those who practice immoral acts to protect our own political future; or
2. We can associate with those who have oppressed (and murdered) us in the past (and who we fear will oppress us in the future) to make illegal an activity that we agree is immoral; or
3. We can decline to publicly involve ourselves in this dispute and adopt an institutional policy of silence while not actively opposing civil rights to all.

I would suggest that, as a matter of political expedience and survival, the best path for Religious Jews is to *generally favor (and certainly not oppose) granting civil rights and political freedom to all,* including those whose activity we find religiously repugnant, providing that the prohibited activity is one that is consensual and harms no one other than its voluntary participants; *hand in hand with that, we should seek to prohibit commercial discrimination against people based on factors unrelated to the commercial activity, such as religious affiliation, national origin, marital status, race, or sexual orientation.* This position is based not on the assertion that all such conduct or statuses are acceptable to Jewish law and tradition (they aren't); but on the assertion—borne out by history—that many of those that seek to curtail activity based on a "religious" sense of ethics quite plausibly will seek, when they are in control, to advance the cause of "Christian ethics" in a way that will be incompatible with the continued successful existence of Judaism in the United States. If we do not seek to protect the civil and political rights of those with whom we theologically disagree, we may find these groups will not seek to assist us when our rights are settled. At the very least, Jewish public policy should not publicly and institutionally oppose granting civil and political rights to all. The exact details of this approach are left to be spelled out later and it certainly does have some limitations. It is clear to this author that Jewish public policy need not favor the legalization of prostitution and pornography in the name of (religious) freedom; as a general matter, activity entered into purely for financial gain creates a different set of issues unrelated to this one. So too this approach should not be understood as preventing systemic governmental (financial) assistance to *all* religions in some of their charitable or educational acts. For example, governmentally sponsored tuition tax credits or payment vouchers to parochial day school—a governmental policy that would vastly increase Jewish education and thus continuity—is certainly proper under this rationale (and should be supported by all those concerned with the future of the Jewish community).

42. For example, in response to a number of European countries banning *shechita* (kosher slaughter) in the early part of this century, Judaism sought and Congress passed a law which states "No method of . . . slaughtering shall be deemed to comply with the public policy of the United States unless it is humane. Either of the following two methods of slaughtering and handling are hereby found to be humane: . . . or (b) by slaughtering in accordance with the ritual requirements of the Jewish faith"; see 7 U.S.C. §1902. If we adopt the principle of refusing to support legislation that explicitly violates any provision of Jewish law, can we really expect others to support our legislative needs that violate their ethical norms?

43. 494 U.S. 872 (1990).

44. RFRA is found at 42 U.S.C. §200bb-1. It was struck down in *City of Boerne v. Flores,* 117 S.Ct. 2157 (1997).

45. *Goodridge v. Department of Public Health*, 798 N.E.2d 941 (Mass., 2003).

46. "Hollywood Report: The 'Passion' Payday," *The Wall Street Journal*, Friday, March 12, 2004. (Mel Gibson is on track to reap at least $350 million in personal profits from his controversial "The Passion of the Christ"—one of the biggest individual windfalls in Hollywood's long history of oversized payouts.)

6

Changing Conceptions of Gentiles at the Threshold of Modernity: The Napoleonic Sanhedrin

Jay R. Berkovitz

In the summer of 1806, one hundred twelve delegates representing Jewish communities throughout the French empire were invited to Paris by Napoleon Bonaparte to answer questions concerning the alleged incompatibility of Jewish law with the obligations of citizenship. Granted civic equality in 1790–1791, the Jews of France had failed to satisfy the lofty, though often unrealistic, expectations of social and economic transformation that many within French society had envisioned for them. Napoleon was certain that this failure was the unfortunate result of well-entrenched religious motivations that were at the heart of the Jewish tradition, and that no satisfactory resolution would be achieved until they were confronted directly.

By most accounts, the dramatic convocation of the "Assembly of Jewish Notables," which was reconstituted early in 1807 under the rather portentous name "*le Grand Sanhédrin*," was a thinly veiled effort to pressure Jewish leaders to acknowledge that strict adherence to traditional Jewish law precluded the fulfillment of duties incumbent upon them as citizens of the state and as members of society at large. It was widely believed, both by proponents of the ideology of Haskalah, and by gentile observers as well, that the future of French Jewry depended on its resolution of the apparent incongruity between Judaism and citizenship. Most historians maintain that under such circumstances it was virtually impossible to represent the demands of Halakhah honestly and forthrightly. The responses of the Assembly of Jewish Notables are generally presumed to be a classic case of *apologia*, clearly intended to construct a positive image of Judaism vis-à-vis the general world at almost any expense. In the most extreme case, the Assembly's pronouncement on the feasibility of intermarriage according to Jewish law appears to have been nothing less than a rebuff of the halakhic tradition.[1]

In the analysis that follows, I intend to reconsider the prevailing evaluation of the Sanhedrin by carefully examining the conceptions of gentiles and gentile culture that had emerged among a number of respected halakhic authorities in the two centuries preceding the Paris convocation. Evidence of a more positive view of gentiles in the halakhic literature of the period appears to have crystallized by the turn of the nineteenth century, suggesting that the much-maligned Paris body did not deviate from the Jewish legal tradition—as it stood at the time—to the extent that is generally assumed. This argument is rooted in the present effort to locate the Sanhedrin within a broad historical and halakhic framework. It also rests on the assumption that the halakhic decision-making process, by its very nature, involves the critical and selective engagement of legal sources and traditions. A number of factors, including the *posek*'s own methodological and interpretative approach to Halakhah, and his understanding of the relevance of contemporary social, economic, and political circumstances, account for the wide range of halakhic rulings on any particular issue.

THE HISTORICAL BACKGROUND

The decision to convene the Assembly of Jewish Notables owed its origins to a fateful meeting in January 1806 between Napoleon and Alsatian farmers in Strasbourg, following the emperor's return from Austerlitz. Persuaded by complaints that their progressive impoverishment was the result of extensive indebtedness to Jewish moneylenders, Napoleon came to view the Jews as "a nation and not a sect . . . a nation within a nation," and as the "vilest of all nations."[2] Their unique circumstances demanded that they be judged "according to political and not civil law."[3] He therefore concluded, against the nearly unanimous opposition of the legislative section of the Council of State, that exceptional legal measures were necessary in order to put an end to Jewish usury and to the humiliation of the French people.[4]

Though hardly novel, these accusations assumed an unprecedented urgency in the revolutionary era. In the years immediately preceding the Revolution, public discussion centered on the claim that the Jewish religion upheld a dual standard of morality that purportedly freed Jews, in their relations with gentiles, from ethical obligations routinely required in dealings with fellow Jews. This contention threatened to undermine the emancipation project in its entirety. Judaism's authorization of usurious rates of interest on loans intended for non-Jews, alongside the charge of social exclusiveness, were taken as proof of its professed hatred of the non-Jew and, generally, of its policy of moral duplicity.[5]

Inspired by the belief that government intervention was the best hope for restoring economic stability in Alsace, Napoleon issued the Imperial Decree of 30 May 1806, which declared a moratorium on all debts owed to Jews by noncommercial farmers of the northeast. Economic rehabilitation was not the emperor's chief concern, however. Jewish lending practices were understood to be symptomatic of a more fundamental problem—the questionable suitability of the Jews to fulfill the obligations incumbent upon them as French citizens. Economic circumstances in the northeast made it clear "how urgent it is to revive sentiments of civil morality among those who profess the Jewish religion in the countries under our jurisdiction, sentiments which have, sadly, disappeared among a very great number of them due to the state of degradation in which they have languished, a state which it is not at all among our intentions to maintain nor to renew."[6] In Napoleon's view, the transformation of the political status of French Jews demanded intensive efforts to remedy the allegedly deficient "sentiments of civil morality" to which the Jews still stubbornly adhered. He therefore proceeded, in the second section of the Imperial Decree, to order the convocation of a Jewish assembly empowered with legislative authority to resolve the question of the incompatibility of Judaism and civic duties once and for all.[7]

The tactical success of the plan to transform the Jews of the empire demanded that the full endorsement of their leaders first be secured. Napoleon sought formal reassurance that the Jews of the empire were committed to the French civil code and to his program of broad social integration. Twelve questions, focusing on marriage and divorce, attitudes toward non-Jews, civic duties, rabbinic authority, occupational restrictions, and moneylending, were brought before the Assembly. The ultimate goal, as made clear by Napoleon, was to "reconcile the beliefs of the Jews with the duties of Frenchmen, and to transform them into useful citizens, in order to remedy the evil to which many of them apply themselves to the great detriment of our subjects."[8] To accomplish this objective, the emperor convened another body in 1807—the Sanhedrin—to formally ratify the Assembly's responses and place them, by government fiat, "on equal footing with the Talmud, as articles of faith and principles of religious legislation."[9]

A careful look at Napoleon's correspondence reveals that the emperor's ultimate objective was the total assimilation of French Jewry, and failing that, to achieve the means to impose rigorous state control over the Jewish population. One dispatch, written immediately before the convocation, contained a list of the specific answers that he desired, confirming that he expected of the Assembly nothing short of an endorsement of intermarriage, a clear affirmation of the "brotherly" relationship between Jews and other Frenchmen, and an explicit prohibition of usury. More concretely, Napoleon entertained the idea of requiring one of every three marriages involving Jews to be with a Frenchman, while he envisioned that military conscription would effectively bring the Jews into the orbit of French culture and mores.[10]

Undoubtedly aware of the dangers implicit in the Napoleonic initiative, the delegates to the Assembly divided into two principal factions—those whose worldview approximated the ideology of the Haskalah movement, and those who adhered to a traditional halakhic orientation. Despite their differences on the authority of Jewish law and tradition, however, the two groups reached a general consensus on how an ethos of tolerance and respect for non-Jews ought to be formulated. This should not be surprising. Members of each faction were aware of the prevailing social and political realities, and each acknowledged the need to fulfill the obligations that the status of citizenship entailed; civic duties, such as military service, were the most obvious and tangible requirements. The more liberal members of the Assembly were firmly committed to a broadly conceived universalism and were therefore prepared to break with what they understood to be Judaism's overly parochial view of the world beyond the borders of the Jewish community. The traditionalist delegates, despite their complete confidence in the superiority of Judaism over other faiths, tended to follow the teachings of the more tolerant rabbinic authorities of the late medieval and early modern periods. In light of the political, social, and economic transformations that had altered the character of Jewish life in the west, they were willing to consider a new foundation upon which Jewish–gentile relations could be based.[11] To view non-Jewish society with contempt was no longer a plausible position, in light of emancipation and the accompanying expectation that Jews become part of the larger social framework.

Throughout its deliberations, the Assembly displayed an unequivocally positive attitude toward the primacy of the state and its gentile citizens, while it strongly endorsed Judaism's compatibility with civic duties. It denied that any aspect of Jewish religious law, e.g., marriage and divorce, contravened the laws of the state. The reason for questions concerning the realm of personal status is clear: in France marriage was the specific arena where the conflict between religion and state was first waged. In 1792 marriage was brought under the auspices of the civil authorities and Jews were required to abide by the new law, which invalidated the legal standing of the Jewish marriage ceremony. Nevertheless, because the National Assembly had not yet established protocols for non-Catholic unions, Jews continued for some time to marry and divorce "according to the laws of Moses and Israel."[12] Napoleon went a step further, instructing rabbis not to perform the marriage ceremony without proof that the civil ceremony had already been performed before a governmental official. The Assembly of Jewish Notables confirmed that the state's role in establishing the legal validity of a marriage took precedence over Jewish law.[13] Though permitted in biblical Judaism and not expressly forbidden by the Talmud, polygamy had been formally prohibited since the synod of Rabbenu Gershom in the eleventh century. On the matter of divorce, the delegates stated that while "repudiation is permitted by the law of Moses . . . it is not valid if not previously pronounced by the French code." With this answer the Assembly then proceeded to underscore the fundamental principle that guided Jews in all their dealings, i.e., that the law of the state is undisputed: "In the eyes of every Israelite, without exception, submission to the prince is the first of duties. It is a principle generally acknowledged among them, that, in every thing relating to civil or political interests, the law of the state is the supreme law."[14]

The possibility of marriage between Jews and Christians was doubtless the most challenging issue facing the delegates, and it was here that progressive and traditionalist views diverged so widely that no agreement could be reached on a single formulation. Instead, two different answers, representing the opinion of each group, were combined. The first part reflected the view of liberal delegates that intermarriage with Christians was not expressly forbidden by biblical law. Accordingly, the prohibition was limited to the seven idolatrous nations of ancient Canaan only, but did not extend to adherents of modern monotheistic faiths such as Christianity.[15] The second part referred explicitly to the opinion of the rabbinic delegates. It stated that in spite of the foregoing technical permissibility of marriage with Christians, the rabbis could not lend their support to such unions. Their response accentuated the ritual requirements of the marriage ceremony, which were considered indispensable to the religious validity of the union. From the standpoint of Jewish law, then, marriage uniting a Jew with a Christian was not a recognized union. The rabbis did concede, however, that such marriages were valid in the civil sense and that a couple united civilly could dissolve the union without the need for a religious divorce.[16] By this statement the rabbis showed themselves to be resigned to the fact that individuals could now choose to live within the civil sphere, well beyond the authority of Jewish law. Combining two answers into one, the delegates appeared to balance the widely divergent demands of Jewish law and contemporary French culture.

It is important to note that in the case of intermarriage, as in other areas as well, the decision of the Sanhedrin varied substantially from the original response of the Assembly of Jewish Notables. Regrettably, differences between the texts produced by the two bodies have been largely ignored. All in all, the Assembly's responses were more deliberative in tone, and also reflected a wider range of views than the Sanhedrin, which was predominately a rabbinic body. In decision 3 the Sanhedrin stated that although an intermarriage created *civil* obligations, it was, from a religious standpoint, a prohibited act and the *kiddushin* were invalid; the fact that no *herem* would be issued in such instances reflected changes in the governing authority of the Franco-Jewish community.[17] As for the highly unorthodox formulation in the first part of the Assembly's response, it appears to have been little more than a rhetorical ploy intended to curry favor with the Napoleonic commission; it offered no *legal* dispensation from the traditional prohibition against intermarriage.

The failure to notice this distinction has led many historians to exaggerate the delegates' general failure to represent the positions of Jewish law and tradition faithfully. Additionally, the Assembly's effusive declarations of patriotism and brotherhood, especially, have been routinely understood as having broken with inviolable assumptions concerning the collective destiny of the Jewish people. In spite of the intense pressure to which members of the Assembly were subjected, it is not at all clear that they either intentionally misrepresented or offered a tendentious reading of Judaism's view of the state and its gentile citizens. Their responses generally fell within the broad range of the Jewish legal tradition, though they invariably rested on certain opinions that were, certainly in the case of marriage, unconventional. Moreover, a more sympathetic reading of the Sanhedrin is amply supported by two bodies of pertinent evidence that historians have either overlooked or underestimated: (a) literature referring to the status of gentiles in Jewish law in the era leading up to the French Revolution; (b) the published writings of Rabbi Aaron Worms, an important Metz halakhic authority who had served as a leading delegate at the Assembly of Jewish Notables and member of the Sanhedrin.

Before surveying this literature, we shall note three sources that offer additional perspective on the Sanhedrin. The first are the written responses of Rabbi Ishmael Ha-Kohen of Modena, a contemporary Italian halakhist who was invited to participate as a delegate, but was unable to attend because of his advanced age. Left in manuscript, these private views were published for the first time thirty-five years ago. They reveal that the positions advanced by the Assembly delegates corresponded closely to the views of at least one contemporary halakhic authority who was free of the intense political pressures felt in Paris.[18] Second, in a letter to Rabbi Baruch Jeiteles, *av beit din* of Prague, Sanhedrin president Rabbi David Sintzheim expressed satisfaction at having successfully resisted all challenges to the integrity of Jewish law. Third, a more convincing indication of respect for the way that the body performed its difficult task may be adduced from a eulogy pronounced by Rabbi Moses Sofer following the passing of Sintzheim in 1812. Sofer, the undisputed champion of Hungarian orthodoxy, praised Sintzheim for having maintained halakhic standards under extreme pressure. Although no details are provided, one may assume that such an uncompromising opponent of religious reform as the Hatam Sofer would not have praised Sintzheim undeservedly on so crucial a matter.[19] Clearly, however, we may assume that neither of the two foregoing opinions was entirely free of bias.

GENTILES IN EARLY MODERN EUROPEAN HALAKHIC LITERATURE

The sixteenth through the eighteenth centuries witnessed the emergence of substantial common ground between Jews and non-Jews, especially as mirrored in the halakhic literature of the period, though recent historical research suggests that this was not the case in Germanic lands.[20] Before proceeding, we shall first consider the range of ethical obligations toward gentiles within classical halakhic sources. The claim that in Jewish law there was a fundamental inequality between the status of Jew and non-Jew gained considerable notoriety with the publication of Johann Andreas Eisenmenger's *Entdecktes Judentums* in 1699.[21] Although the book was riddled by intentional distortions and errors, it succeeded in calling attention to legal inequities in the areas of theft, robbery, return of lost property, and deception. In Bava Kama 113b, for example, the prohibition against withholding money ("*oshek*") was limited to fellow Jews only, based on the wording of Leviticus 19:13, "You shall not oppress your fellow" ("*lo ta'ashok et re'akha*"). *Re'akha* is understood in this instance, as in most others, to refer specifically to Jews.[22] Maimonides, however, saw the withholding of money earned as the equivalent of robbery, and ruled that the one (*oshek*) is prohibited like the other (*gezelah*).[23] Even so, the position of Maimonides is exceedingly complex, as regards the scope of the prohibition of robbery, and more generally with respect to the status of gentiles in Jewish law.[24]

Several key arguments for prohibiting the mistreatment of gentiles emerge in the classical tradition. The talmudic discussion in *Gittin* 61a envisioned harmonious Jewish–gentile relations within the framework of reciprocal interaction. It is clear that the extensive list of ethical obligations that are required vis-à-vis gentiles was mandated for the sake of social stability, mutual responsibility, and the promotion of peace (*mipnei darkhei shalom*). To these largely prudential-ethical concerns Maimonides offered an additional reason why the abuse of gentiles is objectionable. According to *Hilkhot Genevah* 7:8, one who cheats the idolater performs an abhorrent act—an act of *avel*—which Deuteronomy 25:16 condemns harshly: "For all that do such things, even all that act unrighteously, are an abomination unto the Lord thy God." In his *Commentary on the Mishnah*, Maimonides elaborated this idea further, asserting that no form of "falsification, trickery, deceit, fraud, or subterfuge is permitted; of the idolater [the Rabbis] said it is prohibited to deceive any person, even the idolater, especially in a matter that could cause the name of God to be desecrated . . . [or] will foster in a man degenerate character traits, qualities which God abhors, like those who perform them, as is written, 'even all that act unrighteously.'"[25] Enlarging on *Hullin* 94a, Maimonides here linked the specific proscription against deception (*genevat ha-da'at*) with the general prohibition of the desecration of the divine name (*hillul Hashem*), and defined the latter in terms of its inexorable moral implications.[26]

Distinctly different from the Maimonidean view was the approach of R. Menahem Ha-Me'iri of fourteenth-century Provence. Me'iri established a new principle of ethical obligation toward non-Jews, based on the premise that adherents of monotheism were ethically responsible and therefore deserving to be considered as peers.[27] More than any of his predecessors, he formulated a clear distinction between idolaters and those he called "nations restricted by the ways of religion." This distinction permitted a rigorous classification of *halakhot* that applied to the low standing of gentiles in the ethical system of Judaism, on the one hand, and the removal from that inferior category of all those who were members of a monotheistic faith. Concerning the return of lost property and the prohibition of robbery, Me'iri argued that the principle of inequity did not apply to "nations restricted by the ways of religion," who were to be considered as full-fledged Jews.[28] Moreover, he argued that those gentiles who are restricted by the ways of religion ought to be included in the term *amitekha*, therefore entitling them to ethical treatment comparable to a Jew. His principle extended to the ban on excessive profit, equal compensation for property damage, and equality of punishment for bloodshed. The result, theoretically at least, was the collapse of many of the traditional distinctions between Jew and gentile in the civil—though not ritual—realm.[29]

Although the vast majority of Me'iri's writings were unavailable until the twentieth century, his contributions to the idea of tolerance were known to some medieval authorities and indirectly influenced the evolution of Jewish legal thought. In the writings of early modern authorities, the essence of his approach frequently appeared together with the view of Maimonides, combined into a single, comprehensive approach to the treatment of gentiles. For the latter, the fulfillment of ethical obligations toward non-Jews, even idolaters, was essential for the perfection of moral character, irrespective of who the beneficiary might be. Fundamentally inner-directed, the Maimonidean view contrasted with Me'iri's outer-directed approach, which centered on the identity and status of civilized gentiles and their entitlement to equal treatment.[30] These two distinctly different viewpoints each found expression in the positions of respected halakhic authorities in the early modern period.

Important structural changes not only account for the transformation of Jewish political status in modern Europe, but also triggered significant cultural shifts as well. In the last decades of the seventeenth century, expanding commercial activity in western and central Europe set the stage for major changes in the Jewish community, as is evident from the wider distribution of wealth and greater availability of imported fabrics and other luxury products. The transition from agrarianism to an economy based on capital investment, international commerce, manufacturing, and free enterprise went hand in hand with urban growth,[31] creating novel opportunities for Jews to become involved in a wider range of activities in general society. New commercial venues encouraged greater interaction between Jews and non-Jews, which, in turn, accounted for the proliferation of questionable business practices. Concern that deception against gentiles would cause harm to the Jewish community was perennially voiced within the context of warnings of *hillul ha-Shem*. However, increasingly in the seventeenth and eighteenth centuries condemnation of such behavior as "ugly deeds" ("*ma'asim mekhuarim*") on their own account, and not simply for the dangers they posed to the Jewish public, can be found in the halakhic literature.[32]

The legal writings of Rabbi Moses Rivkes of seventeenth-century Lithuania stand out with respect to their heightened concern with ethical justice in dealings with non-Jews. In *Be'er ha-Golah*, his commentary on *Hoshen Mishpat*, Rivkes affirmed and reaffirmed the medieval legacy of ethical teachings. He echoed Maimonides' warning that the mistreatment of gentiles would be injurious to Jewish character development, and he cited traditions strongly commending exemplary behavior toward idolaters, such as the return of lost property, "in order to sanctify the Name and to glorify Israel, so that they will know that they [the Jews] are men of faith."[33] His comments also manifested the clear distinction between pagan and civilized nations that figured so centrally in the halakhic system of Me'iri. Rivkes affirmed that the Halakhah had intended to exclude only idolaters from the category of those deserving ethical treatment, "but not the peoples under whose protection we are exiled."[34]

Evidence of a more positive orientation toward contemporary gentiles and gentile culture is contained in several responsa authored by R. Ya'ir Hayyim Bacharach of seventeenth-century Worms. He viewed Christianity as a non-idolatrous religion[35]—certainly not an uncommon position in his day—but appears to have taken this several steps further than his predecessors. In one ruling, a responsum on abortion, Bacharach referred to moral values that he believed were shared by Jews and Christians. Bacharach was asked to rule on the halakhic feasibility of abortion in the case of a woman who had become pregnant during an adulterous affair. Despite his having reached the conclusion that abortion was, in theory, halakhically permissible, Bacharach refused to grant authorization to terminate the pregnancy because of "a clear consensus [*minhag*] between us and them [the gentile community] in the interest of curbing promiscuity and immorality."[36]

Bacharach's positive evaluation of German legislation and of the law-abiding tendencies of contemporary gentiles is evident in a ruling on legal extradition. Most halakhic authorities were reluctant to deliver Jewish criminals to general courts because of the tense nature of Jewish–gentile relations, the extensive anti-Jewish discrimination, and the injustices that Jewish defendants were likely to face in the non-Jewish court system. Nevertheless, in the seventeenth century one may discern a growing effort to build upon medieval talmudic law. Against the plain meaning of *Tosefta Terumot* 7:20, R. David Ha-Levi, author of the *Turei Zahav*, ruled that an individual may be turned over to the government if he violated a law of the local authority, assuming that this could endanger the community.[37] His father-in-law, R. Joel Sirkes, had gone a step further, stating that if an individual is accused of a crime against the general authorities, even though it is not known if indeed he committed the crime, it is permissible to extradite him so that he may be tried by the general court system.[38] In two separate responsa, Bacharach concurred with the famous ruling of R. Joel Sirkes permitting extradition to gentile authorities. As a clear response to concerns about fairness in the general justice system, Bacharach distinguished sharply between the anti-Jewish prejudices rampant among the masses and the enlightened views of the governing bodies. His conclusion rested on the presumption that a non-Jewish court was capable of conducting an honest investigation and reaching a just verdict.[39]

The foregoing developments in the realm of Halakhah corresponded to changes in Christian and Jewish iconography in early modern Europe. Evidence of a new sense of religious tolerance, despite ongoing tensions, had become more common in central and western Europe. Christian portrayals of Jews had begun to soften the severely negative anti-Jewish stereotypes of the medieval era, preferring to depict them in a more humane and objective manner. No less significantly, in a departure from the earlier tendency to emphasize the Jews' alien character, Christian art had begun focusing on Jewish religious rites. The depiction of daily life in Johannes Alexander Böner's paintings suggests that Jewish–Christian interaction was not a rarity and that Christian interest in Jewish celebrations, such as weddings, was keen; his work gives expression to the emergence of a public arena where sectarian tensions did not prevail. In the same period, Jewish art aspired to portray to Christians both the inner world of Jews, and the public face of Judaism as a rational religion deserving of respect.[40]

THE ASSEMBLY OF JEWISH NOTABLES AND THE PARIS SANHEDRIN

Two facets of the responses advanced by the Assembly of Jewish Notables suggest that the body was perhaps more conservative than has hitherto been assumed. Conceptually, the Assembly did not break any new ground, as virtually each of the substantive issues discussed at the Assembly of Jewish Notables—intermarriage, Judaism's attitude toward non-Jews, rabbinic authority, and moneylending—had already been debated by government officials or by Franco-Jewish leaders in the years immediately preceding the Revolution, and during the subsequent debate on citizenship.[41] In fact, the Malesherbes Commission, in the course of inquiring into the feasibility of Jewish citizenship in 1787, first addressed many of the same issues with respect to both Sephardic and Ashkenazic communities. Initially, seven questions were formulated to clarify Judaism's position on divorce, choice of occupations, and rabbinic authority, among others. Subsequently, a slightly longer questionnaire, consisting of thirteen questions, was submitted to the Bordeaux delegates. These included questions about Sabbath restrictions, moneylending in Alsace-Lorraine, military service, and the status of syndics.[42] A comparison between the twelve questions posed by Napoleon and those taken up by the Malesherbes Commission indicates that after twenty years the issues defining the Jewish question remained largely unchanged. Although political conditions had changed dramatically during the two decades, the decision to convene the Sanhedrin represented a direct challenge to the fact of Jewish emancipation. In effect, the delegates were asked to formally reaffirm their coreligionists' acceptance of the original terms upon which citizenship had been granted in 1790–1791. The 1806–1807 deliberations belonged to the discourse of the preceding twenty years, as indicated by the fact that the old guard, consisting of French *maskilim,* community leaders, and rabbis, were all well represented among the delegates to the convocation.[43]

Second, it has now become clear that crucial halakhic positions adopted at the Assembly were forged under the influence of Metz dayyan and *posek* R. Aaron Worms (1754–1836). The halakhic writings of Worms, arguably the foremost rabbinic scholar in Alsace-Lorraine in the era of Jewish emancipation, provide the basis for a more complete analysis of the Paris deliberations. A student of R. Aryeh Loeb Günzberg, author of the Shaagat Aryeh, Worms played a key role at the Paris meetings. His halakhic discourse on gentiles in Jewish law, which he delivered to fellow delegates at the Assembly, is mentioned in several sources but was never included in the official transactions. Fortunately, Worms decided to publish a summary of the address amid his talmudic novellae twenty-five years later, in the final volume of his major opus, *Me'orei Or* (Metz, 1789–1831).[44] Contained in this discourse are the underpinnings for the Assembly's declarations of loyalty to France and her citizens; however, as one would expect, Worms's presentation was far more complex. The fact that throughout his presentation he never referred to the potential harm that the mistreatment of gentiles could bring upon the reputation of the Jewish community—the concern for *hillul ha-Shem*—is consistent with the new direction taken by the early modern halakhists, and reflects their self-assurance in asserting a more favorable status for non-Jews.

Four central claims were at the core of Worms's address. He opened with an appeal to morality, referring first to the biblical identification of *avel* with cheating others (Leviticus 19:35), then to Maimonides' unqualified objection to deceitful behavior, even toward the idolater. His second argument reflected an appreciation for advances in the legal system of post-revolutionary France. French society's rigorous commitment to the ideal of legal equality virtually erased earlier distinctions in the status of gentiles and Jews.[45] It followed that Jewish law could scarcely maintain inequitable standards in its ethical system. Legal parity was closely related to Worms's third claim concerning the important differences between the status of idolaters and *b'nei Noah*. By disassociating contemporary non-Jews from the pagan nations of antiquity, Worms was able to set aside talmudic sources permitting what modern society understood to be unethical behavior. In the concept of *benei Noah*, he found a talmudic analogue to the law-abiding gentile citizens of modern Europe who were bound by a moral code proscribing murder, theft, and lechery. Worms thereby placed himself squarely within the liberal tradition advanced by Me'iri, though the latter was presumably unknown to him. "Only among the nations of antiquity were there true heretics," Worms asserted, "[but today] there is no distinction between Jew and gentile"; [accordingly,] "we are obligated to physically save the gentiles of today, and their money is prohibited as is any Jew's." Like Me'iri, Worms insisted that the talmudic warning (in Sanhedrin 76b) against returning a lost object to a non-Jew "does not apply to the nations of the world in our day. One announces their lost objects, as in the case of a Jew."[46]

Worms's final argument was predicated on the ideological and social foundations of the Revolution. His vision appears to have been modeled after the Aristotelian *societas civilis*, a community of citizens bound together as free and equal participants and whose ethical responsibilities are grounded in the principle of reciprocity. These ideas governed Worms's selection of sources and the interpretations he chose to highlight, particularly those reflecting a broad universalist thrust. For example, he cited the position advanced in *Seder Eliyahu Rabbah*, against Bava Qama 111b, that the proscription "*lo ta'ashok et re'akha*" (Leviticus19:13) was the basis for banning the use of property stolen from a gentile (*gezel ha-goy*). From there he proceeded to demonstrate painstakingly that each time the term *re'a* appears in biblical texts, its intended referent is humanity at large.[47] This line of reasoning corresponded to the efforts of talmudic sages and Maimonides to apply the Torah's injunction against deception (*genevat da'at*) to Jew and gentile alike.[48]

Elaborating on the distinction between idolatrous and monotheistic nations that relegated much of talmudic law to desuetude, Worms applied the general principle to lending money on interest. He went well beyond his predecessors, adopting an independent position where no precedent could be found. With respect to moneylending, even Me'iri could find no justification to overlook the essential difference between Jew and gentile, and therefore did not apply his principle of "nations restricted by the ways of religion." Worms, however, averred that interest on loans extended to "a believing gentile is only permitted in accordance with the law of the land, [while] interest from a Jew is permitted by the partnership of *heter 'isqa*." This formulation reflected the central claim of Worms's Paris address: that Jewish law envisioned the establishment of virtual parity between Jews and gentiles in the civic arena. The case of moneylending reveals the great importance attached by Worms to regulating the scope of halakhic permissibility within limits imposed by *dina d'malkhuta*.[49]

Considered from the standpoint of Worms's other halakhic writings, the aforementioned views reflect a keen sensitivity to the pressures stemming from modernity. For example, he permitted haircuts in the afternoon preceding the Passover holiday,[50] although the practice was routinely prohibited according to most authorities, including the *Shulhan Arukh*. Citing a lenient tradition concerning those who feared adverse effects on their livelihood, Worms asserted that "in our day it is not customary to go out in long, unkempt hair among the gentiles, who also do not resemble those of former times." Hardly limited to the economic argument advanced by medieval halakhists, Worms's ruling was grounded in the dictates of early nineteenth-century French society and culture and their implications for Jewish–gentile relations. This, we may assume, was also the basis for his ruling permitting men to go bareheaded.[51] These and similar decisions suggest, in contrast to the considerable number of cases of ritual law where Worms ruled stringently, that in his estimation normative Jewish behavior in the civil sphere ought to be governed by a flexible approach to Halakhah.[52]

It is evident from the responses of the Assembly of Jewish Notables that the delegates followed the guidance provided by Rabbi Worms, particularly with regard to the exclusion of Christians from the category of idolaters.[53] The demands of the emancipation era were far more challenging. If the Jews of France were to maintain their position in post-revolutionary society, they would need to dispel all notions of religious superiority and social exclusiveness routinely attributed to Judaism. Still lacking, however, was a general principle justifying positive relations with non-Jews. The Assembly arrived at such a formulation first by asserting, particularly in its answers to questions four, five, eleven, and twelve, that loyalty to the state and its citizens was an indisputable category of religious devotion. Further, the delegates affirmed that "France is our country, all Frenchmen our brothers, and this glorious title, while honoring us in our own eyes, becomes a pledge of which we shall never cease to be worthy."[54] The delegates were thus willing to concede that a redefinition of brotherhood was required in light of the new social and political reality of post-revolutionary France. The bonds of fraternity could no longer be defined solely in terms of religious affiliation; citizenship had emerged, above all else, as the principal basis for uniting members of the French nation. Accordingly, the Jews of France declared themselves "Frenchmen of the Mosaic persuasion."[55]

This declaration did, in theory, signify a revolutionary departure from the assumptions underlying the collective identity and destiny of the Jewish people, but its real significance should not be overstated. Not all sectors of western Jewry understood citizenship in these terms nor did they all redefine the nature of their affiliations according to the Assembly's pronouncements. Most, in fact, would continue to maintain the strongest attachments to their coreligionists, in France and abroad, for most of the century. The social and cultural barriers that continued to separate Jew and Christian, particularly outside of the major urban centers where traditional associations were more easily preserved, inevitably reinforced the ethos of Jewish solidarity. Members of the Assembly were undoubtedly aware of the tenacity of these social realities but also understood the urgent need for clarification of the role of Jewish law in the modern state. At the apparent expense of traditional Jewish solidarity, they affirmed French Jewry's allegiance to the *patrie* by asserting that they would fight Jews of other countries with which France was at war.[56]

Still to be resolved was the question of whether the theoretical compatibility of Judaism with duties toward the state and its citizens could accommodate the Jewish law of moneylending. After initially attempting to neutralize the overwhelmingly negative evaluation of moneylending, the Assembly tackled the much tougher issue of the alleged double moral standard. In this area, too, the delegates followed Worms's lead. The Assembly emphatically denied the claim by asserting that Jewish law was unconcerned with the identity of the borrower. Crucial to this argument was the distinction it drew between two types of loans, commercial and charitable. The delegates asserted, as did Worms, that there was no practical distinction between Jewish and gentile borrowers. Their contention rested on the premise that in Jewish law there were two categories of transactions, commercial loans and charitable loans. In discussing the case of commercial loans, where interest was permitted, the delegates based their argument on the fiction of the *heter 'isqa* explained by Worms, though they made no explicit reference to it. Through this legal device, designed to circumvent the prohibition of taking interest from a fellow Jew, interest became a share in the profits that accrued in the temporary business "partnership."[57] Building on the twin claims that the right to charge interest depends on the religious faith, not affiliation, of the borrowers, and that the purpose of the loan is determinative, the Assembly argued that the Jewish law of moneylending reflected virtual parity between gentile and Jew. Therefore, interest, even among Jews, was lawful in commercial operations, as it was for gentiles.[58] In the case of charitable loans (i.e., those intended for food, clothing, or shelter), the Assembly argued that interest was forbidden, whether the borrower was a Jew or a gentile. Finally, the Assembly endeavored to present the foregoing legal interpretation as consistent with the plain meaning of Deuteronomy 23:21, the source text for the prohibition against taking interest from a fellow Jew. Because the verse makes no explicit reference to Jews, but only proscribes the taking of interest from "your brother" [*ahikha*], the delegates declared that the term *ahikha* ought to be understood broadly to refer to all fellow French citizens.[59] By so doing, the Paris body virtually erased the difference between Jewish and gentile borrowers. This conception of brotherhood—defined by citizenship, not religious affiliation—was an unprecedented departure from the historical identity of the Jewish people, and posed a most serious challenge to Jewish survival in the modern era.[60]

To compensate for the fact that the Assembly of Notables had no official standing in the Jewish community, Napoleon ordered the convocation of a religious body charged with the task of converting the responses to the twelve questions into authoritative doctrines "that would be placed next to the Talmud and [would] thus acquire, in the eyes of all Jews in all countries for every century, the greatest possible authority." Like the ancient Supreme Court in Jerusalem after which it was named, the Grand Sanhedrin was composed of seventy-one members, though only two-thirds were rabbis. On 4 February 1807 the Sanhedrin met for the first time, and over the course of five weeks issued decisions that were binding both from the standpoint of French law and Halakhah. The body sought to define the relation between Jewish law and the modern state without altering any rituals or doctrines of Judaism. More far-reaching in the long run was the distinction that the Sanhedrin drew between the political and the religious realms of Judaism:

> Let us declare, then, that the divine law is complete, [and that] the precious inheritance of the community of Jacob contains [both] religious provisions and political provisions; that the religious provisions are by their nature absolute and independent of circumstances and times; that this is not the case for political provisions, that is, for those that made up the government and were destined to direct the people of Israel in the land of its inheritance, when there was a king, high priest, and magistrates; that these political provisions can no longer be applicable now that Israel no longer forms a national body.[61]

The separation of the two realms profoundly imprinted itself on the consciousness of French Jewry during the next several decades. This was accomplished thanks to the persistent efforts of the consistorial leadership to make the Sanhedrin decisions a regular part of the Jewish school curriculum, and to require that every child be examined by the departmental grand rabbi before becoming a bar or bat mitzvah.[62] Evidence of the impact of the depoliticization of Judaism and, generally, of the importance of the Sanhedrin, is also found in school textbooks, in the views of scholars such as Salomon Munk and Adolphe Franck, and in rabbinic sermons and writings of the 1840s and 1850s. Certainly by mid-century the idea was embraced by broad sectors of the Franco-Jewish community.[63]

The Paris Sanhedrin owed both its prominence and notoriety to the role it played in endorsing the revolutionary concept of *fraternité* as the exclusive mediating principle between the Jewish religion and French society. In this regard the body was able to rely on the Mendelssohnian proposition calling for cooperation between Judaism and the secular state and, as we have shown, on a liberal halakhic tradition that viewed non-Jews in a favorable light.[64] The Paris body affirmed that seemingly irreconcilable conflicts between the religious obligations of Judaism and the duties demanded of citizens by the state were to be resolved in favor of the latter, since loyalty to the modern state was defined as a supreme religious value. Not all French rabbis agreed on the religious status of patriotism. Some worked vigorously to infuse emancipation with religious significance; others had misgivings about how far the practical halakhic implications of republican Judaism might be taken.[65] Leaving nothing to chance, the newly formed Consistory would soon take measures requiring rabbis to emphasize the lessons of the Sanhedrin in their sermons, while the text of the decisions was reproduced in every textbook approved for use in Jewish schools. For the Napoleonic regime, as for Jewish communal leaders, the Sanhedrin provided the authoritative interpretation of emancipation; its answers and doctrinal decisions formed a new and central text for subsequent generations.

One cannot overlook the fact that although the Sanhedrin was enveloped in stunning drama, extensive publicity, and acute political pressure, the Paris meetings involved serious debate on matters of great substance. Historically, the Sanhedrin was the first *public* organization of Jews to articulate a positive attitude toward the state and its gentile citizens, and to draw a clear distinction between the national and religious components of Jewish identity. Considering the fulsome rhetoric and hyperbolic style demanded by the occasion, and in view of its halakhic background and social historical context, the Sanhedrin may be said to have voiced a far more moderate position than is normally assumed. Changing conceptions of gentiles and gentile culture in the preceding two centuries, including a growing respect for gentile law and a progressive disassociation from certain discriminatory views of gentiles, permitted the rabbinic leadership that assembled in Paris to draw boldly on those classical traditions it felt corresponded to the new conditions facing emancipated Jewry. But it must be emphasized that the Sanhedrin, following R. Aaron Worms's lead, was careful to maintain a sharp distinction between the ritual and civil spheres. The civil sphere encompassed the full range of Jewish–gentile relations and duties to the state, whereas the ritual sphere, it was agreed, remained largely inviolate.

Quite apart from the debates themselves, it is important to emphasize that the decisions of Sanhedrin shaped the discourse of modernization for decades to come. This is most apparent in its iconic image as having defined the limits of the transformation that French Jewry needed to undergo in order to be worthy of the title "citizens." The absence of any explicit mention of religious reform, either in the questions addressed to the Assembly or in its responses, confirmed for contemporaries and their descendants that political loyalty and a commitment to social integration alone were the basis of French citizenship. Even fifty years after the convocation, the authority of the Sanhedrin was still in force among all sectors of the community, although its deliberations inescapably invited conflicting interpretations. Religious reformers and staunch conservatives alike found in the Sanhedrin's decisions clear proofs to bolster their respective positions. For all intents and purposes, however, the Sanhedrin removed the question of ritual reform from French Jewry's communal agenda, and thus undercut the movement to reform the Jewish religion.[66]

In the end, the Sanhedrin played a crucial role in shaping a distinct Franco-Jewish identity. Delegates from all corners of the French empire came together in common purpose to address the issues put before them by Napoleon. Cultural, ethnic, and religious differences were bridged, and a tenuous unity was forged. In the process, local leaders such as Abraham Furtado of Bordeaux and Rabbi David Sintzheim of Strasbourg were transformed into prominent national leaders. Their messages were no longer intended for their former constituencies alone but were directed at the broader population of French Jewry.[67] By reconfirming French Jewry's acceptance of the terms of citizenship, the Sanhedrin was instrumental in setting down the rudiments of an ideology of emancipation; this would prove essential to the ideological and programmatic foundations of Jewish modernization in France. At the Sanhedrin, the foundation for a new vision shared by all sectors of French Jewry, irrespective of ethnic heritage, geographical origin, or religious orientation, was secured. In the century-long debate over the challenges posed by emancipation, the founding premises and myths established in Paris served as the starting point for all future discussion.

NOTES

The author wishes to thank Marc Stern for his helpful comments on an earlier draft of this paper.

1. See, for example, Simon Dubnow, *History of the Jews*, trans. and ed. by Moshe Spiegel (South Brunswick: Yoseloff, 1967–73) vol. 4, pp. 552–55; Simon Schwarzfuchs, *Napoleon, the Jews, and the Sanhedrin* (London: Routledge and Kegan Paul, 1979). On the Reform movement's positive view of the Sanhedrin, see David Philipson, *The Reform Movement in Judaism* (New York, 1931), pp. 149–63. For the view of an early Zionist thinker who condemned the Sanhedrin, see Peretz Smolenskin, "The Haskalah in Berlin," in Arthur Hertzberg, *The Zionist Idea* (New York: Doubleday, 1959), pp. 154–57.

2. Maurice Liber, "Napoléon," *Revue des études juives* [*REJ*] 72 (1921): 21.

3. Schwarzfuchs, *Napoleon, the Jews, and the Sanhedrin*, p. 49.

4. Ibid., pp. 46–49. Also see Jay R. Berkovitz, *The Shaping of Jewish Identity in Nineteenth-Century France* (Detroit: Wayne State University Press, 1989), pp. 77–84, and idem, "The French Revolution and the Jews: Assessing the Cultural Impact," *Association for Jewish Studies Review* 20 (1995): 25–86.

5. See, for example, Agricole Moureau, *De l'incompatibilité entre le Judaïsme et l'exercise des droits de cité et des moyens de rendre les Juifs citoyens* (Paris, 1819), pp. 37–60.

6. Shimon J. Maslin, "Selected Documents of Napoleonic Jewry," unpublished paper, Hebrew Union College (Cincinnati, 1957), Document I-A.

7. Imperial Decree, 30 May 1806.

8. Jean Vaillant, *Correspondance de Napoléon 1er* (Paris, 1858–70), 12:700–711, no. 10537, cited in Schwarzfuchs, *Napoleon, the Jews, and the Sanhedrin*, p. 55.

9. Letter from Napoleon to M. Champagny, Ramboulliet, 23 August 1806. Reprinted and translated in Simeon Maslin, ed., "Selected Documents," Document I-B (Cincinnati: Hebrew Union College, 1959).

10. *Correspondance de Napoléon,* vol. 13, pp. 101–2, and 584.

11. Jacob Katz, *Exclusiveness and Tolerance: Studies in Jewish-Gentile Relations in Medieval and Modern Times* (London: Oxford University Press, 1961), p. 193.

12. This was certainly the case in Bordeaux. See Malino, *The Sephardic Jews of Bordeaux: Assimilation and Emancipation in Revolutionary and Napoleonic France* (Tuscaloosa: University of Alabama Press, 1978), p. 66.

13. See Abraham Freimann, *Seder Kidushin ve-Nissuin ahare Hatimat ha-Talmud [Betrothal and Marriage Procedures after the Talmudic Era]* (Jerusalem: Mosad ha-Rav Kuk, 1944), pp. 325–27.

14. Diogène Tama, ed., *Transactions of the Parisian Sanhedrin*, trans. D. Kirwan (London, 1807), p. 152.

15. The question whether the prohibition was limited to the seven Canaanite nations or extended to all non-Jews was debated among *rishonim*. Compare Maimonides, *Mishneh Torah*, *Hil. Issurei Bi'ah* 12:1–2, where no distinction was made, and R. Jacob b. Asher, *Arba'ah Turim*, *Even ha-Ezer* 16:1.

16. Ibid., pp. 154–56. For a brief discussion of the legal aspects of intermarriage, and the citation of several striking precedents, see Dov Frimer, "Israel, the Noahide Laws and Maimonides: Jewish–Gentile Legal Relations in Maimonidean Thought," *Jewish Law Association Studies* 2 (1986): 96–97. Frimer cited R. Joel Sirkes, *Bayit Hadash*, *Even ha-Ezer* 16, where it was assumed that Maimonides recognized the possibility of a marriage of a Jew to a gentile; and R. Jacob Reischer, *Resp. Shevut Yaakov*, pt. 1 (Halle, 1710), no. 20, for a possible halakhic implication of this view as it relates to the disposition of leaven before Passover. Although Reischer conceded that the union of a Jew and non-Jew had no halakhic validity, "it appears that this is a *de facto* marriage in many respects." For Frimer's own explanation of Maimonides' position, see p. 97.

17. Barukh Mevorakh, ed., *Napoleon u-Tekufato* (Jerusalem: Mosad Bialik, 1968), pp. 92–93.

18. "The Responses of R. Ishmael b. R. Avraham Yitzhak ha-Kohen," in Judah Rosenthal, *Mehkarim u-Mekorot* (Jerusalem, 1966), vol. 2, pp. 513–32.

19. See Schwarzfuchs, *Napoleon, the Jews, and the Sanhedrin*, pp. 115–16, and N. M. Gelber, "La police autrichienne et le Sanhédrin de Napoléon," *REJ* 83 (1927): 138–40.

20. Elisheva Carlebach, "Early Modern Ashkenaz in the Writings of Jacob Katz," in *The Pride of Jacob: Essays on Jacob Katz and His Work*, Jay Harris, ed. (Cambridge: Harvard University Press, 2002), pp. 65–83.

21. Johann Andreas Eisenmenger, *Entdecktes Judentums* (Frankfurt, 1699).

22. Also see Bava Kama 111b.

23. Moses Maimonides, *Mishneh Torah*, *Hilkhot Gezelah va-Avedah* 1:2.

24. In *Hilkhot Gezelah va-Avedah* 1:1, Maimonides used language that limited the prohibition of robbery to another Jew (*havero*), whereas in 1:2 he ruled that the prohibition of robbery pertains to a gentile (idolater)'s money as well. For efforts to re-

solve the apparent inconsistency, see *Kesef Mishnah*, ad loc.; Ezekiel Landau, *Resp. Noda be-Yehudah* (Prague, 1776), vol. 1, Yoreh De'ah, no. 81, and Frimer, "Israel, the Noahide Laws and Maimonides," p. 98. Maimonides' view of gentiles deserves a major monographic study, as it touches on complex halakhic and philosophic issues. See, generally, Menahem Kellner, *Maimonides on Judaism and the Jewish People* (Albany: State University of New York Press, 1991).

25. Maimonides, *Commentary on the Mishnah*, Kelim 12:7. Cf. Yosef Kapah's edition (Jerusalem, 1968), vol. 6, p. 126, where the word "*goy*" appears instead of "*akum*." Also see *Hilkhot De'ot* 2:6 and *Hilkhot Mekhirah* 18:1.

26. For a parallel formulation concerning the prohibition against inflicting pain upon animals, see Maimonides, *Guide for the Perplexed*, pt. 3, chapter 17. On the perfection of moral character, see Isadore Twersky, *Introduction to the Code of Maimonides (Mishneh Torah)* (New Haven: Yale University Press, 1980), pp. 356–514.

27. See article by David Berger in this volume.

28. For his general principle of tolerance, see Menahem Ha-Me'iri, *Beit ha-Behirah, Avodah Zarah*, ed. Abraham Sofer (Jerusalem, 1965), p. 59, and specifically with regard to lost property, see *Beit ha-Behirah*, Bava Kama, ed. Kalman Schlesinger (Jerusalem, 1961), p. 330. In the scholarly literature, see Katz, *Exclusiveness and Tolerance*, pp. 114–28; Ephraim E. Urbach, "R. Menahem Me'iri's Principle of Tolerance: Its Origin and Limits" [Hebrew], in *Chapters in the History of Jewish Society in the Middle Ages and Modern Period, Presented to Professor Jacob Katz* (Jerusalem: Magnes Press, 1980), pp. 34–44, and Katz's reply in *Zion* 46 (1981): 243–46; Gerald Blidstein, "Me'iri's Attitude towards Gentiles: Between Apologetics and Internalization" [Hebrew], *Zion* 51 (1986): 153–66; and Moshe Halbertal, *Between Torah and Wisdom: Rabbi Menahem Ha-Meiri and the Maimonidean Halakhists in Provence* (Jerusalem: Magnes Press, 2001), ch. 3.

29. In *Beit ha-Behirah*, Schlesinger, ed., p. 219, Ha-Me'iri understood "*amito*" (Lev. 25:17) as referring to non-idolatrous gentiles. Cf. *Sefer Hasidim*, no. 355, where it is stated in the name of R. Judah He-Hasid that a gentile who accepts the seven Noahide laws is to be treated as a brother with respect to the return of lost property. Cf. Landau, *Resp. Noda be-Yehudah*, preface. For a characterization of Ha-Me'iri's principle of tolerance as apologetic, see Michael J. Broyde and Michael Hecht, "The Gentile and Returning Lost Property According to Jewish Law: A Theory of Reciprocity," *The Jewish Law Annual* 13 (2000): 31–45. For an illustration of Ha-Me'iri's insistence that the distinction between Jew and gentile be firmly maintained in the ritual sphere, see Jacob Katz, *The Shabbes Goy: A Study in Halakhic Flexibility* (Philadelphia: Jewish Publication Society, 1989), pp. 224–25.

30. See Ha-Me'iri, *Beit ha-Behirah*, Bava Kama, p. 330, where the obligation to return an idolater's property is denied, but upheld in the case of one restricted by the ways of religion.

31. Philip Benedict, ed., *Cities and Social Change in Early Modern France* (London: Hyman, 1989), pp. 29–32.

32. Katz, *Exclusiveness and Tolerance*, pp. 156–57.

33. *Be'er ha-Golah*, *Hoshen Mishpat* 348.

34. Ibid., 425:5, cited in Katz, *Exclusiveness and Tolerance*, p. 165. Note the striking similarity to the view of R. Judah Loew ben Bezalel, in his own *Be'er ha-Golah* (Prague, 1598), pp. 143–46, S. Honig, ed. (Jerusalem, 1971).

35. For Bacharach's view that Christians are not idolaters, see *Resp. Havvot Ya'ir*, no. 1.

36. *Resp. Havvot Ya'ir* (Frankfurt, 1699), no. 31. In the medieval period, Christians were occasionally cited as exemplars of moral behavior and piety, in family relationships and in prayer. See R. Shelomo Yitzhaki, *Teshuvot Rashi*, Israel S. Elfenbein, ed. (New York, 1943), no. 207, where Rashi chastised a man who wished to divorce his ill wife by citing the higher ethical behavior of men toward their wives in Christian society. Also see the criticism leveled against idle conversation and levity during prayer, as compared to Christians who pray quietly, in R. Isaac of Corbeil, *Sefer Mitzvot Katan* (Satmar, 1935), p. 18. Also see the comments of R. Jonathan Eibeschütz, *Ya'arot Devash* (Metz, 1789, repub. in Jerusalem: *Makhon Yerushalayim*, 1984), sermon dated 25 January 1745, recommending that Jews learn from the admirable behavior of nobles and dukes whose devotion to the King enables them to overcome their ordinary desires.

37. *Tosefta Terumot* 7:20 refers to a group of marauders who threaten to kill many people unless one member of the group, or a particular individual whom they single out, is handed over to them. See J.T. *Terumot* 8:4 where R. Johanan and Resh Lakish dispute the meaning of the Tosefta text. For R. David Ha-Levi's view, see *Turei Zahav, Yoreh De'ah* 157:8.

38. *Resp. Bayit Hadash*, no. 43. For an equally positive assessment of the fairness of the general court system, see no. 44. For a full-scale treatment of Sirkes' position, see Elijah J. Schochet, *A Responsum of Surrender: Translation and Analysis* (Los Angeles: University of Judaism Press, 1973).

39. See Bacharach, *Resp. Havvot Ya'ir*, ibid., nos. 139 and 146, and compare the similar conclusion drawn by R. Jacob Emden, *Resp. She'elat Yaavetz*, pt. 2, no. 9. According to *Shulhan Arukh, Hoshen Mishpat* 388:9, it is prohibited to surrender a Jew, or his property, into the hands of non-Jews, even if he were an evil person or a criminal. However, one who harasses the community may be handed over to non-Jews in order to beat, imprison, or fine him, but this does not include one who harms an individual (sec. 12). Cf. Moses Isserles, *Hoshen Mishpat* 425:1. Even in the case of a non-believing gentile printer, his status as a human being who "breathes the breath of life through his nostrils" was taken by Bacharach to preclude the diminution of the sanctity of the biblical books. See *Resp. Havvot Ya'ir*, no. 184.

40. Richard I. Cohen, *Jewish Icons: Art and Society in Modern Europe* (Berkeley: University of California Press, 1998), pp. 52ff.; Azriel Shohat, *'Im Hilufe Tekufot: Reshit ha-Haskalah be-Yahadut Germania* [*The Beginnings of Haskalah in Germany*] (Jerusalem: Mosad Bialik, 1960), pp. 49–63.

41. In addition to the writings of Bing, Hourwitz, and Berr, treated below, see also a letter of the Abbé Grégoire to a Jew from Lunéville, in which he sought clarification whether, in light of their distinctive laws concerning marriage customs, divorce, age of majority, inheritance, etc., "their customs are in opposition to ours"; published in *Archives israélites* 91 (1930): 182.

42. Zosa Szajkowski, "The Diaries of the Delegates of the Bordeaux Jews to the Malesherbes Commission (1788) and the National Assembly" [Hebrew], *Zion* 18 (1952): 40; also see Schwarzfuchs, *Du juif à l'israélite*, pp. 81–87.

43. See Tama, *Transactions of the Parisian Sanhedrin*, pp. 133–34. Berr Isaac Berr was one of the most influential members of the Assembly; his son, Michel, secretary of the Sanhedrin, identified with the *régénérateur* movement and made several con-

tributions in the realm of religious instruction. Zalkind Hourwitz, though not at the deliberations of the Assembly, consulted regularly with members, and according to Robert Anchel, *Napoléon et les Juifs* (Paris, 1928), p. 181, he even advised Champagny. On the continuity of the communal leadership in general, with particular reference to the Sanhedrin, see Michael Graetz, *From Periphery to Center: Chapters in the History of Nineteenth Century French Jewry* [Hebrew] (Jerusalem: Mosad Bialik, 1982), pp. 25–26.

44. The seven volumes of *Me'orei Or* were published under the following titles: *Me'orei Or*, vols. 1–3 (Metz, 1790–93); *Be'er Sheva* (Metz, 1819); *Od la-Mo'ed* (Metz, 1822); *Bin Nun* (Metz, 1827); *Kan Tahor* (Metz, 1831). On Worms's biography and scholarly career, see: Nahum Brüll, "Ner la-ma'Or" [Hebrew], *Otzar Ha-Sifrut* 1 (1887): 20–31; Moshe Catane, "R. Aharon Worms and His Student Eliakim Carmoly" [Hebrew] *'Areshet* 2 (1960): 190–98; and Jay Berkovitz, "Authority and Innovation at the Threshold of Modernity: The *Me'orei Or* of Rabbi Aaron Worms," *Me'ah She'arim: Iyunim be-Olamam ha-Ruhani shel Yisrael bi-Yimei ha-Beinayim le-Zekher Yizhak Twersky* (Jerusalem: Magnes Press, 2001), pp. 249–85.

45. Worms's Sanhedrin address was reproduced in *Kan Tahor* (*Me'orei Or*, vol. 7), pp. 10b–11b, *novellae* to B.T. Sanhedrin 58b; also see *Bin Nun* (*Me'orei Or*, vol. 6), pp. 106a and 111a. Cf. the views of Jacob Emden, *Resp. She'elat Yavetz* (Altona, 1739–1759), no. 41, and the general discussion by Shohat, *'Im Hilufe Tekufot*, pp. 68–9, and nns. 152–67.

46. See *Kan Tahor* 11a and 16a. On the position of Me'iri, see Halbertal, *Bein Torah le-Hokhmah*, pp. 88–89.

47. *Kan Tahor* 11a, where citations include B.T. *Hullin* 94a and *Tanna de-vei Eliyahu*, ch. 16. For a discussion of the broader meaning ascribed to *re'a*, see Worms's discussion of Sanhedrin 93a. For a comparable view of *gezel ha-goi*, see Landau, *Resp. Noda be-Yehudah*, vol. 1, Yoreh De'ah, no. 81.

48. See *Kan Tahor* 10b–11b; *Bin Nun* 106a and 111a. Worms's position rested on Maimonides, *Mishneh Torah*, Hilkhot De'ot 2:6 and *Shulhan Arukh*, Hoshen Mishpat 228 and 231.

49. See Ha-Me'iri, *Beit ha-Behirah*, Bava Metzia, p. 267, Schlesinger, ed. Also see Richard Emery, *The Jews of Perpignan in the Thirteenth Century* (New York, 1959), p. 28.

50. See *Od la-Mo'ed* 29a–b.

51. See *Be'er Sheva* 15b.

52. On his refusal to permit the use of imported sugar on Passover unless there was a rabbinic statement attesting to its being absolutely free of any admixture of flour, see *Od la-Mo'ed* 28b–29a. Cf. Moses Sofer, *Resp. Hatam Sofer* (Pressburg, 1855), no. 135, where a more lenient ruling was issued. Also see Worms's remarks in *Od la-Mo'ed* 27a where he was highly critical of efforts to abolish the prohibition of legumes (*kitniyot*) on Passover, and his criticism of the contemporary failure to appreciate and observe the finer technical aspects of *heter isqa*, in *Od la-Mo'ed* 26b.

53. Katz, *Exclusiveness and Tolerance*, pp. 24–36, 106–28.

54. Tama, *Transactions of the Parisian Sanhedrin*, pp. 76–80.

55. See Schwarzfuchs's note on the dissatisfaction of the commissioners with this answer, in *Napoleon, the Jews, and the Sanhedrin*, p. 206, no. 3.

56. Tama, *Transactions of the Parisian Sanhedrin*, pp. 194–96.

57. Katz, *Exclusiveness and Tolerance*, pp. 182–93.

58. Tama, *Transactions of the Parisian Sanhedrin*, p. 200.

59. Ibid., pp. 199–200. Cf. Me'iri's similar formulation in his definition of "brother"; see *Beit ha-Behirah*, Bava Metzia, ed. Nissan Alpert (New York, 1959), p. 329.

60. Cf. Halbertal, *Bein Torah le-Hokhmah,* ch. 3, no. 25.

61. Prologue of Sanhedrin decisions, in Mevorakh, *Napoleon u-Tekufato*, p. 89.

62. See Graetz, *From Periphery to Center*, p. 60.

63. Ibid, pp. 56–59. For two popular textbooks that referred to the Sanhedrin's doctrines, see Elie Halévy, *Instruction religieuse et morale* (Paris, 1820), pp. 74–75, 83, 98–101, and Salomon Ulmann, *Recueil d'instructions morales et religieuses à l'usage des jeunes israélites français* (Strasbourg, 1843), preface. For the views of Munk and Franck, see *Archives israélites* 2 (1841): 383–85; Munk, *Palestine*, p. 99, and Graetz, loc. cit., pp. 63–65. On the rabbinic embrace of depoliticization, see Lazare Wogue, *Guide du croyant israélite* (Paris, 1859), pp. 77–79, 352–57, 386–95, 495–97; Mahir Charleville, *Réponse de M. le rabbin de Charleville, aux questions de la commission consistoriale, publiée à la demande d'un grand nombre de notables* (Paris, 1847), pp. 1–5.

64. For a discussion of Mendelssohn's views, see Alexander Altmann, *Moses Mendelssohn: A Biographical Study* (Tuscaloosa: University of Alabama Press, 1973), pp. 465–68.

65. See Jay R. Berkovitz, *Rites and Passages: The Beginnings of Modern Jewish Culture in France, 1650–1860* (Philadelphia: University of Pennsylvania Press, 2004), ch. 9.

66. One example of reliance on the Sanhedrin's decisions by opponents of religious reform is a letter from Rabbi Salomon Klein to the Minister of Instruction Publique et les Cultes, in *Archives nationales* F19 11037, 31 December 1856. Klein argued that in recommending certain reforms, the 1856 Paris rabbinic conference had violated the religious status quo as set forth by the Sanhedrin and subsequently confirmed by the Napoleonic regime.

67. Graetz, *From Periphery to Center*, pp. 31–34.

7

Jews and Judaism in an Egalitarian Society: Traditionalist Responses in Historical Perspective

Edward Breuer

In one sense, the fundamental issues being addressed in this volume are extraordinarily broad. Questions regarding Orthodoxy and its response to the principled egalitarianism of our time, after all, are integrally connected to the Jewish confrontation with modernity and the complex relationship of modern Jews to western democratic societies. In this regard, the scope of the discussion would appear to encompass nothing less than the story of European and then American Jewry as it has unfolded over the past two centuries. From the end of the eighteenth century, as Jewish civic equality was variously debated and attained across Europe, the question of how Jews were to function in the new socio-political order—as individuals and/or as a community—loomed large. Few individuals, of course, confronted these issues quite so directly or explicitly. But in their words and deeds, in their perceptions and fears, and in their hopes and aspirations, all Jews were forced in one way or another to react to the far-reaching changes.

The reference here to *all Jews* is deliberate, for although the problems wrought by modern developments clearly challenged traditional Jews in a particularly acute fashion, Jews who abandoned normative halakhic practices and beliefs had no less of a challenge in grappling with their role *qua* Jews in western society. For non-Orthodox Jews, navigating the boundaries between one's religious/communal/ethnic identity and one's participation in society was, if anything, even more vexing and complex.

At the same time, a discussion of the historical background of Orthodoxy and its confrontation with egalitarianism can also be a rather limited endeavor. If we focus on issues regarding egalitarianism that may trouble us today—issues framed in terms of privacy rights and protection against discrimination (abortion, gay rights, etc.)—we obviously have little historical precedent upon which to reflect. Earlier generations of halakhically committed Jews had occasion to worry about societal morality and its deleterious effect upon Jewish mores, but none were as thoroughly integrated and deeply engaged in the world around them, and therefore none had to consider the issues as carefully as we do today. The unique confluence of political and social trends that prompted this very forum—that of a community benefiting from a remarkably open society confronting the halakhically problematic consequences of that openness—clearly sets this moment of Jewish history apart from earlier periods.

If, however, we address ourselves to the early political and social notions of egalitarianism, those manifest in the promise of emancipation and the granting of citizenship to Jews across Europe, then an examination of Orthodox responses may be useful and historically substantive. As with any study of this kind, the value of historical perspective rests upon the possibility of capturing the shifting and dynamic nature of the moment, particularly one fraught with such accelerated change, expectation, and pressure. Our hope would be to move beyond a simple typification of traditionalist reactions that came to be known as Orthodoxy, and towards a better appreciation of the disorienting nature of contemporary historical realities.

The pressures on those who sought to maintain inherited rabbinic traditions differed in Western, Central, and Eastern Europe, and underwent change between the late eighteenth and late nineteenth centuries. The differing strategies adopted in response are well known, and from the vantage point of the twenty-first century appear natural and clear. But in historical context, we must bear in mind that beyond their steadfast refusal to abandon halakhic norms, little else was clear. Traditionalists had to struggle to make sense of contemporary events, just as they had to struggle to find an effective voice, and to calibrate their responses with an eye towards fending off the burgeoning Reform movement and addressing the communal needs of a group that still functioned as a distinct minority.

This paper will limit its scope to the historical and geographical parameters of West-Central, Central, and Eastern Europe of the late eighteenth and nineteenth centuries. The story of these Jews—encompassing the *kehillot* of the Habsburg Empire, Prussia, and Russia (i.e., the lands constituting the former Polish commonwealth of the eighteenth century)—offers a century-long confrontation with modernity, from the earliest changes of governmental policies to the attainment of partial or complete civic equality. Because the integration of Jews in these lands was an ongoing and unresolved issue that lingered for decades and even generations, rabbinic and lay leaders had ample opportunity to reflect upon and grapple with the desirability and costs of emancipation.

These *kehillot*, of course, also boasted an impressive number of outstanding rabbinic figures, representing not only the breadth and sophistication of nineteenth-century Jewish learning but its full range of spiritual sensibilities. Given the complexity and problematic nature of Jewish integration into European society, the writings of these well-published and outspoken traditionalists would appear to offer a particularly rich body of literature upon which to draw. It should also be evident that this paper is concerned primarily with the Jewish confrontation with the realities of political and social egalitarianism, and thus deals far less centrally with the Orthodox reactions to such disparate phenomena as the Haskalah or the growth of Reform Judaism.

I

We begin by making a number of broad historical observations regarding the Jews of Western and Central Europe that should serve as background to our discussion. The profound changes that we associate with modern Jewish history—increased tolerance of Jews and Judaism, new social, educational, and economic opportunities, and expanded political access and participation—were all manifestations of complex forces sweeping through Europe. Whether the proximate cause for these changes was primarily socio-economic, cultural-religious, or political is a matter of ongoing scholarly debate, but the implications for the individual and communal status of the Jews were apparent all the same. By the late eighteenth century, European rulers, government officials, and the intelligentsia were seriously engaged in contentious debate over what became known as the "Jewish question." For all its impact on Jewish life, however, the reordering of European society was not about Jews, but about European society itself. To whatever degree they joined the public discourse or dutifully petitioned for their rights, Jews could only respond to, and marginally affect, the broader course of events reshaping their lives.

The impact of political and economic emancipation—or, as the case would often be, the prolonged movement towards emancipation—would thus make itself felt in many ways, whether or not Jews and their *kehillot* wanted it. The same was true, in differing degrees, with regard to the impact of European culture and ideas, and even habits and mores. Although the Haskalah that coalesced in Berlin and Königsberg in the 1780s actively embraced certain aspects of European culture and sought to introduce them into their communities, the process of acculturation that would significantly impact upon European Jewry began before the advent of the Haskalah and took root in communities without any movement of its kind.[1]

In the case of the German communities, for example, it appears that by the 1760s and 1770s many urban Jews from upper-class families were reading and writing German and absorbing European literature and ideas; with one or two notable exceptions, none of these individuals were associated with the Haskalah, even in Berlin.[2] In their growing anxiety regarding those who make "the [study of] French and other foreign languages their central preoccupation and [their] study of Torah secondary," the writings of some eighteenth-century rabbinic scholars yield similar evidence of the same process of acculturation.[3] By the end of the century, rabbinic writings also document a perceived increase in laxity of ritual observance and even a brazen public flaunting of halakhic norms.[4] Again, these social and religious changes appear to have taken place independent of the Haskalah, and certainly before and separate from the beginnings of Reform. It is significant, in this light, that the first concerted traditionalist attack on Reform in 1818–1819 was focused far less on the *fact* of deviant behavior as on the attempt to justify new religious actions with halakhic arguments, and the challenge to rabbinic authority evident in the incorporation of these ideas in a public service.[5]

At its beginnings, then, the new historical dynamic operative among nontraditional Jews was for the most part a movement from social and economic reality to ideology, from new patterns of behavior to new articulations of Judaisms. Notwithstanding real cases of religious skepticism and crises of faith, most Jews were drawn by social and economic opportunity into a society which foresaw the possibility of a public domain that was confessionally neutral and pluralistic. Soon enough, with the acceleration of political and public policy changes throughout Europe, all Jews and Jewish communities found themselves overtaken by these new realities.

The pressures wrought by modernity were surely amplified and exacerbated by the creation of new Jewish movements, modes of study, ideologies, and notions of religious and nationalist identity, but it was the fundamental structural changes—with their concomitant political, social, and cultural ramifications—that shifted the ground on traditional Judaism. The question then, as now, was not whether Jews could seriously effect changes in the course of broader societal developments; it was, and remains, the ability of Jews to make sense of, orient themselves within, and respond to a world which is itself constantly shifting and redefining itself.

II

It is telling, though not entirely surprising, that the individual who provides something of a counterpoint to the picture drawn above was also the first to appreciate the far-reaching implications of the changes at hand. In his writings and public advocacy of Jewish civic equality, Moses Mendelssohn (1729–1786) immediately grasped that the issue central to the nascent debate, namely separation of civil and religious authority, would irrevocably alter the Jewish communal life. Simply stated, Mendelssohn recognized that on a legal and political basis, a move to lessen or end social and economic discrimination had to be predicated upon the notion that the state was to execute its judicial and administrative functions without regard to personal faith. In his analysis, this could not be merely a matter of governmental restraint; rather, evoking the discourse of early modern political philosophy, it had to be argued that the right to pass judgment on matters religious never fell to the state or, for that matter, to any civil authority.

That there should no longer be any legal basis for the public distinction of Christian and Jew was clear; Mendelssohn, however, also understood that there would be no more basis for a legally incorporated community of Jews, thereby spelling the end to Jewish self-government and all its social and religious prerogatives. Given his antipathy for religious coercion and his abiding respect for the privacy of conviction or belief, there were aspects of this that he was not unhappy about. In the final analysis, Mendelssohn correctly understood that the compelling logical and structural forces would transform the *kehillah* into a voluntary association.

Mendelssohn, at the same time, was acutely aware that a society that wholly or even partially rid itself of religious barriers was one that would exert more, not less, pressure on traditional Judaism. In midst of his campaign for Jewish civic equality, Mendelssohn himself was publicly challenged by an Enlightenment-minded German to explain how he could eschew religious coercion, given that the texts and teachings of Judaism were replete with punitive measures and various means of ensuring compliance. At its core, the challenge to Mendelssohn focused on the fact that Judaism itself did not appear to recognize a distinction between religion and society.

On one level, the very fact that Mendelssohn was able to reconceive Judaism was seized upon as an indication of Judaism's ability to accommodate itself to contemporary realities. The issue, in practical terms, was quite simple: if European society was going to treat Jews as equals, then Jews would have to take some responsibility for their exclusion. Jews, in other words, would have to adapt their own traditions in order to enjoy the full measure of civic equality. Moreover, since rabbinic Judaism had affirmed the suspension of certain laws and otherwise demonstrated an historically conditioned response to foreign subjection, was it not unreasonable to expect changes in other areas of Jewish practice—particularly rabbinic—in accordance with new political and historical realities?[6] On another level, if the radical separation of religion and society was neither true to Jewish traditions nor, from a German perspective, good for the integrity and well-being of society, then European society had every right to expect some degree of Jewish conformity to prevailing modes of religion and spirituality. Societal equality was manifest here not as an inviolable principle, but as a function of the Jewish ability to successfully integrate—read: reshape—their religious traditions into European (Christian) society, all in the interests of societal cohesion.

Jewish particularism and the pressures of emancipation stood here in conflict, as they would for most of the next two hundred years. These pressures, however, were sharpened by a distinctly eighteenth-century expression of non-judgmentalism. Perhaps the best articulation of this was Gotthold Lessing's *Nathan the Wise*, in which he put forth—in the mouth of the Jew, no less—a determinedly liberal critique of religious triumphalism and exclusivity. From this enlightened vista, all religious traditions were understood to be striving to embrace the same Father in Heaven, and allowing for any reasonable or objective criteria, it was impossible if not ludicrous to distinguish the superiority of one particular set of revealed truth-claims over another. The only genuine claim for chosenness, in fact, was predicated upon the attainment of the love and admiration of others, an ideal that gave social-humanistic succor to Enlightenment values. Rather than blunting Jewish particularism by pressuring for Christian-oriented reform, such an approach envisioned the mutual recognition of core religious truths and the shedding of particularism in the interests of some universalist faith.[7]

This is not the place to launch into a full assessment of Mendelssohn's *Jerusalem* and its response to these and other challenges, however insightful, provocative, and controversial this treatise may be. What is noteworthy from our perspective is not just *Jerusalem*'s historical standing as an early and direct confrontation with modernity, but Mendelssohn's acute realization that contemporary notions of *egalité* and non-judgmentalism had to be rebuffed if traditional Judaism was to survive intact. His particular approach was to use contemporary Enlightenment sensibilities and ideas in the formulation of ideas regarding the preservation of *halakhah* in all its rabbinic particularism.

Jews, Mendelssohn argued, could never give up the distinctiveness of Jewish practices, for the true knowledge of God was preserved and sustained by the full extent of the *halakhah*. Drawing upon Maimonidean conceptions in *Hilkhot Avodat Kokhavim*, Mendelssohn framed his understanding of Jewish law as the providentially ordained means of fending off idolatry, here provocatively underscoring the superiority of Judaism as a *mitzvah*-oriented tradition, one whose focus was on doing rather than merely believing (i.e., Protestant Christianity).[8] Mendelssohn, moreover, vehemently criticized universalist views of revealed religion as misguided and even dangerous, for the creation of a new set of symbols would either be so broad as to be utterly meaningless, or, if carefully defined and circumscribed, a new source for oppression, intolerance, and ultimately persecution.[9]

In the end, one of the most notable features of these ideas is Mendelssohn's attempt to respond to the perceived pressures of an open society by designing universalist arguments for the preservation of a Jewish particularism. Challenged to sacrifice that which made Jews and Judaism distinct, Mendelssohn tried to argue that a shared belief in a common humanity and a set of basic universal values should not undermine Jewish particularism, but rather, in the true spirit of tolerance, allow for all its rituals and practices, however disagreeable they may be to European eyes.

Despite the forcefulness and conviction of these ideas, there is something in Mendelssohn's statements at the end of *Jerusalem* that conveys a vague sense of apprehension, notable in the pleading tone of his final comments. To fellow Jews, he counsels fortitude: "Adapt yourselves to the morals and constitutions of the land to which you have been removed; but hold fast to the religion of your fathers too. Bear both burdens as well as you can! . . . Persevere; remain unflinching at the post which Providence has assigned to you." Having outlined his arguments regarding the superiority of a traditional ritual-based spirituality, he still felt the need to reinforce the immutable authority of *halakhah*. "I cannot see how those born into the House of Jacob can in any conscientious manner disencumber themselves of the law." To contemporary Germans, he bravely, if perhaps not altogether realistically, pointed to the clear limits to the process of integration: "if civil union cannot be obtained under any other condition than our departing from the laws which we still consider binding on us, then we are sincerely sorry to . . . declare that we must rather do without [it]."[10] Mendelssohn, for his part, did not believe that such a trade-off was at all necessary, but his remarks betray an anxiety regarding the abandonment of traditional observance as Jewish communities essentially became voluntaristic associations and confronted the constraints commensurate with the age of civic equality.

III

Mendelssohn, of course, did not hold rabbinic office nor consider himself a religious leader. European *rabbanim* of the late eighteenth century, for their part, were far less immersed in the world of European letters and intellectual discourse, and they exhibited an appreciably different measure of the societal changes under way. The Maskilim, the early proponents of *Wissenschaft des Judentums*, and the first generation of religious reformers each tended to view the events of their day as an historical turning point of notable if not momentous proportions. Well into the nineteenth century, however, most leading traditionalist rabbis were simply not inclined to see contemporary political and socio-economic developments in epoch-making terms. For all the drama of political-military developments (the French Revolution and the conquests of Napoleon), and with the less spectacular but equally important formulation of new governmental policies towards the Jews (in Prussia, the Austro-Hungarian Empire, and other German-speaking or German-dominated lands), the impacts of these happenings were surely noticed and felt, but largely as matters of practical and material import.[11]

From the 1780s onward, rabbinic scholars took note of the new laws designed to foster the study of German and general subjects among Jewish schoolchildren; while some rabbinic leaders went along only reluctantly, others were more approving, evidently recognizing that these skills would allow Jews to benefit from new economic opportunities.[12] There were, to be sure, cautiously voiced concerns regarding new policies that sought to erase centuries of communal independence, with particular apprehension that the suspension of Jewish juridical autonomy in Habsburg lands would lead to a decline in the quality of Jewish life.[13] On the whole, however, European *rabbanim* publicly lauded the many kindnesses shown the Jews, and any doubts and fears about the new social and political order then emerging were left unspoken.[14]

This remained true, significantly, even as the numbers of Jews abandoning Judaism began to grow and the first generation of Jewish reformers came to the fore in the 1810s. These reformers, as we know, were quick to exhibit a sensitivity to the political implications of nationally focused sentiments regarding redemption, especially the fear that such expressions would undercut Jewish claims for full citizenship; and it was precisely these sentiments that motivated them to eliminate liturgical references to messianic redemption.

Traditionalists immediately addressed themselves to the heart of the political issue, and their response was instructive. In their 1819 pronouncement against the establishment of the first reform synagogue, published as the preface to *Eleh Divrei ha-Berit*, the Hamburg *beit din* asserted that traditionally formulated Jewish messianic beliefs "did not at all impugn the honor of the kings and officers with whom we find protection, for they all know that we believe in the coming of the messiah and the ingathering of the exiles; then as now, no one objected to this belief of ours, for they know that we are obligated to pray for the welfare of the states that have extended their protection to us."[15] The responsum of R. Moses Sofer (1763–1839) reiterated the same notion, but it was clear that he was insistently ignoring the present in favor of the broadest realities of Jewish existence. "We are like captives (*ki-shevuyim*) of the war of destruction [of the Second Temple]," he wrote, and as such, Jews must be profoundly grateful to the nations for "the great kindnesses that they have extended to us these two thousand years."[16] R. Sofer and others, it seems, were entirely comfortable invoking the traditional historical and theological models of *galut* because they did not—or would not—appreciate the ramifications of new socio-economic and political realities, including broad expectations that Jews would adapt themselves to European society in more than superficial ways. This posture, of course, was itself one response among many, and certainly no less legitimate or wise. But whether or not such an approach was a discerning and calculated move, the fact remains that the effect of such a response was to preclude any serious confrontation with the challenges of emancipation and the social effects of equal rights. Even with the acknowledged surge in "deviant" Jewish behavior, rabbinic leaders did not initially connect this with broader societal developments, and hence saw no need to formulate a response to the fundamental changes beginning to unfold.

It is interesting to note that something of the same posture was embraced by leading *rabbanim* even when the social and political changes were indeed acknowledged. In his *Minhat Kena'ot*, a long excursus against the Reform conferences of the mid-1840s, R. Zvi Hirsch Chajes (1805–1855) stated clearly that any student of Jewish history would recognize that "our age is unlike earlier ages with regard to the position of the Jews," noting that persecutions and expulsions had ceased.[17] In most of Western Europe, he went on to add, "Jews are treated like citizens without the slightest difference."

Later on, R. Chajes returned to this point and wrote that most governments have liberated their peoples and now even treat Jews with respect; "they extend to [the Jews] the laws of all citizens without distinguishing them from others."[18] What is interesting is the broader argument employed here: "Despite the fact that we Jews have never been accorded more respect," R. Chajes was saying, "some Jews have impetuously, and unnecessarily, raised the flag of dissention and heresy." The Jewish attachment to their homeland was well known and fully accepted by European rulers, and was not an impediment to good political relations.[19] In fact, traditional Jewish beliefs, positing a sense of separateness, bred a far more respectful attitude towards Jews than the assimilationist tendencies of German Jewry, which seemed only to garner more and more hatred and anti-Jewish schemes.[20] In R. Chajes' view, whatever changes had been instituted appeared to affect only the material conditions of the *kehillot*; and since he did not see any social or religious ramifications to these developments, there was clearly no need for substantive response.

Perhaps the most striking, if idiosyncratic, illustration of these attitudes came from a far lesser known scholar rabbi serving in the Burgenland region of the Austro-Hungarian Empire, R. Abraham (Shag) Zwebner (1801–1876). Noting the recent annulment of some special taxes directed exclusively at Jews, R. Zwebner delivered a sermon in 1846 that voiced appreciation for this repeal, but he went out of his way to justify the original—and even continued—levying of such taxes. In R. Zwebner's thinking, all peoples living in Habsburg lands could consider themselves residents and enjoy all the rights and privileges extended by the empire; everyone, that is, except the Jews. Given their hopes for national redemption, Jews could only regard themselves as wayfarers or long-term visitors, and as such, should naturally be subject to special fees and taxes imposed on all temporary residents. In a telling move, R. Zwebner went further and even reprimanded those Jewish officials who sought such tax relief for not consulting with rabbinic leaders in advance, reminding them that unlike other societies, Judaism brooked no clear distinction between religious belief and politics.[21]

For R. Chajes and R. Zwebner, and, it appears, for many European rabbis, there was simply no new role or position for the Jews to consider. These traditionalists were fundamentally unmoved by the pressures for modernization, remaining unaware of, or ignoring, the fairly explicit understanding on the part of many European officials and intellectuals that Judaism itself would have to change if Jews were to gain civil equality. It is not surprising, of course, that as many Jews clambered for full emancipation, those now emerging as the "Orthodox" were generally nowhere to be seen, apparently content to accept whatever rights or equalities would be extended to them. As far as they were concerned, civil equality or the revocation of special duties were gracious favors that changed little of the fundamental relationship between Jews and the European societies within which they lived. All these rabbis bewailed the Jewish abandonment of observance and what they saw as pernicious moves on the part of Reform, but in denying that contemporary socioeconomic or political developments necessitated substantive changes, they also averted any serious consideration of those developments.

IV

The smaller number of nineteenth-century traditionalist rabbis who chose to see the events of their day as significant and potentially far-reaching did indeed recognize that Jewish membership in the new societies taking shape would necessitate a rearticulation, if not reorientation, of certain aspects of Judaism. A pluralistic society extending the possibility of equal rights would at the very least demand a certain degree of civic commitment, or perhaps an assertion of a shared belief in a common humanity and universal values.

This was precisely the approach taken by the rabbi of Emden, R. Abraham Löwenstamm (d. 1840), as he too sought to discredit the earliest attempts at justifying religious reforms. In the last section of *Tzeror ha-Hayyim*, as he took on the question of whether the perpetuation of traditional messianic beliefs would cast aspersions on Jewish patriotism, R. Löwenstamm's first move was to insist that the messianic idea was a notion that was shared by all mankind, Jew and non-Jew alike, precisely because it so fundamentally defined our humanity.[22] His idea of the messiah, as one might surmise, was essentially an "enlightenment of the eyes" and "purification of the hearts," and even within this muted messianism, he insisted that Jews were to remain thoroughly passive; an embodied Redeemer-King would wield not a sword, but *mussar* and *hokhmah*. R. Löwenstamm went on to insist that "the essence of what a man mourns for in *galut* is the *galut ha-Shekhinah*." *Galut* and redemption are thus naturally complementary, addressing the alienation and ultimate recovery of God's immediate presence.[23] While many of these ideas found their source in earlier rabbinic and medieval literature, there is little doubt about their significance and intent. R. Löwenstamm was fully cognizant of the contemporary social and political meaning of his notion that the attainment of the messianic age would be a day of universal beneficence, and that a yearning for this day only "strengthens our attachment to [our sovereign],"[24] as if the brotherhood evident in his messianism was somehow manifest in the bonds of temporal political arrangements. R. Löwenstamm seemed sensitive to a certain parity that was naturally suggesting itself, a parity between a society that was beginning to make room for Jews, and the need for Jews to express some commensurate expression of belongingness.

A decade and a half later, in the mid-1830s, the individual who would eventually inherit R. Löwenstamm's position in Emden went further in his own reflection upon the place of Jews in modern society. In his *Neunzehn Briefe über Judentum* [Nineteen Letters on Judaism], the young R. Samson Raphael Hirsch (1808–1888) wrote of exile and diaspora in somewhat traditional, albeit romantic terms, describing it as part of Israel's fate, a stage in the fulfillment of its mission, and a means of making Israel into a better nation.[25] Some pages later, in a letter that addressed the issue of emancipation, R. Hirsch put forth a different model of Jewish diaspora existence, one clearly responsive to the new realities of his age.

> Those rejections and restrictions in the paths of life are not an essential condition of exile; on the contrary, it is our duty to attach ourselves to the degree possible to the state which admits us, to further its goals and to consider our own well-being as inseparable from that of the state.[26]

Contrasting harsher times to the new milder one, R. Hirsch fully expected Jews to "take advantage of every alleviation and improvement of his condition open to him in an honest way." More than any other traditionalist of his generation, he could speak eloquently and passionately of the new position Jews would find themselves in:

> I bless emancipation when I notice that no spiritual principle, not even one of foolish fanaticism, stands in its way. . . . I rejoice when I perceive that in this concession of emancipation, regard for the natural rights of men to live as equals among equals is freely extended without force or compulsion, but purely through the power of their own inner truth.

At the same time, however, he would strike a cautionary tone, one that was cognizant of the toll these new conditions had begun to take—and, he feared, would increasingly take—on commitments to Jewish traditions.

> But with regard to Israel, I only bless it if, at the same time, there is awakened in it the true spirit which strives to fulfill the mission of Israel whether or not there is an emancipation, to elevate and ennoble ourselves, to implant the spirit of Judaism in our souls, in order that it may generate a life in which that spirit shall be reflected and realized. I bless it, if Israel will regard emancipation not as a goal of its vocation, but only as a new condition of its mission. . . . But I

> would grieve if Israel . . . would welcome emancipation as the aim of *galut* . . . merely as a means of securing a greater degree of comfort in life.[27]

In *Horeb*, a project that actually preceded and prompted the writing of the *Neunzehn Briefe*, R. Hirsch plainly stated his apprehensions regarding the fallout of a society committed to the principles of non-discrimination. With the new "spirit of humanity" and the "loosen[ing] of fetters," young Jews were mistakenly seeing their deliverance and redemption.[28] It was hardly coincidental that R. Hirsch assessed the dangers of emancipation most directly in the context of discussing Jewish strictures against intermarriage.

> The more friendly, the more considerate, the other people become to the Jews, the greater the fund of affection which the Jews gratefully store in their hearts for prince and country, the closer the intercourse becomes between Jews and non-Jews . . . the greater becomes the importance of these laws; for the danger becomes the danger of Jews going over to the other camp.[29]

And yet, even decades later, R. Hirsch continued to support the continued struggle for equal rights and the concomitant integration of Jews. He would, of course, declare that "if our religion indeed required us to renounce that which men call civilization and culture, we would be ready to do so."[30] But just as there was ultimately no cultural conflict, he insisted in impassioned terms that there should be no friction between the enjoyment of full civic equality and the continued adherence to Jewish particularism. Faithful, traditional Jews, in fact, would make the best citizens, "play[ing] a role of great significance also in the broader concerns of our future as men and as citizens," while Judaism—and note here the echo of a certain messianism—would "serve as a building brick for the increasingly evident progress toward the salvation of all mankind." The only real problem standing in the way of this utopian realization was not any problem inherent in the process of integration, but the growing Jewish indifference to the dictates of the Torah. The task at hand was to convince fellow Jews not to allow "human civic concerns to make us forget the concerns of specifically Jewish character."[31] "Do not regret," he instructed his fellow Jews, "that today's nations, in their struggle for enlightenment, have also invited the sons of Jewish Law to participate in their social aspirations." The Jew had not a little to contribute, for the truths drawn from Jewish Law "are by no means the least significant contributions he could bring . . . when he enters into the life of the nations."[32]

V

The situation in Eastern Europe, of course, was markedly different from that of Western and Central Europe. The late eighteenth and early nineteenth centuries saw a disruptive set of political reconfigurations, which began with the *kehillot* under Polish rule being divided and absorbed into the Prussian, Austro-Hungarian, and Russian Empires. In 1807 some of the *kehillot* taken over by Prussia became part of the Napoleonic-controlled Duchy of Warsaw, and in 1815 the same communities passed into the control of the somewhat autonomous Kingdom of Poland ("Congress Poland"), only to be absorbed into Russia in 1830–1831. Each of these governments struggled to determine its own policies towards the Jews, though none of them were seriously committed to civic equality or integration in concrete terms. These first few decades of the nineteenth century were highly unsettling, and Jewish leaders, both rabbinic and lay, could hardly see through the immediate uncertainties and communal needs to reflect upon the broader import of these developments.

As one attempts to plumb early nineteenth-century literature for attitudes towards these events—and here, I can only claim to have scratched the surface—it is difficult to glean contemporary attitudes in meaningful or substantive terms. The Napoleonic wars appear to have elicited much confusion and uncertainty, though there appear to have been strongly felt expressions of excitement and opposition as well. One rabbinic figure, R. Menahem Mendel of Rymanow (1745–1815), has been identified in various Hasidic traditions as being openly sympathetic to the French cause, viewing these wars as nothing short of the apocryphal battles of Gog and Magog.[33] Whether one saw in these wars the beginning of the ultimate redemption or further exilic tribulation, the stories and traditions attributed to R. Menahem Mendel and other early Hasidic masters had a thoroughly mythic and apocalyptic quality to them, and they nowhere suggest an evaluation (positive *or* negative) of new policies towards Jews, or socio-political expectations of any kind.[34] Similarly, various statements attributed to R. Menahem Mendel regarding the need for Jews to remain apart from the gentile nations (with emphasis upon the importance of maintaining distinctive garb) are sufficiently vague and ahistorical as to qualify their usefulness as a contemporary source.[35]

Perhaps the clearest statement about the socio-political implications of a Napoleonic victory came from a letter of R. Shneur Zalman of Lyady (1745–1813). Writing shortly before his death, R. Shneur Zalman stated that

> if Bonaparte should win, Jews will increase their wealth and their stature, but their hearts will become distant and estranged from their father in heaven; but if our monarch Alexander should win, Jews will become impoverished and their stature will decline, but their hearts will be bound and dedicated to their father in heaven.[36]

Clearly, such a letter would appear to associate French rule with a particular socio-economic order, and offers a remarkably clear-eyed view of the costs of such integration to Jewish spiritual life. There is little doubt that the existence of such a straightforward evaluation of contemporary realities is intended to suggest a profound understanding of modernity and a kind of prophetic view of what in fact lay ahead in the nineteenth century. The letter, it must be said, comes across as a little too perspicacious, and its pithy if casual quality may betray the advantage of some historical hindsight.[37] Whatever the authenticity of this text, it is noteworthy that a letter dated only a year later and attributed to his own son and successor, R. Dov Baer (1773–1827), interprets the Napoleonic wars in kabbalistic terms, echoing the mythic quality of other Hasidic reactions.[38]

In the decades that followed, the large numbers of Eastern European Jews concentrated under Russian rule lived under a succession of Tsars and a shifting set of attitudes and approaches towards modernization in general, and Jewish integration in particular. While the Russian government took its "Jewish problem" no less seriously than European states to the west, a combination of intractable socio-economic problems, aggressive Tsarist tactics, and Jewish insularity created a very different set of dynamics and expectations. As in German-speaking Europe, there is evidence that the early intellectual and cultural processes of modernization preceded and paralleled the advent of the Haskalah, particularly in Lithuania.[39]

But whereas the German Haskalah, which effectively disappeared by the 1810s, was one manifestation of the broader trajectory of acculturation and integration, the parallel Jewish effort to effect change in Eastern European lands proceeded along very different lines and reflected the far more complex set of realities. In Russian territories, where the pressures for change were neither widely nor evenly rooted in socio-economic or cultural developments, the integrationist designs of the Tsarist government were largely imposed from above and applied in a rather oppressive manner. Those Jews who sought to effect educational, cultural, or economic change were caught between a government to which they turned for support and which in turn used them to further its own aims, and a traditional Jewish leadership that quickly came to view most things Tsarist—and Maskilic—with suspicion and hostility.

These various pressures and challenges forced some Hasidic and Mitnagdic leaders into a level of direct political activity that surpassed that of their rabbinic counterparts in Central Europe. In the complex of political and economic realities that constituted Eastern Europe, the rabbinic involvement with Russian governmental policy was born of necessity and motivated by the desperate desire to protect Jewish interests, both religious and material. Much rabbinic and lay attention, naturally, was focused on local issues and matters of immediate and practical import: taxation, military conscription (begun in 1827), the establishment of state-run Jewish schools, and sundry other disputes and points of tension.[40]

This intense awareness of new political policies and their effect on patterns of Jewish life was everywhere a concern, and the fear and anxiety that it evoked is evident in the cultural and religious history of the period. Yet ironically, though not altogether surprisingly, this engagement with integrationist pressures did not immediately manifest itself into a body of rabbinic writings reflecting or commenting upon the broader meaning and consequence of Jewish integration. In some ways, the manifold suspicions and fears were so palpably evident, and the benefits of civic equality so remote, as to obviate the need for articulation.

Later in the nineteenth century, however, one does find a number of outstanding Lithuanian Mitnagdic figures forcefully articulating their views of Jewish integration. R. Yosef Baer b. Yitzhak Ze'ev ha-Levi Soloveitchik (1820–1892), author of the *Beit ha-Levi*, utilized the well-worn midrashic and medieval leitmotif of Jacob and Esau as a figurative representation of the relationship of Jews and gentiles. Commenting upon Genesis 32:12, "Deliver me, I pray, from the hand of my brother, the hand of Esau," R. Yosef Baer noted the apparent redundancy of "the hand of Esau" ("my brother" could here only be referring to Esau) and suggested that Jacob was equally afraid of Esau's hostile intentions as he was of the prospect of putting aside enmity and living in brotherly peace.[41] R. Yosef Baer went on to state that this dual fear was operative in Jewish history as well; while their gentile overlords initially wanted to destroy them outright, they now sought to reside peacefully with Jews, thereby intending to distance them from their rituals and beliefs. The latter, of course, was no less destructive than the first.

> Jacob feared this [later] exile more than the first, for it is human nature to succumb [to its pressures]. This is why Jacob referred to this first when he said "Deliver me, I pray, from the hand of my brother" and only after added "from the hand of Esau." The reason for this is because the first [exile] has only physical subjugation, but the second has both physical and spiritual subjugation, since its benefits accrue only to one who forsakes the *mitzvot*.[42]

Two years later, in 1886, R. Yosef Baer's contemporary R. Naftali Zvi Yehudah Berlin (1817–1893) published an essay titled *She'ar Yisrael* in which he struck a variant of the same theme.[43] Citing Jacob's exile to Aram and his troubled relationship with his father-in-law Laban, R. Berlin suggested that Laban's animosity prefigured a providential feature of exilic reality. "There arises the occasion to think that our secure settlement among the nations indicates their love for us and their desire for us to sustain and satisfy ourselves from the bounty of their land." The Biblical narrative concerning Laban, he wrote, serves to warn us against this dangerous delusion, first by insisting that "in each generation the enemies of Israel are ready to destroy us," and then by recognizing that it is only by God's protection that we are saved. But providence, although salutary, also provides the very instability that R. Berlin viewed as the natural and constant characteristic of Jewish existence. "In every age, even those that appear to be good, wherein enmity is subdued and unheard, [the desire to destroy us] is still a hidden danger that is ready to be actualized when the hand of Providence wishes to chasten us."[44]

Throughout *She'ar Yisrael*, then, R. Berlin emphasizes the fact that Jews are meant to live apart from the nations of the world, even if, as he goes out of his way to point out, they are to offer the world their wisdom and morality as embodied in the Torah.[45] For this Lithuanian *rosh yeshivah*, the improvement of socio-economic conditions, and perhaps even civic equality, were not in and of themselves objectionable, inasmuch as Jews could still maintain their separateness. The two, in his mind, were not mutually exclusive, and he embraced this very possibility as a promising feature of contemporary developments: "Indeed, today there are many among the great nations of Europe who do recognize the truth and love us; we do hope that their numbers increase."[46] The problem of the nineteenth century, however, was that Jews themselves had failed to recognize their appointed mandate to live "alone and separate from others," with the unfortunate providential repercussions:

> It is, therefore, understood what happens when Israel tries to break out of its aloneness and imitate others, ending in the removal of its religious tradition of Judaism. How does the Holy One return them to their structured purpose? Animosity for Israel is stirred up among the nations; they are pushed away from their activities and dwellings until, inevitably, the uniqueness of Israel is recognized, and the word of God is reestablished forever.[47]

In the end, the perspective offered by R. Berlin circumvented the need for a reasoned or calculated evaluation of modernity and its integrationist realities. The intrinsic structures of Jewish existence, after all, were a function of a metahistorical covenantal relationship, thereby superseding the particular socio-political challenges of the day.

VI

In both Eastern and Western Europe, attitudes towards socio-political integration and notions of egalitarianism could find expression not only in the kind of comments cited above, but, somewhat indirectly, in halakhic discourse and *piskei halakhah* taken by various rabbinic authorities. At one level, the application of halakhic principles to new conditions and the reexamination of traditional practices in light of new realities would appear to provide a wealth of historical insight into the manifold pressures wrought by emancipation and attempts at integration. Indeed, there were numerous cases of this kind, including questions such as the permissibility of school attendance on Shabbat,[48] the necessity of a *get* where a couple had a civil marriage but no *kiddushin*,[49] questions regarding traditional head-covering practices (relating separately to both men and women),[50] and the permissibility of circumcision for a child born to a Jewish father and non-Jewish mother.[51] These issues reflected the stresses and strains to which Orthodox Judaism was subject, and while they highlight the various stratagems adopted by rabbinic authorities in response to the distinct challenges of modernity, they do not generally allow us to garner substantial insight into the issues we are dealing with here. By their very nature, writings of this kind limited themselves to the halakhic issues at hand, and though decrying the abandonment of normative practices, they ultimately yield little regarding the broader demands of civic equality and integration.

There are, however, a number of halakhically framed issues, including some that recur in other chapters of this volume, that were more intrinsically attuned to the implications of civic equality and the expressed values of mutual respect and ethical reciprocity. Clearly, in an age when laws mandating special social and economic treatment of European Jews were being rescinded, discriminatory rabbinic strictures regarding non-Jews, especially with regard to ordinary matters of property, pecuniary obligations, and the delivery of health-care, would seem to be discomfiting.

No less delicate was the matter of how Jews were to perceive the religious rituals and symbols of Christian neighbors, a matter with practical import that would also test, however symbolically, the limits of mutual toleration. Nineteenth-century discussion of these issues would naturally unfold within the halakhic parameters of earlier codes and *teshuvot*, so the question is whether, or to what degree, one can delineate contemporary sensibilities in the handling of some of these questions. The three issues examined below will be dealt with briefly and without the benefit of a full analysis of the underlying texts and principles; they are not intended to exhaust the pertinent halakhic matters of the day, but rather, are cited here for their ability to illustrate a variety of approaches and responses.

One issue with a long history of halakhic discourse is that of differing standards of legal obligation in matters of property and money, as for example the halakhic principle that required a Jew to return the lost property of another Jew but exempted him or her when the item lost can be presumed to have belonged to a non-Jew.[52] Despite the obvious sensitivity that such an issue would presumably elicit, a preliminary review of nineteenth-century texts appears to indicate that there was not much discussion of this matter, and little that moved beyond earlier articulations.

In a short German monograph that attempted to deflect entrenched prejudices against the Talmud, R. Abraham Löwenstamm expressed an acute self-consciousness concerning pecuniary discrimination against non-Jews and the negative light it cast on rabbinic morality. Asserting once again that this was a propitious time to work against all inequalities "on the path to a united humanity," R. Löwenstamm set out to defend the rabbinic position as one of common sense and true morality.[53] Drawing on the position articulated by a number of medieval halakhists, he argued that the laws guiding the relationship of Jew and gentiles were determined not by Jewish law, but by that of the nations in which Jews lived; as such, Jews would certainly uphold all the property rights enjoined upon them as residents of a gentile state, but could not be expected to extend their own laws regarding property rights and obligations to gentiles when these gentiles themselves had no such legal provisions.[54] In his presentation R. Löwenstamm seemed content to work within the fairly well-worn categories set down by earlier rabbinic authorities and limit his discussion to the treatment of pagans and the distinction between pagans and those—like contemporary Christians—who upheld the seven Noahide laws. Despite his clear acknowledgment of the unique historical moment at hand, there appeared to be little attempt to build upon the more far-reaching medieval positions of Maimonides or R. Menahem Meiri or later authorities who affirmed their views.

Few other Orthodox rabbinic figures seemed interested in addressing the question. R. Samson Raphael Hirsch, for example, glossed over this entire question without the slightest acknowledgment of the moral difficulties that inhered in some rabbinic texts.[55] At the other end of the century, and much further to the east, R. Barukh Epstein (1860–1942) offered a slightly broader articulation of inherited views on this subject, arguing that the only salient distinction regarding the Jewish obligation to return lost property was whether or not the society in which one lived upheld the Noahide laws. Societies which did not respect these laws were fundamentally lawless, and no property was secure; but those who upheld such laws, "and this includes most contemporary nations and all enlightened states, are beyond all doubt equal to Jews with respect to these laws."[56]

Another issue, one that received substantially more attention, was whether a Jew may transgress sabbath laws in order to save the life of a critically ill non-Jew in the same way he or she was mandated to do for a fellow Jew.[57] Towards the end of the eighteenth century, scholars like R. Joseph Teomim of Lemberg (1727–1792) and R. Shneur Zalman (at this time still residing in Lyonza) upheld the normative *halakhah* that, under normal circumstances, prohibited a Jew from providing even life-saving medical assistance to a gentile on the sabbath when such aid entailed violations of sabbath laws; R. Shneur Zalman, in fact, quite clearly insisted on maintaining the medieval position that this stricture was in effect not only with regard to pagans and idolaters, but all gentiles.[58] In the nineteenth century, however, rabbinic authorities moved towards a far more permissive stance on this matter, in good measure by expanding the Talmudic notion of allowing certain proscribed activities out of fear of gentile hostility (*mi-pnei eivah*) and its consequences.

In a responsum dated 1839 dealing with the classical Talmudic case of a Jewish midwife delivering the babies of gentile women, R. Moses Sofer argued that the halakhic interdiction against providing assistance to a gentile woman in labor on the sabbath applied only to violations of Biblical laws, but not rabbinic ones. As such, he suggested that a Jewish midwife delivering a baby should have a gentile cut the umbilical cord (a deed Biblically prohibited), but he added that "if there is [the possibility of gentile] hostility, this is tantamount to fear on account of mortal danger (*sakanat nefashot*), and one may permit even proscribed Biblical labor."[59]

A few years later, in his commentary on the Mishnah, R. Israel Lipschütz (1782–1865) noted that the Mishnaic statement prohibiting a Jewish midwife from assisting with the labor of a non-Jewish woman was suspended in times of gentile hostility, but added that this exemption would not appear to apply on the sabbath. "However, in our day," he went on to say, "when the authorities severely punish any midwife or doctor who refuses to attend to a gentile when called, or any non-Jewish doctor who refuses to attend to a Jew, it is possible to be lenient."[60] In the decades that followed, other rabbinic authorities appeared entirely comfortable in accepting this position.[61]

The most expansive treatment came at the hands of R. Aryeh Leib Broda of Lemberg (1840–1928) who wrote a responsum not only affirming the position of R. Sofer, but building on it in at least two significant ways. First, since the duty of saving human life overrode the sabbath laws for both Jews and those considered a *ger toshav*, he extended this broadly to any non-Jews who observed the Noahide laws, a category into which he then appeared to place all contemporary Europeans. Second, he suggested that if the reason for allowing Jewish doctors to treat non-Jewish patients on the sabbath was concern for gentile hostility (*eivah*), then this should be allowed even when the patient was not critically ill (falling into the category of a *holeh she-ein bo sakanah*).[62]

Most striking, however, was his analysis of Talmudic Jewish–gentile relations in comparison to his own day. In late antiquity, he pointed out, hatred for Jews was so fierce that Jews would hardly gain more enmity by refusing care for an ill gentile, and as such, there was little justification to violate the sabbath. In modern times, when governments

> protect us from all harm to our persons and property, and provide medical care without making any distinction between Jews or gentiles who are ill, and care for the well-being of the Jewish people—it is evident that the slightest trace of hostility and strife is to be viewed as a danger. We are required to employ any pretext to remove ourselves from this like the "distance of a bowshot [Gen. 21:16]."[63]

R. Broda saw clearly that the egalitarian principles of modern society had already sharpened the discriminatory implications of such *halakhot*, making the utilization of notions like *mi-pnei eivah* more indispensable than ever.[64]

In light of these sensitivities, it is also historically interesting to note that halakhic pronouncements aside, there is evidence that the practice of providing medical assistance to gentiles on the sabbath had already become part of the accepted reality of Jewish life in nineteenth-century Europe. R. Hayyim Halberstam of Sanz (1793–1876) agreed in principle that one could never violate a Biblical injunction out of fear of hostility, but noting that "it was the custom of doctors to be lenient," he sought to legitimate such action by basing it—without textual corroboration—on what he referred to as "*takkanot artzot*."[65] Right at the end of the nineteenth century, R. Israel Meir ha-Cohen (1839–1933) wrote similarly that "[Jewish] doctors of our time, even the most upright, are not at all concerned with this issue, for they regularly travel many miles to cure gentiles," although in this case he made no attempt to legitimate their actions and condemned them as intentional desecrators of the sabbath.[66] In either case, it was clear that halakhically committed Jews already internalized the need to adjust their actions to new social and professional realities; whatever their response, rabbinic authorities were not, in this instance at least, in a position to control Jewish practices on the basis of halakhic norms.

A final issue, the last we will consider here, concerns the nineteenth-century rabbinic assessment of Christianity, particularly the varieties of Trinitarian beliefs and the role played by Jesus in the Christian understanding of God. The question, from a halakhic perspective, was whether Christian devotional practices or beliefs should be regarded as *avodah zarah*, or whether they could be regarded as some kind of *shittuf* (associated deity), thereby allowing for the possibility that for gentiles, such beliefs and practices are to be considered a non-idolatrous and hence permissible form of worship. Early modern Ashkenazic *poskim* were divided on this issue. Some argued that even when gentiles prayed (or swore) to other gods, they really had the "Creator of Heaven and Earth" in mind, and that such *shittuf* was not prohibited to them (*einam muzharim al ha-shittuf*).[67] Other rabbinic authorities critiqued this view and rejected it, essentially contending that the prohibition against idolatry applies in its fundamentals to both Jews and gentiles, and would thus preclude such an allowance.[68]

Early nineteenth-century European scholars remained divided, and the halakhic analysis on both sides of the issue seemed unconcerned and unaffected by contemporary developments. R. Wolf Boskowitz (d. 1818), who served various communities in Moravia and Hungary, argued at length that the Noahide prohibition against idolatry did not include a commandment to believe in the unity of God; it followed, therefore, that non-Jews should be allowed to believe in deities that properly constitute *shittuf*.[69] R. Samuel Landau (d. 1834), the head of the rabbinic court in Prague, did not cite R. Boskowitz by name, but he affirmed that this view had gained wide currency. Nevertheless, he could not concur, and insisted—without specifically addressing the issue of Christianity—that gentiles no less than Jews were enjoined from any form of worship that included *shittuf*.[70] R. Akiva Eger was similarly aware of the widespread leniency on this matter, and he too argued that *shittuf* was prohibited to gentiles.[71]

As the century progressed, those arguing that *shittuf* was an acceptable form of gentile worship tried to advance their position in new ways, and their writings began to yield some recognition of contemporary realities. In his *Ha-Ketav ve-ha-Kabbalah*, R. Jacob Zvi Meklenburg of Königsberg (1785–1865) took up the most important medieval and early modern rabbinic views on the matter, but asserted throughout that a careful reading of the relevant Biblical texts strongly supported the position that *shittuf* was not prohibited to non-Jews. At the end of this rather lengthy discussion, R. Meklenburg felt compelled to add that "everything written about this subject is in reference to earlier nations, in which heretics denied the creation of the world and the like. This is not the case with contemporary nations in whose lands we find shelter; we are obligated to seek their welfare and to pray for their peace."[72]

A much more involved analysis of the issues was written in a responsum by R. Marcus Horovitz (1844–1910), the Orthodox chief rabbi of the Frankfurt-am-Main Jewish community (over and against R. Hirsch's secessionist *kehillah* of the same city). Asked in 1891 whether a Jew could contribute to the building fund of a Catholic church, he began by expressing his discomfort with rabbinic authorities who would allow such donations for socially pragmatic reasons (*mishum darkhei shalom* or *mishum eivah*) despite their theoretical-halakhic inclination to view *shittuf* as a form of idolatry prohibited to all gentiles.[73] Acknowledging, perhaps, the morally unsatisfying nature of such solutions, R. Horovitz wanted nothing less than a principled position that would allow for contributions of this kind. After subjecting all the classical sources and responsa down to the nineteenth century to a thorough analysis,[74] he concluded that there would be no halakhic prohibition whatsoever to making such a donation. But making a bold and possibly unprecedented assertion, he went further and insisted that Jews regard contributions to a Catholic church fund as a "mitzvah of sanctifying God's great name."

> All the nations will see that we are faithful Jews, always ready to exert ourselves with love in sanctification of God's name that there be one God with one name [Zech 14:9]; and that we are ready to cast all our burdens and all our honor in this world on behalf of our sacred beliefs. We recognize that this *mitzvah* rests upon us and not another nation, but also that a non-Jew could be among the great and righteous individuals and worthy of the world to come if he observes the seven universal Noahide Laws.[75]

R. Horovitz's responsum is remarkable for its appreciation of the social and religious ramifications of this question, and the premium placed upon mutual respect and acceptance as Jews were being integrated into European society.[76]

VII

For all the willingness of some rabbinic leaders to embrace the attendant realities of this new age, their vision of Jewish integration into European society rarely dealt in any concrete fashion with some of the thornier challenges of modernity and their ramifications for Orthodox Judaism. The problem was not only the gossamer quality of their writings on this subject, but, ironically, their rather limited bearing on real contemporary conditions. Jews living in Western and Central Europe did not see the full measure of rights until the 1860s and 1870s, and this after a protracted and often discomfiting political process; Jews living further to the east had far less to show. Throughout most of the nineteenth century, then, Orthodox Jews were still living with the effects of social and political separateness, not to mention an abiding intolerance and hostility.

It is important, in this regard, to note the real ambivalence of Orthodox leaders, lay and rabbinic, towards the attainment of complete equality, even when it had already been achieved in Western and Central Europe. In a blunt statement, the weekly Orthodox journal *Israelit* pronounced in 1874 that since the state could not be expected to meet the special needs of halakhically observant Jews, and since such Jews would not be able to make use of certain rights, complete equality was anyhow an impossibility.[77] In 1906, the same publication could unabashedly state that while true civil equality was an admirable goal, "for us, as for Orthodox Jews in general, [it] is a secondary consideration, one of the various means by which . . . the obligations set by the Torah [are] advanced."[78]

Traditionalists contributed relatively little to the campaign for civil equality, partly because the cause of equality had been so closely identified with reformist and assimilationist tendencies, partly out of a distaste for activism and its potential to incite a gentile backlash, and partly because some degree of separateness allowed the Orthodox to maintain a distinctive social and religious space they could minimally control.[79] Even when Orthodox Jews were politically involved, either through representation in one of the legislative or consultative assemblies of Europe or through advocacy and lobbying, their time and energy were devoted not to a principled consideration of the implications of emancipation, but to preserving their beleaguered interests.

While some Orthodox Jews, mainly German and urbanized, saw themselves in terms of the grand vision articulated by R. Hirsch, most nineteenth-century traditionalists continued to perceive notions of equality and emancipation in far more limited terms. A rabbinic leader like R. Esriel Hildesheimer could sincerely declare that, if necessary, he was ready to sacrifice emancipation for the sake of *halakhah*,[80] but daily life generally did not admit such grandiloquent gestures. Orthodox Jews struggled with a variety of practical problems and the challenges of adapting halakhic observance to new realities;[81] they sought to build and sustain their religious and educational institutions, either within or without the structures of the broader Jewish community; and they endeavored to stem the steady abandonment of Jewish observance and to fight back against the intellectual and scholarly onslaught of the Reform and Positive-Historical schools. In all this, Orthodox Jews were guided by distinct ideals and principles, but these were focused, rather defensively, on the immediate religious needs of the moment.

Even in our day, some, mainly *haredi*, communities, continue to voice a certain provisionality to their place in western democracies, viewing governmental action as conditioned upon the tolerant and benevolent disposition of the current office-holder, and inclined towards the traditions of *shtadlanut* to achieve their ends. In one sense, of course, such communities are fully consonant with modernity; modern democratic societies, after all, allow for their citizens to form distinctive communities, including communities that reject the very values that allow for this pluralism. But these *kehillot* do not see themselves as embracing pluralism. Rather, like most traditionalists of the early nineteenth century, they simply do not recognize the changes wrought by modernity as anything more than a periodic and temporal shift in Jewish fortunes.

It is only in the past generation or two that a new set of perceptions have taken root among Orthodox Jews, and it is this shift that has brought about qualitatively different confrontation with modernity. In the past three or four decades, the long sought-after benefits of emancipation were made readily available to large numbers of Jews, and as the last vestiges of societal resistance gave way, members of the Orthodox community advanced socially, economically, and politically in ways far more concrete and meaningful than those ever imagined.

As some earlier scholars and leaders understood, the pressures to conform to the religious norms and sensibilities of European society were not simply the price for civic admission, and would not cease with the attainment of emancipation. The real challenge and struggle would revolve around the ability of Jews to maintain their traditional halakhic commitments when such traditions could only be preserved by some degree of purposeful disengagement or differentiation from non-Jewish society. For the first time, Orthodox Jews have come to view themselves as full and equal members of the societies in which they dwell, a reality that is indicated not so much in vague words or declarations as in a wide variety of behaviors, assumptions, and expectations.

Two centuries after the beginnings of the Jewish experience of modernity, Orthodox Jews have broadly internalized the reality that something fundamental has changed, that the society in which one resides belongs to the halakhically observant Jew no less than any other religious or ethnic group. It is this unprecedented integration into western society, of course, that serves as the framework and predicate for this volume; and it is in addressing this moment in time that we properly move out of the realm of the historical into the less certain terrain of the present and future.

NOTES

I wish to express my gratitude to Rav Moshe Soloveichik for sharing his wealth of knowledge regarding the issues and texts addressed in this paper. My thanks also to Prof. Alan Brill for his references to Eastern European sources.

1. The best example of this in Western Europe is the case of British Jewry, documented in Todd Endelman, *The Jews of Georgian England, 1714–1830: Tradition and Change in a Liberal Society* (Philadelphia: Jewish Publication Society, 1979), pp. 118–165. For Eastern Europe, see the discussion below.

2. The social and cultural changes affecting Berlin Jewry have been well documented in Deborah Hertz, *Jewish High Society in Old Regime Berlin* (New Haven: Yale University Press, 1988), pp. 35–47, 86–95, 147–203. See also Steven M. Lowenstein, *The Berlin Jewish Community: Enlightenment, Family, and Crisis, 1770–1830* (New York, 1994), pp. 46–54, and passim; Dolf Michaelis, "The Ephraim Family," *Leo Baeck Institute Year Book* 21 (1976): 201–228; and Miriam Bodian, "*Ha-Yazamim ha-Yehudim bi-Berlin, ha-Medinah ha-Absolutivit, ve-Shippur Matzavam ha-Ezrahi shel ha-Yehudim be-Mahtzit ha-Sheniah shel Me'ah ha-18,*" *Tziyon* 49 (1984): 176–182.

3. This quotation is from Zvi Hirsch Koidonover, *Kav ha-Yashar* (various editions), chapter 82; see also R. Jonathan Eibeschutz, *Yecarot Devash* (Jerusalem, 1983), 1:23 (sermon of 1743); and vol. 2:33 (sermon of 1748); R. Ezekiel Landau, *Ahavat Tziyon* (Jerusalem, 1966), pp. 5b (sermon of 1762) and 7a (sermon of 1764); and R. Joseph Steinhardt, *Zikhron Yosef* (Fürth, 1773), introduction, p. i [unpaginated in the original]. The first two sources are discussed in Mordechai Eliav, *Ha-hinukh ha-Yehudi be-Germaniyah bi-Yeme ha-Haskalah ve-ha-Emantzipatziyah* (Jerusalem, 1960), pp. 16–17.

4. See, for example, R. Eleazar Fleckeles, *Olat Hodesh* (Prague, 1785), pp. 77a–79a. R. Zvi Hirsch Horowitz, *Lahmei Todah* (Offenbach, 1816), pp. 19b–20a, 69b, 115a, 124a.

5. This is explicitly acknowledged in the opening paragraphs of the Hamburg *beit din* pronouncement of 1819 against the local reformers and the opening of their Temple; see *Eleh Divrei ha-Berit* (Altona, 1819), iii.

6. These arguments were addressed to Mendelssohn in a pamphlet titled *Das Forschen nach Licht und Recht . . .* (Berlin, 1782); reprinted in *Moses Mendelssohn Gesammelte Scriften Jubiläumsausgabe*, ed. F. Bamberger, A. Altmann, et al. (Stuttgart: Friedrich Frommann Verlag, 1971–) [henceforth *GSJ*], 8:73–92; see, on the issue of rabbinic Judaism, pp. 83–85. The distinction between "pure" Biblical Judaism and its rabbinic accretions was everywhere assumed in contemporary European discourse about Judaism; see my "Politics, Tradition, History: Rabbinic Judaism and the Eighteenth Century Struggle for Civil Equality," *Harvard Theological Review* 85:3 (1992): 357–383.

7. See Gotthold Ephraim Lessing, *Sämtliche Schriften*, ed. Karl Lachmann (Stuttgart, 1887), pp. 91–95. The relevant scene, Act Three, Scene Seven, is reprinted in English translation in Paul Mendes-Flohr and Jehuda Reinharz, eds., *The Jew in the Modern World* (Oxford: New York, 1995), pp. 64–67.

8. *Jerusalem, oder über religiöse Macht und Judentum* (Berlin, 1783), reprinted in *GSJ*, 8:99–204; see pp. 165–191. For an English translation, see *Jerusalem, or On Religious Power and Judaism*, trans. Allan Arkush (Hanover, NH: New England University Press, 1983), especially pp. 97–125. See also the excellent analysis of Lawrence Kaplan, "Maimonides and Mendelssohn on the Origins of Idolatry, the Election of Israel, and the Oral Law," in *Perspectives on Jewish Thought and Mysticism*, ed. by Alfred L. Ivry et al. (Amsterdam: Harwood, 1998), pp. 423–455.

9. *Jerusalem, GSJ* 8:203 [Arkush translation, pp. 137–138].

10. *Jerusalem, GSJ* 8:198–200 [Arkush translation, pp. 133–135].

11. In his recounting of the Napoleonic assault on Pressburg in the summer of 1809, for example, R. Moses Sofer's ample anxieties were nowhere directed at the social and political ramifications of French rule. To the degree that he had any broader political concerns, it was with what he perceived as the military-political arrogance of the Habsburg strategy. See his *Sefer ha-Zikharon* (Pressburg, 1879).

12. See the sermon dated 1782 in R. Yehezkel Landau, *Derushei ha-Tzelah* (Jerusalem, 1966), p. 53a; the 1816 sermon of his son, R. Samuel Landau, *Ahavat Tziyon* (Prague, 1827), p. 27a [reprinted with *Derushei ha-Tzelah*, p. 19a]; the part-testament, part-manifesto of R. David ha-Cohen Friesenhausen, *Mosdot Tevel* (Vienna: Anton Strauss, 1820), pp. 76a–77a, 89b, where he affirmed that idealized education aside, all Jewish children would benefit from a basic knowledge of vernaculars and a general curriculum; and the letter of R. Aaron Fuld, apparently written around 1824, in Simhah Asaf, *Mekorot le-Toldot ha-Hinukh be-Yisrael* (4 vols.; Tel Aviv: Dvir, 1954), vol. 1, pp. 275–276.

13. See Abraham Trebitsch, *Korot ha-Ittim* (Brünn, 1801), p. 30a. It is not surprising that here too, worry about the far-reaching costs of integration was linked to a clear perception that something significant had changed in the 1780s.

Other expressions of concern on the part of rabbis serving within the Habsburg Empire at this early juncture are sufficiently vague as to be of limited historical value. For example, in a collection of sermons titled *Ma'amar Ester* (Ofen, 1832), p. 12b, R. Wolf Boskowitz (d. 1818) spoke out against Jews who adopted the dress of their gentile neighbors. He cautioned that rather than fostering the acceptance of Jews, such attempts to alter external appearance would only lead to resentment, for it would be taken as a sign of Jewish arrogance. Europeans, R. Boskowitz added, were less interested in the Jews' external appearance than in their conversion. Although this sermon was dated 1808, and R. Boskowitz had spent his entire career serving *kehillot* in Bohemia, Moravia, and Hungary, there is really little in such statements that indicate an apprehension particular to the policy changes of late eighteenth- and early nineteenth-century Europe.

14. See, for example, R. Eleazar Fleckeles, *Olat Hodesh*, introduction, wherein he discusses Jewish attitudes towards contemporary European peoples and their rulers, especially in light of the reforms promulgated by Joseph II: "In particular, in times such as these, it is incumbent upon us to commend and praise them, to honor 'exalt and raise them [Isa 63:9],' since a king has arisen, one who is good and beneficent to

all, 'who conducts his affairs with equity [Ps 112:5]' . . . [He established] 'one judicial standard [Lev 24:22]' for all, applied equally to everyone whether distinguished or lowly. Everyone is free to engage in any area of commerce, trade, or craft, and permission is given to each people to observe and fulfill all the decrees and laws according to their religion and beliefs."

15. This appeared as the preface to *Eleh Divrei ha-Berit*; see p. iv.

16. Ibid., p. 9.

17. *Minhat Kena'ot* (Zolkiew, 1849), p. 2b.

18. Ibid., p. 14b.

19. Something of the same point was made by R. Chajes' contemporary, R. Shlomoh Yehudah Rapoport, in his own missive against the Reform conferences of the mid-1840s. See *Tokhahat Megulah* (Frankfurt, 1846), p. 21.

20. *Minhat Kena'ot,* p. 21b.

21. *Derashot ha-RASH* (Jerusalem, 1904), # 82, pp. 77a–b.

22. *Tzeror ha-Hayyim* (Amsterdam, 1820), pp. 70a–71a.

23. Ibid., pp. 75a ff.

24. Ibid., p. 81b.

25. *Iggrot Tzafon: Neunzehn Briefe über Judentum* (Altona, 1836), pp. 41–45 [letter 9].

26. Ibid., p. 79 [letter 16].

27. Ibid., pp. 81–82.

28. *Horeb, Versuche über Jissroels Plichten in der Zerstreuung* (Altona, 1837); see the English edition, published as *Horeb: A Philosophy of Jewish Laws and Observances*, trans. I. Grunfeld (2 vols.; London: Soncino, 1962), 1:126 (§ 220).

29. Ibid., 2:379 (§ 503).

30. *Die Religion im Bunde mit dem Fortschritt* (Frankfurt, 1854); translated into English by Isidor Grunfeld as "Religion Allied to Progress," *Judaism Eternal* (2 vols.; London: Soncino, 1956), 2:234–235.

31. *The Collected Writings* (8 vols.; New York: Feldheim, 1984–1995), 6:11.

32. Ibid., 8:325.

33. See *Sefer Tiferet Menahem* (Warsaw, 1926), pp. 18–20; and the two versions cited in Baruch Mevorah, ed., *Napolion u-Tekufato* (Jerusalem: Mosad Bialik, 1968), pp. 186–187. In contrast to the sources used in earlier sections of this paper, those cited here are not drawn from R. Menahem Mendel's own writings, but are teachings related by colleagues and students; this alone would appear to account for the different versions that come down to us. Such sources certainly represent a set of Hasidic attitudes towards the Franco-Russian wars, though whether they are truly R. Menahem Mendel's is a much larger methodological issue.

34. See also the other Hasidic sources cited in Mevorah, *Napolion u-Tekufato*, pp. 184–185, 188–189; and Azriel Frenk, *Yehudei Polin bi-Yemei Milhamot Napoliyon* (Warsaw: Hatzefira, 1912), pp. 13–14, 18–19.

35. Comments of this sort are evident in the sermons and Biblical commentaries collected by his student R. Ezekiel Panet and published as *Menahem Tziyon* (Tchernowitz, 1851). See the Jerusalem, 1991 edition, pp. 36–37, 51, 98.

36. This letter was first published in Hayyim Meir Heilman, *Beit Rebi* (Berditchev, 1902), pp. 93–94. It has been reprinted numerous times, with some variation in its language; cf. *Iggrot-Kodesh* (Brooklyn, 1980), pp. 150–151, 454–455.

37. On the general issue of reliability of extant material regarding the life of R. Shneur Zalman and other nineteenth-century leaders of Habad, see Roman A. Foxbrunner, *Habad: The Hasidism of R. Shneur Zalman of Lyady* (Tuscaloosa: University of Alabama Press, 1992), pp. 41–45, 216–217. Cf. also the discussion of R. Shneur Zalman in Frenk, *Yehudei Polin bi-Yemei Milhamot Napoliyon*, pp. 51–55.

38. See Heilman, *Beit Rebi*, pp. 95–102. Cf. also his sermon of 1827 in Joshua Mondshein, *Migdal Oz* (Kfar Habad, Israel: 1980), pp. 399–407.

39. See the discussion of nineteenth-century Vilna in Joshua Levisohn, *The Early Vilna Haskalah and the Search for a Modern Jewish Identity* (Unpublished Ph.D. Dissertation, Harvard 1999), pp. 10–16 and passim. Cf. also Steven J. Zipperstein, *The Jews of Odessa: A Cultural History, 1794–1881* (Stanford, CA: Stanford University Press, 1986), pp. 13–15.

40. See the broad-ranging discussion in Eli Lederhendler, *The Road to Modern Jewish Politics* (New York: Oxford University Press, 1989), pp. 58–83.

41. R. Yosef Baer applied the same twofold fear in his reading of Genesis 32:8, "Then Jacob was greatly afraid and was distressed."

42. *Beit ha-Levi al Derush u-Mile d'Aggadeta* (Warsaw, 1884), pp. 17a–17b. For an earlier alternative historical reading of the same Biblical passage, see Frenk, *Yehudei Polin bi-Yemei Milhamot Napoliyon*, p. 14.

43. This essay, along with R. Berlin's commentary to *Shir ha-Shirim*, was published in 1886 under the title of *Rinnah shel Torah*.

44. *Rinnah shel Torah* (Kfar Hasidim, 1993), pp. 199–200. The English translation here is taken from *Why Antisemitism?* trans. Howard Joseph (Northvale, NJ: Aronson, 1996), pp. 12–13.

45. R. Berlin made the same point regarding the Jews' mandate to live separately in his *Ha-Amek Davar* to Num. 23:9, first published in Vilna, 1879–1880.

46. Ibid., p. 209; *Why Antisemitism?* p. 35.

47. Ibid., pp. 206–207; *Why Antisemitism?* p. 28. See also his *She'elot u-Teshuvot Meishiv Davar* (Warsaw, 1894), #44, pp. 27a–b.

48. See David Ellenson, *Rabbi Esriel Hildesheimer and the Creation of a Modern Orthodoxy* (Tuscaloosa: Alabama University Press, 1990), pp. 64–65; R. David Zvi Hoffmann, *Melammed le-Ho'il* (3 vols.; Frankfurt, 1926–1932), vol. I, no. 58.

49. Hoffmann, *Melammed le-Ho'il*, vol. III, no. 20.

50. R. Esriel Hildesheimer, *She'elot u-Teshuvot Rabbi Azriel Hildesheimer* (2 vols.; Tel Aviv, 1969–1976), vol. I, *Yoreh De'ah*, no. 231; vol. II, *Even ha-Ezer*, no. 36; Hoffmann, *Melammed le-Ho'il*, vol. II, no. 56; Eric Zimmer, "Men's Headcovering: The Metamorphosis of a Practice," in Jacob J. Schacter, ed., *Reverence, Righteousness and Rahamanut: Essays in Memory of Rabbi Dr. Leo Jung* (Northvale, NJ: Jason Aronson, 1992), pp. 340–347; and Breuer, Modernity Within Tradition, pp. 7–9.

51. See the exchange of R. Zvi Kalischer and R. Hildesheimer in *She'elot u-Teshuvot Rabbi Azriel*, vol. I, *Yoreh De'ah*, nos. 229–230; and R. Marcus Horovitz, *Matteh Levi* (Jerusalem, 1979), Part II, *Yoreh De'ah*, nos. 54–55.

52. For a recent article citing some of the most pertinent halakhic sources, see Michael J. Broyde and Michael Hecht, "The Gentile and Returning Lost Property According to Jewish Law: A Theory of Reciprocity," *Jewish Law Annual* 13 (2000), pp. 31–45.

53. See *Der Talmudist, wie er ist; oder wir sind alle Menschen* (Emden, 1822), pp. 3, 7–8.

54. Ibid., pp. 28–41.

55. R. Hirsch wrote very briefly and only in vague terms about the obligation to deal honestly with all people, whether or not they were Jewish. In his *Horeb*, 1:228 (§337), R. Hirsch cited the *Shulhan Arukh*, *Hoshen Mishpat* 348, and wrote that "it is immaterial from whom you may steal, filch or withhold, be it an Israelite or a non-Israelite, a heathen or idolater. . . . in every case you have transgressed against a Divine prohibition and are in sin until you have restored it." While this statement reflected the view of R. Joseph Karo and others, R. Hirsch clearly tried to keep his presentation straightforward and unambiguous by ignoring the far more problematic statement of R. Moses Isserles, loc. cit. More troubling was his statement in *Horeb*, 2:418–19 (§ 558-220), where R. Hirsch spoke of the obligation for Jews to return the lost property of their brothers, while conveniently neglecting to discuss whether or not this extended to non-Jews. Many decades later, in an essay published as *Über die Beziehung des Talmuds zum Judenthum und zu der Sozialen Stellung Seiner Bekenner* (Frankfurt: J. Kauffmann, 1884), p. 18 [printed in English as "The Talmud and Its Teachings on Social Virtues, Civic Duties, and Commercial Integrity," in *Judaism Eternal: Selected Essays from the Writings of Rabbi Samson Raphael Hirsch*, trans. I. Grunfeld (2 vols; London: Soncino, 1956), 2:168], R. Hirsch similarly glossed over all kinds of problems by suggesting that there were no categorical differences between Jewish obligations to pagans, non-Jews who abided by the Noahide Laws, and fellow Jews. This approach may also be evident in his handling of the far more public issue of monetary interest in loans to non-Jews; see the discussion in Noah Rosenbloom, *Tradition in an Age of Reform: The Religious Philosophy of Samson Raphael Hirsch* (Philadelphia: Jewish Publication Society, 1976), pp. 344–347.

56. *Torah Temimah* (Vilna: Romm, 1904), to Deut. 22:3, note 22. He wrote this commentary between 1887 and 1901.

57. For a review of the relevant halakhic sources, see R. Ovadyah Yosef, "*Tipul Refui be-Nokhri be-Shabbat*," in Moshe Hirschler, ed., *Sefer Halakhah ve-Refuah* (Jerusalem: Regensberg Institute, 1980), pp. 147–150; and Avraham Avraham, *Nishmat Avraham* (Jerusalem: Erez, 1983), *Orah Hayyim* §330(2), pp. 225–226.

58. See R. Teomim's *Pri Megadim*, *Eshel Avraham* to *Orah Hayyim* § 330, note 5; and R. Shneur Zalman's *Shulhan Arukh*, to *Orah Hayyim* §330(2).

59. *She'elot u-Teshuvot Hatam Sofer* (3 vols.; Jerusalem: Mekkor, 1970), Part II (*Yoreh De'ah*), no. 131. R. Hirsch might well have appreciated this approach and shared it in practice, but in contrast to R. Sofer, chose to gloss over the issue entirely; see *Horeb*, 1:76 (§149).

60. *Mishnayot . . . im Peirush Tiferet Yisrael* (Danzig, 1845), *Avodah Zarah*, II:1, *Tiferet Yisrael* note 6.

61. See R. David Judah Leib Silberstein, *Shevilei David* (Przemysl, 1880), *Yoreh De'ah* §154; and the Rebbe of Munkacs, R. Zevi Hirsch Shapira, *Darkhei Teshuvah* (1893), *Yoreh De'ah* §154, where cites both R. Lipschütz and R. Silberstein approvingly.

62. *Sefer She'elot u-Teshuvot Mitzpeh Aryeh Tinyana* (Lemberg, 1911), Part I, *Orah Hayyim*, no. 10, pp. 6b–8b. R. Broda fully appreciated the radical implications of his position, as is evident in his wondering aloud how it was that a Jew could not violate the sabbath for a fellow Jew who was not critically ill, but that he could do so for a non-Jew in a similar medical condition. The question was left unanswered.

63. Ibid., p. 7a.

64. For a critical, though empathetic, analysis of R. Broda's position, see R. Isaac Herzog, *Pesakim u-Ketavim* (3 vols.; Jerusalem: Mossad Ha-Rav Kook, 1989), vol. II, no. 63. Although the twentieth century has its own dynamics and realities and should receive separate treatment elsewhere, it may be noted that R. Herzog's responsum explicitly acknowledges that while nowadays far less personal harm will befall a Jew who refuses to aid a non-Jew on the sabbath, such a refusal would have immeasurably broader reverberations and dangers.

65. *Divrei Hayyim* (Lemberg, 1875), Part II, *Orah Hayyim*, no. 25.

66. *Mishnah Berurah* (Warsaw, 1892–1898), §330, note 8.

67. See the gloss of R. Moses Isserles to *Shulhan Arukh*, *Orah Hayyim* §156(1); R. Shabbetai Cohen, *Siftei Kohen* to *Shulhan Arukh*, *Yoreh De'ah* §151(1), note 7; and R. Samuel b. Joseph of Cracow, *Sefer Olat Tamid* (Amsterdam, 1681), to *Shulhan Arukh*, *Orah Hayyim* §156(1).

68. See R. Ephraim b. Ya'acov ha-Kohen, *Sha'ar Ephraim* (Sulzbach, 1688; Lemberg, 1886), no. 24; and R. Jonah Landsofer, *She'elot u-Teshuvot Meil Tzedakah* (Prague, 1757), no. 25. See also the responsum of the late-eighteenth-century chief rabbi of Hamburg, R. Raphael ha-Kohen, *Ve-Shav ha-Kohen* (Altona, 1792; reprinted Brooklyn, 1969), no. 38. For a listing of other sources, see J. David Bleich, *Contemporary Halakhic Problems* (New York, 1983), v. II, p. 213.

69. *Sefer Seder Mishnah* (Prague, 1820) to Maimonides, *Yesodei ha-Torah* I:7; and see above n. 13. Although not writing in a halakhic vein, Mendelssohn put forth a similar notion, suggesting that it was entirely natural that the nations of the world would worship God through various divine intercessors; this might, in fact, have been natural for Jews as well, were it not for God's guidance and express injunction. By dint of their special encounter and relationship with God, this nation was uniquely instructed to worship without the use of celestial intermediaries. See his *Sefer Netivot Ha-Shalom* (Berlin, 1780–1783) [reprinted in *GSJ* vol. 16], *Biur* to Ex. 20:2.

70. His responsum is published with those of his father; see R. Ezekiel Landau, *Noda bi-Yehudah-Mahadura Tinyana* (Prague, 1811), no. 148. This view is cited approvingly in R. Abraham Zvi Hirsch Eisenstadt's *Pithei Teshuvah* to *Shulhan Arukh*, *Yoreh De'ah* §147, note 2 (first printed in the Vilna, 1836 edition).

71. *Sefer She'elot u-Teshuvot Rabbi Akiva Eger* (Jerusalem, 2002), Part IV, no. 43. This volume of responsa is comprised of his writings that appeared among the work of his rabbinic colleagues, in journals, or had remained unpublished; as such, this particular responsum does not appear in the earlier published responsa of R. Eger.

72. *Ha-Ketav ve-ha-Kabbalah* (Königsberg, 1852) to Deut. 4:19, and cf. also his commentary to Exodus 20:3. This Biblical commentary was first published in Leipzig, 1839, but this comment (among many others) was added only in the second edition of 1852.

73. *Matteh Levi*, *Yoreh De'ah*, no. 28.

74. One of his more interesting arguments is that rabbinic authorities who argued that *shittuf* was a form of idolatry, and hence prohibited even to gentiles, erroneously cited the first chapter of Maimonides' *Mishneh Torah*, *Avodat Kokhavim* to this effect. R. Horovitz maintained that Maimonides' historico-philosophical presentation of the history of idolatry was purely expository, and was not written with halakhic distinctions or assertions in mind; hence, no such deductions could be derived from this text.

75. *Matteh Levi, Yoreh De'ah*, no. 28; the quote appears on page 85. R. Horovitz ends the responsum on a sobering note, warning his correspondent that such contributions to a church were only permissible if there were no Jewish converts who were members of that church, particularly if the church was the only one in its vicinity. The problem, of course, was a straightforward one of *lifnei iver*. A reader of his comments, however, cannot but help being struck by the contrast between his congenial attitude towards Catholics and his unbridled hostility and resentment towards Jewish converts.

76. This question was also addressed by R. David Zvi Hoffmann in his *Melammed le-Ho'il*, vol. II, no. 148, where he states that such donations are prohibited. It is evident from this responsum and no. 55 of the same section that R. Hoffmann agreed that gentiles may engage in a form of worship that includes *shittuf*; his issue here was that since Jews were strictly enjoined from such practices, permitting donations specifically designated for a church building fund was tantamount to allowing a Jew to participate in the building of an idolatrous temple. R. Hoffmann, however, saw no problem in allowing donations of a more general nature, even if they were then appropriated for church construction. R. Hoffmann also addressed these questions at length in his *Das Schulchan-Aruch und die Rabbinen über das Verhältniss der Juden zu Andersgläuben* (Berlin, 1885), p. 121.

77. Cited in Mordechai Breuer, *Modernity within Tradition: The Social History of Orthodox Jewry in Imperial Germany*, trans. E. Petuchowski (New York: Columbia University Press, 1992), p. 294.

78. *Israelit* (January 18, 1906), no. 3(1), cited in Marjorie Lamberti, *Jewish Activism in Imperial Germany: The Struggle for Civil Equality* (New Haven: Yale University Press, 1978), pp. 147–148.

79. Ibid., p. 177, and Jacob Toury, *Die politischen Orientierungen der Juden in Deutschland von Jena bis Weimar* (Tübingen, 1966), pp. 20ff, 88.

80. *Gesammelte Aufsätze* (Frankfurt, 1923), pp. 57–58.

81. See the examples cited above, in notes 48–51.

8

Modern Orthodox Jewish Day Schools and Non-Jews

Jack Bieler

DOES A PARTICULAR ARTICULATED EDUCATIONAL GOAL OF JEWISH DAY SCHOOLS EVER BECOME ACTUALLY REALIZED?

A review of many Orthodox day schools' mission statements[1] will reveal that one of the core values to which these schools are ostensibly committed is fostering "good citizenship" within their student bodies.[2, 3] Not only do the Mission Statements express an avowed interest in acquainting students with the wisdom of the Jewish and secular worlds, but they similarly call for those who complete the schools' educational programs to be both practicing Jews and active participants within the society at large.

Milton Himmelfarb,[4] writing at a time when the day school movement was in its relative infancy, although raising questions regarding the quality of the education being provided by these schools, was nevertheless resolute in his defense of the day schools' preparing their students to participate fully in American society. "Though day schools do not give their pupils a school experience with children who are not Jewish, the pupils are apt to be taught respect for others quite insistently. There is research to show that an essential part of the defensive ideology of the day schools,[5] hammered home to their students, is an emphasis on American pluralism. A few years ago, an astute researcher found that as far as he probed in the direction of ultra-Orthodoxy, the day school children he interviewed were fully committed to intergroup pluralism, among the other articles of the American creed."

In a more recent article extolling the accomplishments of day schools, Jack Wertheimer[6] writes, "Not only do they steep young people in Jewish learning, instilling in them the 'habits of the heart' for a lifetime of Jewish experience, they do so without in the least compromising their young charges'

American identity.[7] To the contrary, by communicating in the strongest way possible that it is entirely proper to live as Americans strongly engaged with Judaism and the Jewish people, these schools hold out the promise for a generation equipped as perhaps none other before it to contribute meaningfully to the civic life of its two worlds."

Striving to become good citizens of a secular, non-Jewish state presumes a certain positive predisposition towards the people of that state as well as to the cultural and moral climate extant within it. Increasingly, the Orthodox world is portraying general society as validating mores and lifestyles antithetical to religious values and behavior, and the majority of individuals who comprise that society as fundamentally different and even alien from the type of people who can serve as appropriate representatives of a Divinely created world. In an article reporting on the New Jewish High School in Waltham, MA, an institution that sees itself as a community day school[8] in contrast to explicitly Orthodox day schools, Peter Beinart[9] writes, "The Orthodox community, for its part, has rarely celebrated the melting pot, and generally worries less about total acceptance by the broader culture." Beinart's point is truer of recent years than it was only a few decades earlier. Consider for example the submission twenty-five years ago of Rabbi Shubert Spero[10] to a Symposium entitled, "The Jew in America":

> In one fundamental respect, however, the modern Orthodox American Jew is at one with the earliest Jewish arrivals in Colonial days. Like them, we seek an integrated community and not an isolated one as in the Amish community. Unlike our Hassidic groups in Williamsburg and Crown Heights, we wish to participate not only in the general economic sphere but in the cultural arena as well and even on the social level to a degree compatible with the norms of Halacha. The degree of assimilation sought after by modern Orthodox American Jews (creative involvement in the university, theater, arts, in dress, and living habits) is not a "compromise" we make in order to "make it" economically, but is a well-formed decision based upon a considered judgment as to what is the Torah ideal.

A more contemporary perspective voiced by Emanuel Feldman, the current editor of the journal of Orthodox Jewish thought, *Tradition*, supports Beinart's contention that Orthodoxy posits an ever-increasing alienation from the values and mores of contemporary life:

> So does society slide down the slippery slope of contemporary morality. There are no absolutes. All is relative. Even religion itself is no longer a matter of strong belief and of absolutes, but of preference and choice. I prefer chocolate to vanilla. I prefer Judaism to paganism. Do you wish to know what is right and what is wrong? The answer lies not in your Bible but in the latest polls. In our time, the old joke about Moses and the Ten Suggestions has been apotheosized.

The fact that this is not an isolated view, but represents the perspective of many mainstream Orthodox Jews is powerfully symbolized by the assumptions inherent in one of the questions posed to the thirty-three participants in a 1998 *Tradition*[11] article, entitled, "The Sea Change in American Orthodox Judaism: A Symposium":

> As a believing Jew, what facets of Torah life give you the most personal strength to thrive spiritually as an Orthodox Jew *in a hedonistic environment that is not conducive to Torah values?*[12]

In light of such current assessments, the question must be asked: Can commitment to social action and conscious efforts to advance the quality and interests of such a society continue to serve as an appropriate educational ideal for the Orthodox day school?[13, 14] Furthermore, even if one were to contend that a positive attitude towards seriously engaging general society is both viable and desirable, given the present Jewish educational context, that is, current day school curriculum, personnel, and school structure,[15] is it realistic to anticipate that students will have been encouraged to think and act along these lines? In response to such questions, it is appropriate to reflect upon and investigate (1) whether the aspiration is in fact compatible with Jewish education as it is currently constituted, and (2) what changes could/should be initiated in order to more realistically pursue such a goal, assuming that it is in fact a value that should be preserved in Jewish day schools' missions?

UNDERSTANDING WHAT CONSTITUTES BEING A "GOOD CITIZEN" FROM THE SECULAR PERSPECTIVE

While an argument could be made that being a "citizen" is a matter of right and privilege rather than obligations,[16, 17] which would limit the extent that one would need to actively contribute to the surrounding society, a different connotation appears to traditionally have been applied to the concept in the American context. In the foreword of *The American Citizen's Handbook*,[18] the following code appears:

> To be a good father, mother, sister, or friend,
> To be a dependable, faithful, and skilled worker in home, school, field, factory or office,
> To be an intelligent, honest, useful, and loyal citizen, with faith in God and love of fellowman,
> To recognize the brotherhood of man and to live by the Golden Rule,
> These are the aspirations that have brought happiness and achievement to the America we all love.

Some social critics have argued that in the aftermath of World War II, a change has taken place in the manner that average Americans approach their citizenship.[19] Nevertheless, current advocates of civic education in schools are as insistent as ever regarding what is to be taught concerning the nature of the *responsibilities* of citizenship.[20, 21] Todd Clark[22] writes, "the most important reason for civic education (is) the creation of a sense of membership in one's local community, a knowledge of its institutions, a willingness to participate, and a passion to solve its problems."[23]

While such civic expectations have been usually only implicit for non-Jews at times when the masses were granted rights and privileges within their societies, Jewish minorities throughout their history have been overtly confronted by the need to accept upon themselves clearly delineated social responsibilities vis-à-vis their non-Jewish fellow citizens in order to be accorded the privilege of citizenship.

The first time that the expectations of citizenship for Jews in a non-Jewish country were clearly formulated was during the early stages of the Emancipation, when the French Sanhedrin,[24] attempting to lend credibility to the principles enunciated by the Assembly of Notables, gave the following answers to two of the twelve questions posed to them by the French government:[25]

> that every Israelite is religiously bound to consider his non-Jewish fellow citizens as brothers, and to aid, protect, and love them as though they were co-religionists; that the Israelite is required to consider the land of his birth or adoption as his fatherland, and shall love and defend it when called upon.[26]

The converse of such demands in the form of an anti-Semitic attack is asserted by the Midrash and Targum to have comprised the essence of Haman's argument to Achashveirosh that the Jews not only should not be considered to be citizens of Persia, but should not even be allowed to continue to live.

> There is one nation that is scattered and spread among the peoples, nations, and languages, and a few of them reside in each of the provinces of the kingdom, and the rules of their Torah are different from those of any other people, our bread and cooked foods they refuse to eat, our wine they refuse to drink, our holidays they refuse to observe, and our customs they do not follow, and the decrees of the laws of the king they do not adhere to, and the king gains nothing from them, and what benefit does the king receive from them by allowing them to continue to exist?[27, 28]

We are consequently faced with the question not only of answering the Hamans of the world, but also can (should?) the Orthodox day school be expected to convey the message to its student body that an observant Jew is expected to be a "good citizen" of the non-Jewish state in which he resides, recognizing the tensions that will be created between Jewish religious practices, beliefs, and values and the practices, beliefs, and values of the general society and its constituents.[29]

JEWISH PRIMARY SOURCES ON THE QUESTION OF INTERACTION WITH AND RESPECT FOR NON-JEWISH SOCIETY

The Midrashic interpolation of Haman's canard against the Jews, while painful to read, is nevertheless not without some merit, in light of the primary sources of Jewish tradition.[30] Whether speaking generally, e.g. (Leviticus 20:24,26) "I am *ha-Shem* your Lord, *that separated you from the nations*; And you will be to Me holy, because I am holy *HaShem, and I separated you from the nations to be Mine*," or specifically, e.g. (Ibid., 18:3) "And *like the behavior of the land of Egypt* wherein you resided do not do, *and like the behavior of the land of Canaan* where I am bringing you there, *do not do and in their statutes do not go*[31] the idea is reiterated throughout *TaNaCh* that Jews are to avoid at all costs having more to do with those in the surrounding society than is absolutely necessary. RaShI's (Solomon ben Isaac; 1040–1105) commentary, citing *Torat Kohanim*, on Leviticus 20:24, suggests that the entire system of ritual commandments is designed for no other purpose than to emphasize the separation and difference of Jews from non-Jews.

> "I am the Lord, your God, Who has divided you from the nations."
>
> RaShI: If you are separated from them, then you are Mine; but if not, you belong to Nevuchadnezzar (the Babylonian King)[32] and his colleagues. R. Elazar ben Azarya says: From where is it learned that a person should not say, "I am disgusted by pork, I have no desire to wear mixtures of wool and linen," but rather one should say, "I really want to do these things, but what can I do? My Father in Heaven has decreed upon me (that I not do them)." The Torah teaches "And I will separate you from the nations to be Mine," that your separation from them should be for My Sake, one should separate himself from prohibited activity and accept upon himself the yoke of the Kingdom of Heaven.

Another Midrashic[33] approach to the issue of differentiation, as enunciated in Leviticus 20:26, sees ritual law as not only setting Jews apart, but that these rules actually take mundane actions and force Jews to perform them differently from their non-Jewish neighbors.

> Said R. Levi: All of the activities of the Jewish people are different from those of the nations of the world, with regard to their ploughing, their sowing, their harvesting, their bundling, their threshing, their storing in granaries, their wine pressing, in their counting and in their tallying. (Deuteronomy 22:10) "Do not

> hitch together an ox and a donkey for ploughing"; (Ibid., v. 9) "Do not sow seeds in your vineyard to produce mixed species"; (Leviticus 19:9) "And the droppings of your harvesting do not pick up"; (Deuteronomy 24:19) "And if you forget a bundle. . ."; (Ibid., 25:4) "And you shall not muzzle the ox while it is engaged in threshing"; (Ibid., 15:14) "And you shall surely give (the newly released Jewish servant) from your flock, from your granary and from your winepress"; non-Jews count (their calendar) in accordance with the sun and the Jewish people count in accordance with the moon.

Bilaam enunciates a poetic statement to this effect:[34] "Behold it is a nation that will dwell in solitude, and not reckoned among the other nations." R. Meir Simhah Ha-Kohen of Dvinsk (1843–1926)[35] attributes self-conscious legislation designed to keep Jews separate from the surrounding society to the forefather Jacob. When contemplating the dangers of assimilation and extinction confronting his family once they took up residence in exile, the commentator asserts that the cultural differences that marked the Jewish sojourn in Egypt[36] were actually rules imposed upon the family by the patriarch prior to their leaving Canaan. The commentator suggests that it was obvious to Jacob that "seventy individuals in the midst of a powerful and aggressive nation would assimilate and be nullified, each one being faced with hundreds of thousands (of those unlike him.)"[37] Jacob's legislative response to the specter of the loss of Jewish identity due to having to reside within a hostile majority culture for a significant period of time, was later emulated by Ezra when he made the cornerstone of his program for the restoration of the Jews to Israel following the Babylonian exile the dissolution of intermarriages,[38] as well as by later Rabbinic leaders when they included among eighteen rules declaring off-limits to Jews the bread, oil, wine, and daughters of non-Jews as a deterrent to intermarriage.[39]

Even without availing oneself of Biblical commentaries or Talmudic discussion, an unembellished review of recorded events and laws in the books of the Bible that involve non-Jews readily creates the impression that non-Jews are hostile, pose threats to Jewish continuity, and must be placed under Jewish subjugation in order to alleviate the threats that they pose.[40, 41] While there are sources and traditions within mainstream Jewish thought[42] which could be used to balance, if not refute, the negative impressions associated with non-Jews left by this type of cumulative reading of traditional material, to what extent are these counter sources well known, particularly to those who are not truly conversant with the materials of Jewish tradition? In an educational context like that of a day school, such sources would obviously have to be self-consciously inserted into curricular studies in order to assure some sort of balance in terms of how to relate to non-Jews and non-Jewish society in a fair, evenhanded manner. It is safe to say that for the most part, they are currently not part of the standard day school curriculum. Should they be?[43]

A PSYCHO-SOCIAL RATIONALE FOR EMPHASIZING AND ENGINEERING DIFFERENCES BETWEEN JEWS AND NON-JEWS THAT SUGGESTS THAT MITIGATING THE EFFECT OF DWELLING UPON THE HOSTILITY OF THE NON-JEWISH WORLD MIGHT ACTUALLY BE COUNTERPRODUCTIVE IN TERMS OF JEWISH CONTINUITY

From a psychological and social perspective, the statements, stories, and rabbinic legislation casting a negative light upon the non-Jewish world would appear to be designed to impress upon each Jew that she or he along with his or her people have been and continue to be under siege. Mortimer Ostow[44] writes, "Cohesive groups tend to reinforce their cohesion by elaborating on their common origin. . . . Among the most powerful of such (accounts) are stories of origin and crisis. In the former, the origin of the group is portrayed as a remarkable event that came to pass despite the *hostility* of the environment. In the latter, the existence of the group is threatened by an *enemy* or a natural event. An actual threat to a group impels its members to reinforce their commitment to each other for purposes of defense of the group; a recollected threat exerts similar influence."[45] Ostow's analysis serves as the basis for Lucy Dawidowicz[46] describing how the parental generation of various cultures seeks to inculcate loyalty and commitment to family traditions: "Modern Jewish mothers . . . like mothers in all cultures, classes, and societies, rear their babies into awareness that the world is divided into two camps: We and They. The Italian mother draws the perimeter of We around the family, excluding the rest of the world. The Greek mother extends the community of We to include the village. The Jewish mother enlarges the We to embrace all Jews, those living now and those of the past, those living here, there, and everywhere."

While Dawidowicz and Ostow speak in general terms about the development of Jewish identity, Sol Roth[47] specifically addresses the challenges that in his opinion face Orthodoxy.

> The essential problem to which Orthodoxy must address itself is forming parameters for *Havdalah* (separation) that will assure the transmission of tradition from generation to generation. I do not believe that Jewish tradition can be preserved successfully in the general Jewish community . . . in the face of a policy that recognizes no limits to the extent of Jewish immersion in the life of American society. . . . To encourage the selection of the Jewish option, it is necessary to maximize Jewish life and experience it in the context of a Jewish community in which Judaism is lived intensively, that is to say, it is necessary to stress *Havdalah*.

Although Roth[48] in an earlier article lists "positive" attitudes that contribute to the advancement of a sense of Jewish community, including (a) the love of the members of the Jewish people, (b) a covenantal sense of religion, (c) holiness in terms of a relationship with the Divine, (d) the connection to the land of Israel, and (e) reconciling living Jewishly with the demands of a democratic society and a scientific world, the "negative" attitude with which he *begins* his analysis of how Jewish community can be preserved, is *Havdalah*.

> Judaism urges the Jew, in some important way, to separate himself from the non-Jew. This demand is, at least from a logical point of view, not unreasonable. Every community which sees itself as distinguished in character, and which seeks to preserve itself, must recognize that it is different, and therefore separate from others. Definition logically involves differentiation.[49]

Thus it would appear that a positive case could be made for stressing the differences between Jews and non-Jews from the perspective of Jewish identity and continuity. But what price is paid by such an emphasis with respect to being willing and able to take one's place in the general society in which one lives? Will a point be reached as a result of the emphasis upon not only difference, but also perceived threats and hostility, where a person will be dissuaded from making a whole-hearted effort to engage with the world at large? And since identity formation is an extremely pertinent consideration for students of day school age, particularly adolescents in Middle and High School,[50] to what extent should Jewish identity in general and *Havdalah* in particular be the overarching aim of curricular and extra-curricular day school programming?

CONSIDERING THE DAY SCHOOL SETTING IN LIGHT OF THE *HAVDALAH* ISSUE

While an array of references can be brought to bear with regard to the question of how interaction with non-Jews is discussed in traditional Jewish sources, the manner in which this topic is presented in an educational setting is a related, but nevertheless significantly different, issue. Students on the elementary, middle, and high school levels seldom are confronted with comprehensive, thorough, and scholarly reviews of a given topic in Jewish studies. Curriculum is often designed in disciplines such as Bible, Prophets, Mishna, Talmud, and Jewish law, to cover massive quantities of material in terms of pages, chapters, and verses, combined with some attention devoted to literacy skill development, rather than in-depth thematic approaches to significant topics.[51]

As a result, the impression that students receive regarding an issue such as interaction with non-Jews will usually be based upon side comments made in various classes by diverse teachers reflecting different points of view, and rare prolonged discussions, the latter certainly not lasting longer than a portion of a learning period on a given day.[52] Only within the context of an individual research project would there even be the possibility for a student[53] to investigate a particular issue in-depth. And even under such circumstances, what is to guarantee that the work will be sufficiently thorough to yield an adequate and representative result?

In order to investigate the contexts in which these typically occasional interchanges would arise in the classroom, I carried out an informal survey among my colleagues at the Melvin J. Berman Hebrew Academy in January of this year (2001). I sent each Judaic studies faculty member a letter requesting him or her to share with me in whatever format made him or her most comfortable—verbal or written—experiences that they had where the topic of non-Jews had come up in their classes over the course of the term.[54] I also spoke to the school psychologist, asking that she describe to me conversations that she has had with individuals seeking counseling as a result of issues arising from discussions concerning non-Jews in the classroom.

Since the Judaic studies faculty at this particular day school is comprised of individuals of various ages and social, religious, and educational backgrounds, all adhering to the tenets of Orthodox Judaism, it would appear impossible to generalize with regard to the approach or orientation of the faculty as a whole. Students attending the school run the gamut from Nursery through grade 12, coming from families that could be categorized as ranging from Traditional Conservative to Traditional Orthodox. One would expect a rich assortment of situations and topics to arise.[55]

Most of the responses that I received dealt with themes in Bible and Prophets. One teacher cited a number of topics that were raised during the course of the *Parshat ha-Shavuah* (review of the weekly Torah portion in anticipation of its being read in the synagogue on the upcoming Sabbath) presentation.[56, 57] Another instructor listed a number of classroom discussions taking place in his Prophets class, including the perspectives offered by students in response to the Biblical passages.[58]

Time devoted to current events, particularly those affecting Israel, was another context when discussions would turn to how to relate to non-Jews, and how they in turn relate to Jews in general and religious Jews in particular. Yet another faculty member noted that when he taught the incident of Moses killing an Egyptian taskmaster in defense of a Jew who was being bludgeoned (Exodus 2:11–12), he cited an Halachic source that considers the incident a legal precedent for future physical conflicts between Jews and non-Jews.[59]

The Jewish history teacher asserted that the entire course is in effect a study of how Jews and non-Jews interacted with one another, and for the most part, since Jews have historically been cast in the role of victims, the contexts of non-Jewish activity are overwhelmingly negative. With respect to Talmud, since the entire high school studies the same Tractate, in this case the third chapter of Tractate Sukka, a section lent itself as a test case with regard to the issue of the portrayal of non-Jews. The Talmud presents the situation of Jews purchasing from non-Jews myrtle branches for use in the *Sukkot* festival ritual of holding and waving four species (Leviticus 23:40). Rabbi Huna instructs the purchasers to acquire these branches in a particular manner because it is presumed that the non-Jewish sellers had stolen the land upon which they are growing their merchandise. The issue is further complicated by the textual emendation of RaShI[60] that suggests that there is a qualitative difference between stolen property that was originally a Jew's as opposed to that which was stolen from a non-Jew. Whether an instructor draws attention to this issue and the extent to which he decides to explore its parameters becomes a litmus test for how non-Jews are presented in a Judaic studies class context. It would appear that some classes did take up the matter, while others avoided it.

A Hebrew language teacher remembered that several of the stories in the text *Ivrit Shitatit* (Systematic Hebrew) (Dr.'s Shahar and Rina Yonay, Vol. 1, Shai, New York, 1997) dealt with non-Jews in a positive light, including the case of Dama ben Netina, the individual who exhibited exemplary respect for his father, despite thereby sustaining a significant financial loss.[61, 62] Yet another teacher recorded that he presented R. Akiva's comment in Avot 3:14 dealing with *Tzelem Elokim* (the assumption that man was created in *HaShem*'s Image—Gen. 1:27) as applying to all human beings, including non-Jews.

The school psychologist noted that on a number of occasions students had sought her out after teachers had made disparaging comments regarding non-Jews, particularly when the student was aware of a conversion or an intermarriage in his family or if she or he had non-Jewish friends.

From the responses of faculty members, it was readily apparent that the subject of interaction between Jews and non-Jews generally arose as a reaction to a particular text, subject matter unit, or student query, as opposed to a pro-active, premeditated initiative on the part of the teacher himself or herself. Assuming that this is representative of Orthodox day schools, to what extent should these schools be encouraged to engage in specific programming designed to specifically address this issue?

To obtain a sense of the lasting impressions that were being made on the students in the same school, I asked the students in my Talmud classes, ranging from 7th through 12th grades, to respond to a questionnaire as well.[63] I have to emphasize very strongly that these comments come in response to *anything* that was said, discussed, and/or learned over the course of 7–12 years of Jewish education as presented by various teachers and students. Furthermore, since a significant number of students have transferred into the school from other institutions over the years, they may be citing incidents and/or comments that occurred in venues other than this particular school. Another factor to be considered in evaluating these surveys is that for one reason or another, comments that would have cast a more favorable light on this subject as well as upon certain staff members may have been forgotten or not heard. What is remembered could be an unfair representation of the bulk of these students' experiences.

However one wishes to view the process by which these impressions were obtained, attention has to be paid to these cumulative effects and decisions made as to whether they must be self-consciously addressed. Responses could be categorized as dealing with (1) curricular issues, (2) comments and opinions volunteered by teachers, (3) sentiments expressed by peers, and (4) impressions received by dealing with non-Jewish students in athletic and other out-of-school settings.

1. With respect to curricular matters, students seemed to have difficulty in world studies when other religions and cultures were presented. While the students can be faulted for not being open-minded and intellectually curious, one also has to wonder whether the teachers' presentations were accessible and not oversimplified.

Jewish history was perceived as a basis for confirming that non-Jews were uniformly hostile to Jews. Such a conclusion was reinforced by sources in Torah and Prophets that portray persecutions and discriminations at the hands of non-Jews on the one hand, and the superiority of Jews over non-Jews on the other. Apparently there is a "catch-22" when one attempts to build up Jewish pride and self-esteem by dwelling on the themes of Chosenness and being a treasured people (*Am Segula*) and the implied converse with respect to those that are not so chosen and treasured.

One student was disturbed by what he perceived as a double standard with respect to how Jews as opposed to non-Jews were treated before the law.[64] The line in the prayer "*Aleinu*"[65] that states that others worshipped deities of nothingness and emptiness offended some students, who were upset that teachers went out of their way to insist on the recitation of this line, that had for many years fallen into disuse due to censorship. While some students apparently were ready to include all non-Jews in this negative evaluation, others felt that distinctions had to be made between contemporary forms of religion and those of the ancient past. Students expressed the sentiment that creating an "us–them" dichotomy in so many areas was disrespectful and even counterproductive.

2. Teachers' opinions and side comments also apparently make long-lasting impressions. One student recalled that when someone stood up for non-Jews in a disagreement, the teacher said, "You sound like a non-Jew." Another[66] faculty member stated that non-Jews were unintelligent.[67] Yet another directed invectives against Arabs as a result of the ongoing Israeli situation. Another staff member reportedly opined, "Non-Jews have been torturing Jews for no reason for years." Not surprisingly, more tolerance was evidenced on the part of General Studies teachers than Judaic studies teachers.[68]

3. Comments made by fellow students also generated concern. It appears that some students, particularly those with either non-Jewish relatives or non-Jewish friends and/or neighbors, took particular umbrage when fellow students would make bigoted or racist remarks. Furthermore, students who spent time in public or non-Jewish private schools commented that they were not made to feel self-conscious of their Judaism in those contexts, and therefore it was difficult for them to understand the apparent prejudice that they encounter in a Jewish day school.[69]

It is reported that some students would laugh when non-Jewish teachers would stumble on the Hebrew names of the members of their classes, it being unclear if this was directed only at the teacher's error or an indication of a lack of tolerance for someone coming from a different culture. (There were several comments to the effect that the non-Jewish teachers' interest in things Jewish and their high moral and professional deportment mitigated a great deal of the negative impressions given by the curricular material that was studied in school.)

Students also called attention to fellow students referring to peers attending less religious day schools as "*Goyim,*" suggesting not only a disdain for those students, but also for the group with whom those students are being associated. And it was pointed out that for many day school students, the less they have in common with others, the more intolerant they are, with greatest disdain reserved for racial minorities.

4. The experiences that students have with non-Jews in out-of-school contexts (4) yield mixed results. While some students comment that they are put off by the promiscuity and other aspects of personal behavior that they observe on the part of fans at games or when they participate jointly with non-Jewish schools in a cultural event, others say that they have always been treated with great respect and even enjoy the attention received when students would ask them about the meaning of particular Jewish practices.

Students attending mock trial matches are impressed by the respectful and appropriate behavior evidenced by their opponents and opponents' fans, perhaps suggesting that different populations within a given school will react differently to interactions between themselves and those who adhere to different religions and traditions.

CONCLUSION

Jewish day schools have a complex task to satisfy, among others, two self-contradictory ideals. On the one hand, they are expected to serve as powerful fortifications against the onslaught of Jewish assimilation that is currently taking place in the United States. To this end, time is spent helping students understand the positive aspects of their heritage in order to gain maximum loyalty and commitment to that tradition. Yet, when unchecked, such a presentation can result in students concluding that they not only have nothing in common with the society surrounding them, but that there is no point in attempting to establish any sort of meaningful two-way interaction.

The Jewish mission must simultaneously address not only Jewish identity and commitments and responsibilities to one's co-religionists, but also the responsibilities of participating as a productive member of the society in which one finds him. To this end, the following recommendations are made:

a. All teachers must be regularly sensitized to the effects of their teachings and comments upon their students. The leadership of the school must determine what sort of balance to strike between Jewish and general commitments, communicate these expectations to the entire school community, and hold all school constituents to advancing this policy and outlook.
b. Specific curricular units should be introduced that would counterbalance the more overtly particularistic aspects of the present curriculum in order that students can strike an appropriate balance between these two powerfully competing interests.
c. Individuals, such as non-Jews who sheltered Jews during the Holocaust, members of other faiths who have exhibited extraordinary personal behavior towards not only Jews, but all of humanity, individuals who have accomplished outstanding things in terms of improving general society, should address the student body from time to time, in coordination with Jews who have achieved heroic things in terms of their interactions with the greater society, in order to create an alternate image of how not only Jews can be holy, idealistic, and admirable.[70]
d. Well-controlled social service projects should be undertaken that would allow Jewish students the opportunity to get to know and to appreciate the human qualities that members of other faiths possess.[71]

In this manner our day schools can begin to realize both of the goals that they so proudly proclaim in their mission statements and public pronouncements.

NOTES

1. While educational institutions may write mission statements, there is no guarantee that the schools will attempt to adhere to them. It is the contention of the author that the mission statements ought to be carefully formulated; arrived at by building a consensus of staff, students, parents, and other key constituents; posted publicly throughout the school; and regularly referred to in terms of curricular and program development, as well as with respect to the implementation of everyday school business.

2. E.g., an excerpt from the Mission Statement of the Melvin J. Berman Hebrew Academy, Rockville, MD:

> The MJBHA is an Orthodox Community Torah Day School committed to providing a comprehensive Jewish and secular education within a strong atmosphere of Torah values and academic excellence, as well as inspiring the student body to reach for the highest standards of morality and citizenship. . . . The BHA strives to enable its graduates to become Halachically observant, well-educated Jews who feel comfortable within as well as enabled to contribute significantly to the rapidly changing world in which we live.

An excerpt from the Statement of Philosophy and Objectives of the Ramaz School, New York, NY:

> The Mission of the Ramaz School . . . is to educate its students in the two civilizations of which they are a part. The first is the world of Torah, mitzvot, the Jewish people and its culture, Zionism and the State of Israel. Simultaneously, and with equal emphasis, we teach our students the disciplines and the finest values of western civilization and the American democratic heritage. . . . We also endeavor to develop within our students a commitment to the ideals of freedom, democracy, human dignity, justice, and fairness. We foster a spirit of objectivity, an awareness of and respect for a diversity of views among ourselves and in American society, and an understanding of the equality and dignity of all people and their God-given opportunity to realize their potential.

An excerpt from the Mission Statement of the Kushner Yeshiva High School, Livingston, NJ:

> Western Culture and American democratic values are embraced at Kushner Yeshiva High School as important vehicles in the formation of *Adam HaShalem*—the fully developed individual. . . . They develop a keen sense of justice and are taught to behave as responsible citizens in American society.

An excerpt from the Mission Statement of Maimonides School, Boston, MA:

> To produce religiously observant, educated Jews who will remain faithful to their religious beliefs, values, and practices as they take their place as contributing members of the general society.

3. A possible change in attitude and orientation can be perceived with regard to the issue of citizenship in American society when one notes that the latest forms of the Mission Statements of some schools traditionally associated with Modern Orthodoxy, have, at best, de-emphasized the issue.

An excerpt from the Mission Statement of Fuchs Mizrachi School, Cleveland, OH:

> The school is committed to the unity of the Jewish people, the inculcation of ethical standards and the belief in the dignity of every human being. Of paramount importance is the teaching of values inherent in Torah-based moral practice. A FMS education strives to enable each student to achieve the love of God and humankind, and be imbued with the joy found in these relationships.

An excerpt from the Mission Statement of Yeshiva University High School for Girls, Queens, NY:

The High School offers academic excellence in an atmosphere that encourages the young women to adhere to the traditional ideals and practices of Orthodox Judaism, while finding a place, a niche in the modern world.

4. "Reflections on the Jewish Day School," in *Commentary*, July 1960, p. 32.

5. Could the current de-emphasis upon citizenship in the Jewish day school at least partially reflect a sense of increased security and acceptance on the part of the Orthodox community within American society, whereby it no longer feels that it has to justify its existence to Americans who do not share its beliefs and commitments?

6. "Who's Afraid of the Day Schools?" in *Commentary*, 108:5, December 1999.

7. The assumption that developing the students' American identity is an important aspect of the mission of a Jewish day school located in the United States would appear to contradict another cornerstone of Orthodox day schools' mission statements, commitment to Israel as a Jewish State in which all Jews should aspire to reside. The school should determine whether for this particular school community, living in the United States is a *le-khathilah* (a priori) or *be-di'avad* (a posteriori) concern, and program accordingly.

8. The following excerpts from community day school mission statements reflect their particular ideological orientation:

a. Kehillah Jewish High School, Palo Alto, CA

Kehillah Jewish High School is open to students and families from a wide range of Jewish backgrounds, including those with no prior Jewish day school education. The school welcomes family involvement to build a vibrant Jewish community. Kehillah Jewish High School nurtures the particular religious convictions of every family while emphasizing the covenantal bond shared by all Jews. www.kehillahigh.org/about.html

b. The Jewish Academy of Metropolitan Detroit, Detroit, MI

The Jewish Academy of Metropolitan Detroit affirms that the normative practice of Judaism guided by halacha sanctifies the lives of both individuals and the Jewish community. As our students come from diverse Jewish backgrounds, we seek to inculcate among them a belief in God and knowledge and appreciation of traditional Jewish texts within a pluralistic spirit that transcends denominational boundaries. www.jamd.org/mission.htm

c. Gesher Jewish Day School of Northern Virginia, Fairfax, VA

Gesher is a community Jewish Day School that respects the wide range of Jewish observance, practice and tradition, supported by a strong partnership among students, their parents and the faculty. www.gesher-jds.org/newpage1.htm

9. "The Rise of Jewish Schools," in *The Atlantic Online*, October 1999, www.theatlantic.com/issues/99oct/9910jewishschools.htm

10. *Tradition*, 16:2, Fall 1976, p. 11.

11. Vol. 32 No. 4, Summer 1998.

12. The only response that appeared to qualify the underlying assumption that all things associated with the non-Orthodox world are antithetical to Torah values, was submitted by Walter Wurzburger:

While I recognize that the ethos of modern culture is flawed and poses many challenges to my spiritual integrity, I do not reject it hook, line, and sinker. There are many valuable insights in modern literature, philosophy, and various other branches of the humanities. Torah is not an escape mechanism from the harsh realities of life, but a *Torat hayyim* which directs me, not to withdraw, but to address all facets of human existence. I therefore neither endorse nor reject modernity but confront it critically in the light of my understanding of what Torah demands of me.

13. The case of the "Yale Five" could be viewed as an example of day school products striving to afford themselves a superior secular education, yet avoiding what they perceive as the pernicious aspects of the lifestyle associated with such an education. These students sued the university in order to be exempted from living on campus and thereby being exposed to "the rampant immorality" that pervades the co-ed dorms. When asked why the classroom discussions involving the same students who inhabited the dorms were not deemed equally if not more objectionable, one of the plaintiffs, Batsheva Greer, responded, "When something is said in a classroom, you can listen and write notes and it doesn't make an impression on you. . . . But when you're in an immoral environment, it has a detrimental effect. Actions are just more detrimental than words. They aren't good for one's soul."—quoted in Samuel G. Freedman, *Jew vs. Jew: The Struggle for the Soul of American Jewry*, Simon & Schuster, New York, 2000, p. 261. While a number of factors certainly contributed to the development of these students' decision to challenge Yale in court, schooling must play some role in their decision to adopt the strong stand that they have taken.

14. In addition to observing the reticence exhibited by many day school graduates when it comes to participating fully in campus life, parallel attitudes manifest themselves in terms of the increasing numbers who refuse to attend a secular university, as well as those who are uninterested in obtaining a college education at all. Not only will day school students who do opt to attend university avoid aspects of student life that they deem compromising, but they also tend to prefer pre-professional courses of study, as opposed to exploring the liberal arts. Disciplines such as history, literature, and psychology are all means by which an individual can become more familiar and empathetic with those who comprise general society, and day school graduates who do not engage in such courses of study either reflect their disinterest in, or their antipathy to, the assumptions and values of general society.

15. When the administrators, curriculum developers, and faculty members of day schools are comprised of individuals who themselves are either indifferent, or even hostile, to general societal attitudes and assumptions, and who are lacking general education themselves, the intellectual, emotional, and spiritual atmosphere pervading the school will militate against forming a positive approach towards participation within general society, regardless of what a school's Mission Statement might advocate.

16. "Citizen"—1) an inhabitant of a city, often of a town, especially one possessing civil rights and privileges, a burgess or a freemason of a city. 2) . . . in USA, a person, native or naturalized, who has the privilege of voting for public offices and is entitled to full protection in the exercise of private rights.—*The Oxford English Dictionary*, Second Edition, prepared by J. A. Simpson and E. S. C. Weiner, Clarendon Press, Oxford, 1989, p. 250.

"Citizenship"—The position or status of being a citizen, with its rights and privileges.—Ibid.

17. During my tenure at the Ramaz School in New York City, a number of lectures were presented to my Talmud classes by an attorney conversant with Jewish law, comparing Torah and secular civil law. One of the points that he repeatedly im-

pressed upon the students was that whereas Halacha was concerned with obligations, secular law was mainly focused upon rights and privileges. Although he was addressing high school students and presenting them with a quick overview rather than an in-depth legal analysis of the two systems of law, in light of the assumptions of civics education, i.e., that participation in secular society does in fact entail considerable responsibility and obligation, it is interesting to consider the effect that such a point would make upon the students at whom it was directed, particularly those who do not go on to study law. In an attempt to highlight a cornerstone of Jewish tradition, was general society possibly given short shrift?

18. An anthology of patriotic poems, speeches, hymns, anthems, and stories, published in 1941 by the National Education Association, quoted in Brian Burrell, *The Words We Live By: The Creeds, Mottoes, and Pledges That Have Shaped America*, Free Press, New York, 1997, p. 42.

19. "Postwar Americans tended to regard public concerns much as they did economic interests: in terms of pursuing their advantage, if need be, by striking advantageous bargains with others. Citizenship in practice exhibited the qualities typical of marketing and exchange. Furthermore, as government resources were put to ever new uses, Americans increasingly defined citizenship in terms of the claims they could legitimately argue they had, as individuals and as members of a special category to some of those resources. Claimant politics began to overshadow civil politics."—Robert N. Bellah, et al., *The Good Society*, Vintage, New York, 1992, p. 61.

20. "National Standards for Civics and Government 9–12," distributed by the Center for Civic Education (www.civiced.org/912erica.htm), page 51 ff. Lists the following as *responsibilities* of citizens: *Personal Responsibilities* (taking care of oneself, supporting one's family and caring for, nurturing, and educating one's children, accepting responsibility for the consequences of one's actions, adhering to moral principles, *considering the rights and interests of others, behaving in a civil manner*); *Civic Responsibilities* (obeying the law, being informed and attentive to public issues, monitoring the adherence of political leaders and governmental agencies to constitutional principles, and taking appropriate action if the adherence is lacking, *assuming leadership when appropriate*, paying taxes, registering to vote and voting knowledgeably on candidates and issues, serving as a juror, serving in the armed forces, *performing public service*).

21. Perhaps it is the perception of the change in common understanding of the implications of the concept of citizenship, as well as the sense that students are lacking a sense of responsibility to the greater society, that has spurred on educational leaders to promote courses on civics and citizenship while younger citizens are still attending school.

22. "Rethinking Civic Education for the 21st Century," in *ASCD Yearbook 1999: Preparing Our Schools for the 21st Century*, ed. David D. Marsh, ASCD, Alexandria, VA, 1999, p. 66.

23. An even more radical conception of the duties of citizenship is described by James MacGregor Burns and Stuart Burns (*A People's Charter: The Pursuit of Rights in America*, Knopf, New York, 1991, p. 462):

> Citizenship, rather than merely an "outer frame" of duties such as voting, paying taxes, and obeying laws, would be experienced as "the core of our life," in Michael Walzer's formulation,

which "assumes a close knit body of citizens, its members committed to one another." Such an activist citizenship would express itself through the development of participatory democracy, an ideal crystallized in the 1962 "Port Huron Statement" of Students for a Democratic Society: ". . . As a social system we seek the establishment of a democracy of individual participation, governed by two central aims: that the individual share in those social decisions determining the quality and direction of his life; and that society be restructured to encourage both autonomy and common participation."

24. While it can be argued that the answers that this assemblage produced were exercises in apologetics designed to gain a political end, i.e., citizenship for French Jewry, nevertheless in the words of Professor Jay R. Berkovitz in "Changing Conceptions of Gentiles at the Threshold of Modernity: The Napoleonic Sanhedrin" (p. 144 of the present volume), "the Sanhedrin provided the authoritative interpretation of emancipation; its answers and doctrinal decisions formed a new and central text for subsequent generations."

Professor Berkovitz also notes that the Consistory enacted legislation requiring the answers of the Sanhedrin to be recited in the course of *Shabbat* services as well as requiring reproduction of its text in textbooks approved for use in Jewish schools. It would be difficult to point to parallel educational initiatives in contemporary day schools, at least outside of Israel, in terms of direct and prolonged discussions concerning responsibilities toward the broader society within the context of Judaic studies, as opposed to general history or civics subject matter.

The Washington Institute for Jewish Leadership and Values, directed by Rabbi Sid Schwartz, and utilizing a grant from the Jim Joseph Foundation, has developed a course for day schools, entitled, "Jews, Judaism, and Civic Responsibility." It is being field-tested in a small number of schools and hopefully will become a frequently taught elective, if not a required course, in day schools throughout the country. Further information can be obtained from the Institute, located at 11710 Hunters Lane, Rockville, MD 20852; WIJLV@aol.com

25. Question 5: What conduct does Jewish law prescribe toward Frenchmen not of the Jewish religion?

Question 6: Do the Jews born in France and treated by law as French citizens, acknowledge France as their country? Are they bound to defend it? Are they bound to obey the laws and follow the directions of the civil code?—Quoted in "Sanhedrin, French," in *The Jewish Encyclopedia*, man. ed. Isidore Singer, Vol. 11, Ktav, New York, 1901, p. 46.

26. Ibid., p. 48.

27. Targum on Esther 3:8.

28. In Pharaoh's attribution to the Jews the intention to join any attackers of Egypt in an effort to overthrow the reigning authorities (Exodus 1:9–10), one encounters an even earlier, albeit less detailed, instance of an accusation against the Jews depicting them as a separatist, divisive, and potentially dangerous force, that has to be reined in, before "it is too late." Another Biblical anti-Semitic attack is to be found in Ezra 4 when the opponents of Judah and Benjamin (Samaritans) accuse the Jews of wanting to rebuild the Temple in order to mount a rebellion against the ruling authorities.

29. Whereas certain activities associated with participation in general society could potentially compromise one's religious values and practices, e.g., serving in the armed forces at times that do not qualify as situations of *Pikuach Nefesh* (life and

death), supporting the rights of certain elements within the greater society to pursue lifestyles that are deemed deviant by the standards of Jewish law, or engaging in aspects of citizenship where in order to succeed apparently dishonest practices must be undertaken, etc., other aspects of citizenship should be quite compatible with living a committed Jewish life. Therefore it would be interesting to investigate the extent to which day school alumni vote, serve on juries, and participate in community civic associations as compared to others within the society at large as well as to Jews who did not receive day school educations.

30. See Joshua Berman, "Aggadah and Anti-Semitism: The Midrashim to Esther 3:8" in *Judaism*, Vol. 150, 38:2, Spring 1989, pp. 185–96 for the variations in the Midrashic approach to this verse down through the years, reflecting the range of nuances in these accusations during various historical periods.

31. Rabbinic interpretation, as exemplified in RaShI on Leviticus 18:3, *d.h. u 'be-khukotei'hem Lo Teileichu,* and RaMBaM, *Mishna Torah, Hilchot Avodat Kochavim* 11:1, has expanded the connotation of this verse from merely a rejection of the sexual and pagan mores of the Egyptian and Canaanite societies, implied by the preceding verses, to include issues of dress and cultural activity. A review of various positions taken by Halachic decisors regarding this matter can be found in Rabbi Zvi Teichman, "Chukat Ha'Akum: Jews in a Gentile Society," in *Journal of Halacha and Contemporary Society*, Vol. 1, No. 2, Fall 1981, pp. 64–85.

32. Why *Torat Kohanim*, and subsequently RaShI, should be citing specifically Nevuchadnezzar as the exemplar of the nations of the world, is explained by Avraham Berliner (*RaShI Al HaTorah*, J. Kaufmann, Frankfurt on Mein, 1904, p. 257). He notes that, as in *Pesikta Zutrati*, the text should read "*Harei Atem le-umot ha-Olam*" (Behold you will belong to the nations of the world). Berliner states that out of fear (of repercussions due to censorship) the text was changed in both *Torat Kohanim* and RaShI.

33. *Pesikta Rabbati* 15:5.

34. Numbers 23:9. Since the premise of the prophet's pronouncements assumes that despite his attempts to curse the Jewish people, all that he could muster were blessings, rather than being viewed as a negative trait or imposed punishment, being alone and separate is apparently considered a virtue.

35. *Meshekh Chachmah* on Leviticus 26:44.

36. *Vayikra Rabba* 32:5 lists the defining qualities of the Jews that made them deserving to be redeemed from Egyptian slavery as their not having changed their names or language, their having refrained from reporting on one another to the non-Jewish authorities, and their sexual propriety. *Pesikta Zutra* on Exodus 6:6 adds that the Jews retained distinctive dress as another means for preserving their ethnic identity. (The devotion to these manifestations of cultural uniqueness stands in stark contrast to the implication of commentaries like that of RaShI on Exodus 12:6 to the effect that the people had ceased observing circumcision prior to their redemption from Egypt.) Commentaries such as RaShBaM, *Lekach Tov* and RITVA associate these Midrashic traditions with the interpretation found in *Haggadat Pesach* (Deuteronomy 26:5) "'And they became there a nation'—to teach that Israel was *Metzuyanim* (outstanding, markedly different) there (in Egypt)."

37. *Meshekh Chachmah*, ibid.

38. Ezra 9,10.

39. *Mishna Shabbat* 1:4; *Talmud Shabbat* 17b.

40. In Genesis alone, the following themes can all contribute to a sensibility that surrounding nations are threatening and lacking in basic morality:

Gen. 12:10 ff.	Sara being threatened by Pharaoh. (It is only with the Divine Selection of Abraham and his offspring that the Biblical saga of the Jewish people begins in earnest. Therefore events affecting the likes of Adam, Eve, Cain, Abel, and Noah do not enter into consideration with regard to the particular theme in question.)
Ibid., 13:13; 18:20, 19	The evil of the people of Sodom and Amora.
Ibid., 14	Wars, kidnapping, selfish division of spoils perpetrated by local potentates.
Ibid., 15:13–14	Future exile and suffering at the hands of an alien nation prophesied for the Jewish people.
Ibid., 20:2 ff.	Sara being threatened by Avimelech.
Ibid., 21:25–26	Philistine responsibility for the filling of Jewish wells.
Ibid., 23:16	The exorbitant price exacted by Efron for the grave of Sara.
Ibid., 24:29 ff.; 29:13 ff; 30:27 ff.; 31:2; 32	Lavan's shrewd negotiating first with Eliezer and then with Jacob.
Ibid., 26:7 ff.	Rebecca threatened by Avimelech.
Ibid., 26:15 ff.	Further controversy regarding wells.
Ibid., 26:35, 46; 27:2	Displeasure with Esau's foreign wives.
Ibid., 34	Dinah, Shechem, rejection of intermarriage and assimilation, destruction of Shechemites.
Ibid., 37:36	Joseph is sold to either Ishmaelites or Midianites.
Ibid., 39:7 ff.	Potiphar's wife makes sexual advances towards Joseph, which leads to the latter's imprisonment.

A glaring exception to these examples is the behavior of MalkiTzedek (Gen. 14:18–20), which could be interpreted as serving as a foil to the actions of the King of Sodom (Ibid., 17,21). On the other hand, although Ishmael and Esau begin as siblings to the forefathers Isaac and Jacob, respectively, their hostility eventually symbolizes civilizations, Islam and Rome, which not only compete with, but also attempt to destroy, the Jewish people. Therefore, at a certain point, they too number among the "others" against whom the Jews struggle for survival.

As for the laws of the Bible, negative impressions of non-Jews can similarly be derived:

Exodus 21:20–21, 26–27; Leviticus 25:44–46	Aspects of the institution of non-Jewish slavery. (This is in contrast to Jewish slavery, which appears as a form of indentured servitude rather than total bondage which non-Jewish slavery appears to entail.)
Exodus 23:32–33	The need to banish and not make treaties with former inhabitants of Canaan.

Leviticus 18:27–28	The sexual perversions of which the Egyptians and Canaanites were guilty are not to be emulated by the Jews.
Ibid., 25:47–54	The need to ransom a Jewish slave, particularly from a non-Jewish master due to the latter's possibly in terfering with the former's practice of his religion.
Deuteronomy 7:2	In addition to not entering into agreements with former inhabitants of Canaan, no positive considerations, e.g., gifts, compliments, etc., should be extended to them.
Ibid., 7:3–4	Prohibition against intermarriage, with the explicit rationale that there is fear that the Jewish member of the marriage will become alienated from his or her spouse.
Ibid., 17:16	Returning to Egypt in order to settle must be avoided by Jews at all costs.
Ibid., 20:18-10-18	Inhabitants of Canaan can make peace and remain in their land only in a state of subjugation to the Jews.
Ibid., 21:10–14	The non-Jewish war captive.
Ibid., 23:4–9	The restrictions on dealing with Amonites, Moabites, and Egyptians.
Ibid., 23:21	Interest on loans can be taken from non-Jews.
Ibid., 25:17–19	Eternally remembering how Amalek attempted to destroy the Jews.

41. The depiction of other groups as threatening and deserving of radical intervention on the part of a specific religious community, is not indigenous to any particular religion. Nel Noddings writes,

> violence is part of the history of all major religions, and the desire to destroy the wicked can be easily aroused. For some groups, the wicked must have performed horrible acts in order to qualify as "wicked," thereby deserving retribution. For others, the wicked are simply those who do not believe or believe differently. In the latter case, violence may be direct and physical if religious belief is combined with political power, or, in the absence of such power, it may be threatened at some later date (*Educating for Intelligent Belief or Unbelief*, Teachers College Press, New York, 1993, p. 56).

42. Such themes and approaches include the following:

a. Are the non-Jews mentioned in Biblical sources comparable to non-Jews being encountered contemporaneously? (Views of RaMBaM, *Meiri*, *Tosafot Yom Tov*, *Tiferet Yisroel*, *Torah Temima*, etc., would counterbalance the implications that all non-Jews are to be categorized in the same manner.)
b. Are the nations that inhabit the geographical areas of Egypt, Moab, Amon, etc., the actual descendants of the peoples mentioned in the Bible? (To what extent has this been rendered moot by the Talmudic assumption that no one is any longer living in their indigenous land due to the administrative policies

of Sanherev, King of Assyria ("*Sancherev Ba U'bilbail HaOlam*")—see, e.g., Berachot 28a; Yomah 54a.

c. Jewish responsibility to be a "Light unto the nations" and therefore undertake to participate in the broader world, despite possible risks of assimilation or even destruction (Isaiah 42:6 and associated commentaries and sources).
d. The necessity to perpetrate acts of "Sanctification of the Divine Name" in order to win admirers for God and monotheism (Leviticus 22:31–33 and related materials).
e. Non-Jewish individuals who adhere to the seven Noachide commandments are to be considered among the "righteous of the nations of the world" and merit a place in the World-to-Come, something that can be forfeited by Jews not living up to their ritual responsibilities (RaMBaM, *Mishna Torah*, Laws of Kings).

43. The same charges of apologetics and inauthenticity precipitated by pressures from without that were leveled at the work of the French Sanhedrin could similarly be brought to bear upon positions cited in the previous footnote. On the other hand, it could be contended that at least some of these approaches are legitimate and defensible, if not during all periods of Jewish history, then at least during our current period. However, it is obvious that as long as these perspectives are not formally incorporated into day school curricula, the overwhelming majority of students will never be exposed to them.

An ongoing experience that I have had reinforcing such a contention is the annual presentation that I make to the OU interns, a program that brings to Washington observant college students who spend their summer working in various congressional and senatorial contexts. In addition to their work experience, these interns meet with a number of individuals who discuss with them aspects of the political experience that is unique to Orthodox Jews. For the past four years, I have given a talk based upon sources such as those mentioned above, that I discussed in a paper entitled, "A Religious Context for Jewish Political Activity" (*Tikkun Olam: Social Responsibility in Jewish Thought and Law*, ed. D. Shatz, C. Waxman, N. Diament, Jason Aronson, Northvale, NJ, 1997, pp. 145–58). Although the participants in the OU program, virtually all having attended day school, are obviously self-selecting in terms of being at least somewhat interested in participating in the federal political process, it has seemed to me that they never have previously encountered the Jewish sources that directly address the nature of what they have chosen to do for the summer.

44. "Determinants of Jewish Identity," in *The Israel Annals of Psychiatry and Related Disciplines*, 15:4, December 1977, p. 317.

45. Ironically, the emphasis upon how Jews have had to struggle against their enemies for time immemorial can in some cases have just the opposite effect, i.e., instead of solidifying one's loyalty to his or her people, an individual can be driven to separate himself or herself from them because he or she is unwilling to cast himself or herself as the victim of ongoing oppression. Jerry V. Diller ("Identity Rejection and Reawakening in the Jewish Context," in *Journal of Psychology and Judaism*, 5:1, Fall/Winter 1980, p. 41) writes, "If . . . a person has internalized the majority culture's values, particularly its negative attitude towards one's ethnic group, one may reject one's Jewish identity and the self on the basis of its dictates." See Helen Epstein's fascinating account of the effects of the Holocaust upon the children of survivors in *Children of the Holocaust* (Bantam, New York, 1979).

46. *The Jewish Presence: Essays on Identity and History*, Harcourt Brace Jovanovich, New York, 1978, p. 5.

47. Contribution to "Symposium—State of Orthodoxy," in *Tradition* 20:1, Spring 1982, p. 67.

48. *The Jewish Idea of Community*, Yeshiva University Press, New York, 1977, pp. 17–19.

49. Ibid., p. 17.

50. While teenagers are considered to be most acutely in the throes of identity formation, in light of the following statement by Robert Coles, attention must be paid to elementary students as well in this regard.

> So many younger schoolchildren are eager to embrace the imaginary—indeed their minds are often afire with it. Given a choice, they will leap into one or another scenario, be it historical or contemporary, factual or fictional, and bring to it their very own moral or intellectual assumptions (*The Moral Intelligence of Children*, Random House, New York, 1997, p. 121).
>
> No question, the early school years that precede the onset of adolescence (grades one to six, say) matter a great deal, morally—and not only as a consequence of home life. At this time, the voices and actions of *teachers and coaches* and the parents of friends become alternative examples, complementary and supplementary and sometimes contradictory in nature, to be the substance of what is implied, suggested, enacted, with respect to the values at home. (Ibid., p. 130)

It is notable that a number of responses from students in the student survey that I summarize later in this paper commented that they found teachers in the lower grades more closed-minded and doctrinaire with regard to the issue of interaction with non-Jews compared to teachers in the higher grades. Whether this is age appropriate, a reflection of the types of individuals who are drawn to teach in the different divisions of the school, etc., would have to be considered if this observation is given credence.

51. During 2001, a prolonged interchange on the Bar Ilan University listserve for Jewish education, Lookjed, discussing whether preparing students for confronting the challenges that they might face in general society ought to occupy a significant portion of curricular time in day schools, at the possible expense of further development of Jewish study skills and information acquisition, illustrated the preponderance of thinking among many day school staff members that concern for the more existential and philosophical issues is not a priority. Naturally one could speculate whether this has basis in a true appreciation of the educational context, or whether this has to do with the predisposition of the particular individuals participating as well as their own training and sense of competency with regard to philosophical and theological conundrums.

52. Occasions when comments about non-Jews and non-Jewish society unrelated to specific curricular issues are particularly common are societal celebrations generally deemed pagan in origin and therefore inappropriate for Orthodox Jews, e.g., Halloween, Dec. 25th, Jan. 1st, Feb. 14th, and March 13th. The Halachic controversy swirling around the celebration of Thanksgiving centers around whether or not the commemoration is essentially religious. See Rabbi Michael Broyde, "Thanksgiving: Secular or Religious Holiday" in *The Journal of Halacha and Contemporary Society*, No. 30, Fall 1995, pp. 42–65. Naturally Kristallnacht and Yom HaShoah similarly elicit

presentations and/or comments about general non-Jewish complicity or mere indifference regarding the atrocities perpetrated during the Holocaust.

53. This would usually only involve a single student, since generally different topics are assigned or chosen in order to insure a modicum of originality and independent research.

54. The text of the letter that I sent to my colleagues read:

> I am doing research regarding if and how non-Jews are discussed within the context of Judaic studies in the day school setting. This year, whether you are teaching *Gemora*, *ToshBa*, *Chumash*, *Navi*, *Ivrit*, or Jewish history, there may have been issues that arose either directly from the curriculum, or in the course of classroom discussions that impacts in one way or another on this theme. I would very much appreciate it if you could describe these discussions to whatever extent you are able. If there were occasions where you pointedly avoided bringing the topic up, or told the student that there wasn't time to go into the issue, I would be interested not only in the context in which this happened, but also why you chose to respond in the manner that you did. If you like, you could write your impressions and recollections on this page or send me email at … Thanks for your time and thoughtfulness. Sincerely,

55. My investigation method was unscientific and hardly comprehensive. To better make the case, a more rigorous instrument has to be devised, a higher response rate has to be pursued, and a number of variables have to be taken into account, such as what teachers are likely and/or unlikely to report due to being wary of admitting to extreme positions, what teachers are expecting me to be looking for, teachers' reflectiveness and ability to recall passing conversations over the course of the school year, etc. It would also be significant to compare teacher reports from several different Orthodox schools in different locales, featuring faculties of varying backgrounds, and drawing upon different economic strata in terms of student body. Comparing day schools of different denominations with regard to this issue would also be of interest.

56. The teacher's report mentioned the following examples:

a. *Parshat Chaye Sara*—
   1. (Gen. 23:6) Abraham was respected by the non-Jews that he encountered upon searching for a grave for Sara, due to his reputation for being exceptionally ethical and considerate.
   2. (Ibid., 23:15) Ephron's questionable conduct when selling the burial cave to Abraham.
   3. (Ibid., 25:6) The gifts that Abraham gives to the children of Ketura before sending them away.

b. *Parshat Toldot*—
   1. (Gen. 26:17 ff.) Isaac having to live by his wits to survive in Gerar. "The wisdom required in dealing with non-Jews, including the qualities of patience, courage, and guarded respect. The knowledge of differences between us and them as well as how to handle delicate situations without compromising our beliefs and values. The courage, tenacity, pride, and consistency necessary to earn respect." (*The above is a verbatim rendering of the teacher's submission. It should be obvious that depending upon the tack that the teacher takes, such a lesson could be constructive or destructive in terms of how children will in-*

ternalize the lessons of the Torah vis-à-vis how to approach the non-Jews that they will encounter during their own lives.)

2. (Gen. 26:35) *Morat Ruach* (bitterness of spirit). The attitude of Isaac and Rebecca to their sons' marrying Hittite women.

c. *Parshat va-Yetze—*

1. (Gen. 29:13 ff.) Interactions between Jacob and Laban. The principle of "*Kabdeihu VeChashdeihu*" (respect him but be suspicious of him).
2. (Ibid.) Jacob and Laban's usage of the term "*Ach*" (brother).

d. *Parshat va-Yishlach—*

1. (Gen. 33:12–14) The meeting between Jacob and Esau. *"Harchek mi-Shachen Ra"* (distance yourself from an evil neighbor).

57. The fact that these themes would be addressed as part of the *Parshat ha-Shavua* lesson as opposed to the daily curriculum, lends further credence to the contention that these ideas will more often than not be presented in passing, rather than being well-developed and thoughtfully constructed. If the regular curriculum is based upon the concept of a rapid survey of primary texts and commentaries, the *Parshat ha-Shavua* slot, which might occupy no more than a small portion of the time allotted to Bible study, will usually entail that much more of a quick overview of the material due to time constraints and the pressure to review as much of the Torah portion as possible.

58. The teacher's report mentioned the following examples:

a. Judges 5:31 (the final verse of the Song of Debora): "So shall You cause all of Your enemies to be destroyed, *ha-Shem*." Students defined the "enemies" of today as "Arabs." *(Consider comments by Moshe Greenberg, translated from his* HaSegula VeHaKoach *[Kibbutz ha-me-u'chad, 1986, pp. 15–16]:*

> *The greatest difficulty entailed in teaching the book of Joshua is the danger that the student will apply the message of the book of conquest to our situation today: the Canaanite enemy = the Arab enemy, and the prophetic method of dealing with the situation is expulsion and destruction. This danger is so great that there is room to ask whether it is appropriate for us today to teach this book in our state.*

While the writer obviously has a particular political perspective that causes him to view these Biblical passages with greater concern than many others, nevertheless the red flag that he raises is representative of many parallel issues throughout Jewish primary sources. Even were we not to adopt the drastic course of banning material in our canon from being taught in Jewish schools, the question remains: what precautions can be taken so that lessons inimical to what is being studied will not be derived, in this case concerning contemporary non-Jews?)

b. I Kings 8:41–43: Solomon's request to *ha-Shem* during the course of his consecrating prayer for the newly built Temple that the prayers of non-Jews be heard along with the prayers of Jews. A comparison of verses 39 and 43 interpreted by RaDaK suggests that deserving or not, the Divine Answering of prayers offered by non-Jews will constitute a Sanctification of *ha-Shem*'s Name. Aside from a discussion of the nature of what qualifies as a "Sanctification of *ha-Shem's* Name," students discussed the possibilities for conversion to Judaism and the place of the contemporary synagogue, serving as a substitute for the now-destroyed Temple. The discussion then proceeded to address inviting non-Jews to one's *Bar Mitzva*, what should be expected of these individuals when they attend in terms of headcovering, the concealing of symbols associated with other religions, etc.

59. RaMBaM, *Mishnah Torah*, Laws of Kings 10:6, based upon Sanhedrin 58b, states that a non-Jew striking even a glancing blow upon a Jew, is culpable for the death penalty, since Moses executed the Egyptian who was striking the Jew. While RaMBaM states that this crime is not enforceable in a Jewish court, but rather, in the words of R. Yosef Karo's commentary, *Kesef Mishna*, would only constitute a death sentence in the Heavenly Court, how this was exactly presented to the class is of interest. If the caveat that this is not a practical *Halacha* was not explicitly made, is it likely for students to think that such a punishment should be physically carried out today? Furthermore, the language in the passage both in the Talmud as well as in RaMBaM is "*AKU"M*," the acronym representing "*Ovdai Kochavim u'Mazalot*" (the worshippers of stars and planets, i.e., idolaters). Once it is posited that this is not simply a censor's gloss (see fn. 17 above), to what extent should the statement have been further qualified regarding whether an equation can be made between this particular Egyptian and non-Jews that are encountered today?

60. Sukka 30a, *d.h. Mai Ta'ama Setam AKU"M Gazlei Arata mi-Yisroel Ninhu.*

61. The original source for this story is in Kiddushin 31a. Once again one has to wonder how the content, as opposed to the vocabulary, grammar, etc., was presented by the teacher to the students. Were they given and did they receive the impression that Dama ben Netina was the rule or the exception? Aside from the positive reinforcement of the commandment to act appropriately towards one's parents, what sort of lesson either explicitly or implicitly was learned regarding how to view non-Jews?

62. It would be interesting to investigate whether the decision to place such a story in the text was taken, at least in part, to make the text acceptable to a broader range of schools. In a program for character development, "Project *Derech*," there are six different versions in an attempt to incorporate a school's specific religious outlook within the examples given and lessons drawn. One of my colleagues, once sensitized to my interest, excitedly brought to me a book that one of her students had used upon which was based the *Parshat ha-Shavuah* lesson that the student had presented to her classmates. The story centered around the activities of a righteous non-Jew. Upon inspecting the book, I noted that it was published by the Union of American Hebrew Congregations, Reform Judaism's administrative organization. I once again wondered if casting positive light on non-Jews in educational texts could be demonstrated to be denominationally distinctive.

63. Students were given the following:

> I am currently doing research on the manner in which non-Jews are discussed, dealt with, thought about, etc., in Jewish day schools. I would appreciate it if you would now take a few minutes and jot down some impressions that you have had over the years when you were in either this day school, or some other regarding non-Jews. You may have gained these impressions because of subject matter that you studied, comments that have been made in class by teachers or friends, interactions that you have had while involved in

extra-curricular activities, etc. Your comments will be kept anonymous and you don't have to sign this page if you do not wish to do so. Thanks for your help, Sincerely. . .

64. Examples of some of these issues include the manner in which suits arising from one person's animal injuring another are adjudicated, the relative severity of the punishments applying to the Noachide laws as opposed to the same laws vis-à-vis Jews, the difference in the obligation to give charity to Jewish as opposed to non-Jewish needy, it is permissible to speak *Lashon ha-Ra* (statements of fact designed to place the object of the conversation in a less than flattering light) regarding non-Jews, and the exemption from returning a non-Jew's lost object as opposed to that of a Jew.

65. "*SheHeim Mishtachavim la-Hevel VaRik, u'Mitpallelim le-Eil Lo Yoshia*" in e.g., *The Complete ArtScroll Siddur*, ed. R. Nosson Scherman, R. Meir Zlotowitz, Mesorah Publications Ltd., New York, 1984, pp. 158–59, and see Ibid., fn. *SheHeim Mishtachavim.*

66. Since I did not ask students to identify who was making these specific comments, I suppose that it is theoretically possible that only one or two staff members are volunteering these extreme opinions, and others are not. But I think this unlikely.

67. An Anglicization of "*Goyische Kopf*"?

68. Yet students quoted non-Jewish faculty members to the effect that they feel that they are not as respected as Judaic studies teachers, and that there can be felt an "us vs. them" quality not only throughout the school day, but even during professional days.

69. An interesting approach to address this phenomenon is suggested by the psychologist Beverly Tatum.

> The parts of our identity that *do* capture our attention are those that other people notice, and that reflect back to us. The aspect of identity that is the target of others' attention, and subsequently of our own, often is that which sets us apart as exceptional or "other" in their eyes. . . . People are commonly defined as other on the basis of race or ethnicity, gender, religion, sexual orientation, socioeconomic status, age, and physical and mental ability. Each of these categories has a form of oppression associated with it: racism, sexism, religious oppression/anti-Semitism, heterosexism, classism, ageism, and ableism respectively. In each case there is a group that is considered dominant (systematically advantaged by the society because of group membership) and a group considered subordinate or targeted (systematically disadvantaged). When we think about our multiple identities, most of us will find that we are both dominant and targeted at the same time. But it is the targeted identities that hold our attention and the dominant identities that often go unexamined (*"Why Are All the Black Kids Sitting Together in the Cafeteria?" and Other Conversations about Race*, Basic Books, New York, 1997, pp. 21–22).

Within the day school context, being Jewish is dominant, as opposed to being non-Jewish, leading students to be less introspective about their Jewish identities than they would be were they to attend a public or non-Jewish private school. On the one hand, this is the very reason why day schools have been established, i.e., to afford students the opportunity to feel more natural and uninhibited about their personal identities and Jewish development. But the concomitant result is a particular attitude, sometimes discriminatory and stereotypical, regarding non-Jews with whom they have far less interaction. The question then presents itself as to whether the present balance is the only one possible if it would be concluded that a more even-handed experience would be more educationally and socially desirable.

70. It is not necessary to place a greater emphasis upon presentations dealing with this issue than upon those that serve to reinforce and inspire commitment to Judaism and the Jewish people. All schools should regularly schedule appearances of outstanding individuals who can raise important issues and model exemplary service and accomplishment to their student bodies. The above proposal is merely to advocate that included within these presentations are individuals who have successfully lived in both worlds and who see such lives as meaningful and appropriate.

71. Once again, such projects should not be the only objective of a community service program. Service to exclusively Jewish causes is naturally crucial in the development of *Chesed* (compassion) during the years to come. But serving the general non-Jewish community should also be included and not be belittled.

9

Re-Committing to Our Mission: How Hard an Endeavor?

Gidon Rothstein

Two useful rules should guide our approach to instigating change. First, if it ain't broke (or in clear danger of soon breaking), don't fix it. Tampering or tinkering with existing institutions and responses to life issues requires a high level of confidence that a problem exists that needs correction. Enough areas of public life are broke and in need of fixing that it would be quixotic to alter any that are working reasonably well. Second, the economists' rule that the most successful remedies are those that deal narrowly with a problem can be applied to other areas of life as well. Broad remedies generally carry externalities, unforeseeable and unwanted additional costs.

These rules suggest three stages in planning change to existing behavior, whether personal, social, or institutional—defining areas of concern, considering the level of concern those issues ought to engender, and, finally, searching for the most efficient and narrowly focused way to rectify the problem identified. Only successful execution of all three leads to the most economic and most beneficial responses. Application of these steps is as important to internal Orthodox institutions as it is to general social issues. In each of these areas, Rabbi Bieler's paper, it seems to me, falls short.

HOUSTON, DO WE HAVE A PROBLEM?

When it comes to identifying the problem of training for civic involvement, I question whether Orthodox educational institutions have such a problem; if we do, it is not clear that it is the same one that bothers Rabbi Bieler. By framing the issue as a discussion of how to insure that graduates of Modern or Centrist Orthodox Yeshiva high schools remain committed to a maximal form of "good citizenship," Rabbi Bieler necessarily assumes that Modern and Centrist Orthodox *yeshivot* are now failing to achieve that result. His paper suggests not only that schools give students the wrong messages about these topics, but that the students absorb and accept those messages from their teachers, at the ultimate cost to their active participation in society.

A first problem lies in the definition of good citizenship, which remains murky in Rabbi Bieler's paper. Would a young woman who attends a liberal arts college, works at a career in which she interacts productively with society at large on a daily basis, votes in all elections, writes occasional letters to her representatives, and pays her taxes qualify as a good citizen? If such a woman chooses to spend her volunteer time on visiting the sick in her Jewish community, or feeding the poor within that community, does that lower her standing as a good citizen? Would Rabbi Bieler say the same for an African American who chooses to spend his communal time on civil rights issues? A woman who fights for breast cancer research? A first issue that is not fully defined by Rabbi Bieler and, I feel certain, one where reasonable people could differ, is the kind of good citizenship we want to promote in *yeshivot*.

For the sake of the argument, however, let's suppose that a Jew who does not pay attention to the issues of the day, broadly speaking and not just those that affect that Jew directly, does not qualify for the kind of good citizen badge Rabbi Bieler seeks. We will assume that unless schools are striving to educate their students to be that involved in the community, that they are failing in some of the ways Rabbi Bieler worries about.

Even with such a maximal definition of good citizenship, it is not clear that we have a significant problem. Relying on anecdotal evidence (as, indeed, does Rabbi Bieler) schools seem as committed as ever to having their graduates engage the broader world in a range of ways. Even before September 11, I was approached by students who were selling muffins to benefit refugees in the Balkans, were visiting their local nursing home, were trying to enlist people to join or support various Walks for the Cure. After 9/11, the community mindedness of the schools I know was heightened even more; the importance of active good citizenship in America was stressed to even a greater degree, as was the debt of gratitude Jews owe and continue to owe to this country.

On the career side as well, I do not know of any drop in the numbers of Modern and Centrist Orthodox Yeshiva high school graduates who attend college and enter professions. Rabbi Bieler notes that many head to pre-professional programs (footnote 14) instead of the liberal arts, but I believe that reflects a nationwide trend that has little to do with the students' Jewish background. Without evidence of a change in the results of the education our students are getting, it seems premature to reserve a place at the table of educational reform for the issue of engaging non-Jewish society both academically and socially.

The messages students in high school receive from their teachers is worth discussing for other reasons, as I will note below, but Rabbi Bieler does not investigate how those experiences affected the students' worldview. I suspect that comments of the type he noted only upset the students, reinforcing or creating the impression that their teacher(s)—and possibly Judaism as a whole—are cloistered and medieval (in the negative senses of both of those words). That creates a significant problem in its own right, but it is not the issue Rabbi Bieler identified.

ARE WE THE SOURCE OF THE PROBLEM?

Moving along, for the sake of the argument, to accepting that over the last forty years there has been a drop in the world-participation, academic and/or social, among young Modern and Centrist Orthodox Jews out of proportion to what is happening in society at large,[1] it still would not prove that we have a problem in our high schools. Many of the *yeshivot* in Israel that schools allow and encourage their students to attend espouse a different philosophy on this specific issue than did the home high school. Further, since at least some students go to Israel expecting to "*frum* out," since the institutions in Israel have the students for a much more concentrated period of time with fewer competing attractions than in high school, since the students think of their immersion in *yeshiva* as a more "pure" experience than high school, the year in Israel can enormously influence teenagers' perspectives, often in the exact direction Rabbi Bieler fears.[2]

In my community a couple of years ago, for one example, a young man went to a yeshiva where his *rebbe* asked him what he was doing the next year. When he replied, "I'm going to X college," the *rebbe* smiled and said, "No, you're not." In his case, it turned the young man off to that teacher; for others, the confidence and charisma of the *rebbe* could send the clear message that the "right" way to behave was to avoid college. For many *rebbeim* in Israel, the "right" way would also include rejecting engagement with the world as a whole, involving oneself only with Jewish concerns.

Further, many students return from Israel having adopted modes of dress and conduct that differ not only from their families' practice, but also from the theory of religion reigning in their homes and home communities. These students are not only *more* religious, meaning more concerned and punctilious in their observance of the ideals set forth by their families and rabbis, they are (some self-consciously and deliberately) *differently* religious. That difference might easily include a rejection of the engagement with the outside world they encounter at home (and were taught in school), since they may blame that engagement for the religious lacks they perceive in their families and home communities. The Israel experience is, in my opinion, a first place to look for reasons that students are less engaged with the outside world than we taught them to be.

HOW MUCH SHOULD IT BOTHER US?

Even were we to decide that Modern and Centrist Orthodox Yeshivah high schools have a problem in how they teach students about good citizenship in its broadest sense, I wonder further about how that problem is being created and about how worried it should make us. For example, many such schools are staffed with at least some Judaic studies teachers who personally reject engagement with the secular world, at least to the extent the Modern and Centrist Orthodox world support. If a reduction in students' interest in communal engagement stems from their relationship with those teachers, the serious problem thus created should not cause us to rethink our basic method of transmitting our values and ideas to our students. Rather, it is an example of the challenges that confront Modern or Centrist Orthodox education because of its inability to produce sufficient numbers of like-minded educators to staff its schools.

I know of an extremely charismatic and effective teacher in a Modern Orthodox high school who—during lunchtime discussion groups—openly informs students of his/her distaste for secular studies and mocks the compromises engendered by a life lived in honest engagement with the outside world. That teacher creates a problem for the school, but not one that requires curricular adjustment. It is, rather, a question of finding staff that either shares the school's ideals or can commit to respectfully explaining those ideals to students.

Were we to discover that even teachers who espouse a Modern Orthodox view of the world were making comments that disparage involvement in broader society, in whatever form, our level of concern would still be intimately connected to our feelings about such engagement. Rabbi Bieler assumes that engagement with the world is so clearly a good that he rejects *havdalah*, separation, as the sole (or even, I suspect, the central) guiding factor in developing our attitude to the non-Jewish world.

Yet, in thinking about where we stand on this issue, it is vital to remember that—in the best of times—our engagement with that outside world requires careful balance. Both academically and socially, we always weigh "*hen 'am levadad yishkon*" being "a people that dwells alone"[3] against the responsibility of "*ve-dirshu et shelom ha'ir asher higleti etkhem shama*," "seek the peace of the city to which I have exiled you."[4] For all that we recognize *hokhmah ba-goyim*, wisdom among the nations, we equally reject the possibility of Torah among those nations.[5] We care about providing for non-Jewish poor—in which we might bundle all social welfare issues—but nonetheless give priority to *'aniye 'amkha* and *'irekha*, the poor of our nation and of our cities. In bemoaning failures of engagement, we also would need to clarify exactly what level of engagement we are encouraging, and how far we are falling short. The issue to consider would be not only whether we are falling short, but also by how much.

TORAH AS A COMPETING AREA OF WORRY

Those questions—whether there is a drop in students' engagement with non-Jewish society, whether that drop comes from factors outside of the system, such as the Israel experience or teachers of different philosophical leanings than the school, and, finally, how much of a gap that drop creates between the ideal and the real—should color our concern and attention to this issue. At least in terms of curriculum, we must weigh concern for producing good citizens against the more immediately pressing need to give these students a true sense of *talmud Torah* and a set of skills that will make such study accessible to them. Citizenship can be learned elsewhere; Torah literacy cannot.

That our attempts to improve Torah literacy should probably win out over our concern with promoting good citizenship and active engagement is highlighted by the skills and knowledge that prevail among Yeshivah high school students today. While Rabbi Bieler speaks of a curriculum as designed to "cover massive quantities of material in terms of pages, chapters, and verses, combined with some attention devoted to literacy skill development," the reality is that we generally do not succeed in covering significant amounts of material nor at developing true literacy, except with the very highest performing students.[6]

The need for developing students' knowledge of Torah is more pressing for both theoretical and practical reasons. On the level of theory, insuring graduates' continuing adult engagement with Torah, both its study and performance, is clearly more central to an Orthodox high school's mission than insuring that they will choose to engage the broader world in the most active sense of the word. Without denying the positive value in such engagement as part of an ideal, it is clearly subordinate to the more central ideal.

That theoretical statement becomes important when we consider the practicalities of current Jewish education, where the failures in the Torah realm are so obvious. In the Lookjed discussion to which Rabbi Bieler referred in his footnote 51, an administrator at a Metropolitan New York area high school asserted that such schools can only hope to give their graduates positive feelings towards Judaism and convince them to remain committed to active involvement with their communities as adults. This educator thought that giving these students true literacy, the ability to read and understand

Jewish texts at a level parallel to their English skills, was beyond the reach of high schools. Without judging the accuracy of that view, it certainly suggests a climate in which the question of how to instill a true sense of *talmud Torah* is at least as problematic as the questions Rabbi Bieler raises.[7]

A second factor that should affect schools' approach to this problem is a changed American society. Recognizing these changes, it seems reasonable that educators present that society and how to interact with it in less unequivocally positive ways than previously. Whether or not we have taken the time to adjust our mission statements,[8] our sense of an adult Jew's proper place in this society, could, indeed should, have changed in these years, to reflect those new realities. That we find our students picking up a different sense of non-Jewish society than those of a generation ago is, to some extent, not only necessary but salutary.

Even if we reject every point made until now, if we adopt the same perspective on American society as thirty years ago, if we assume that the old model of engagement remains true, the changes in the American moral climate should at the least mitigate the seriousness of any problem seen in failures to live up to that model. We should never take lightly our falling short of achieving ideals, but in a time when overengagement with the world poses greater dangers and carries greater risks than before, the level of concern about perceived underengagement and rejectionism should be moderated as well.

REVIEWING THE RECOMMENDATIONS

Aside from being more bothered by other failures in our high schools than this one and being less concerned about the problem as Rabbi Bieler defined it, the situation also seems to me to pose a different kind of problem than he suggests. Since, as indicated before, students who hear negative comments about non-Jews often reject both those messages and their bearer, the teachers who make such comments may be contributing to students' learning that they need not take their teachers' opinions seriously. Given students' connection to the host culture in clothing, language, and (very often) the names by which they identify themselves, not to speak of the means of entertainment that they consider the most pleasurable parts of their lives, we should be concerned that we are writing ourselves out of these students' lives, not that we are changing those lives in undesirable ways.

My differing assessment of the issues Rabbi Bieler has raised guide my reaction to his recommendations as well. I agree wholeheartedly with, and would underscore, both parts of his first recommendation, his call for sensitizing teachers to the effects of their comments. I would say that recommendation should be applied broadly speaking, not only in the area we are discussing here. Such sensitivity should be coupled with administrations clearly communicating to staff the "party line," and the tolerable range of differences of opinion on important *hashkafic* issues. While there should certainly be room for individual differences, teachers must recognize that their responsibilities as caretakers of young and impressionable students requires that they speak with sensitivity to the effect of their language at all times, so that their students not absorb the wrong impressions. Avtalyon's warning "*Hakhamim hizaharu be-divreikhem*" applies to all teachers, from those at the youngest ages and up; the danger that our students will drink of the *mayim hara'im*, of the evil waters of whatever heresy rules at a particular juncture in history, is no less true now than it was in the time of Hillel's teacher.[9]

I think Rabbi Bieler also points to an important ethical issue about which teachers must be clear. In accepting employment by an institution, a teacher commits to espousing the values of that institution, in all detectable ways, as at least one legitimate and fully workable expression of a well-lived Jewish life. Contradicting, contravening, or otherwise obstructing the transmission of the messages of the institution constitutes a betrayal of that teacher's responsibilities.

R. Samson Raphael Hirsch, in his explanation of the Talmud's ruling that we cannot condemn a young man as a *ben sorer u-moreh*, a rebellious son, until his parents speak "in one voice," sees the rule as referring to the unity of the value system these parents espouse for their son. Unless they speak in one moral voice, unless they transmit a fully agreed-upon sense of behavior, the child cannot be solely blamed for failing to heed their admonitions.[10]

The jump to a teacher is but a short one, and whether that teacher sees himself or herself as providing students with a more religious, more sophisticated, or more useful set of values, the static created by the mixed messages is deleterious to the students. When I attended the Yeshivah of Flatbush Joel Braverman HS, my teachers adhered (in their personal lives) to a wide range of *hashkafic* and *halakhic* beliefs and observances. And yet none of them (in my perhaps somewhat nostalgic recollection) evinced any discomfort with transmitting and espousing the school's religious message. All schools should ensure such an environment for their students.

CURRICULAR CHANGE AND ITS PROBLEMS

To the extent that the rest of Rabbi Bieler's program envisions significant change from the current Yeshiva high school structure and curriculum, it engenders less of my sympathy. Introducing "curricular units" presumably means taking time from the study of texts that already do not suffice to accomplish relatively minimal goals. In secular settings, I would note, students do not study subject matter until they have basic skills that make them able to do some reading on their own, and even to research a topic further should they so choose.

We could, perhaps, study *Avodah Zarah* with commentators and the relevant scholarly literature about Jews' responses to non-Jews in the medieval and modern periods—Jacob Katz's *Exclusiveness and Tolerance*, my teacher and mentor Haym Soloveitchik's writings on *yayin nesekh* and pawnbroking, Moshe Halbertal's book on the Meiri and similar literature—but teaching that material well is challenging at the graduate school level, and inappropriate for high school.

Perhaps some of Rabbi Bieler's concerns could be met by planning regularly scheduled informal talks on significant topics without any interest in textual study per se. Here, though, I would warn against setting up such talks as a separate part of the curriculum; students develop a relationship with a teacher based, to some extent, on the teacher's being the one who judges their work over the course of a year. To expect harried high school students to connect to yet another teacher, for a period or two a week, on a topic on which they will not be tested, seems utopian.

Two incidents reinforce this impression. When I was a senior in high school, Dr. Joel Wolowelsky taught such an informal course about Jewish attitudes towards death. I enjoyed a close personal relationship with Dr. Wolowelsky at the time and therefore paid attention to the meetings and benefited greatly from the discussions. Without that personal connection, however, I suspect I would have seen the class as pretty much a free period, as did at least some of my peers, with a consequent lessening of the discussions' impact.[11] Several years ago, I was asked to teach a once a week course, in six-week units, about the Rav, ztllh"h, to ninth graders whom I did not otherwise know. The lack of a pre-existing connection, the lack of a formal grading process, and the poor match between subject matter and students combined to make it a frustrating and largely unproductive experience.

Given those impressions, I would suggest that such talks, around this or any other issue, would be more productive if they happen "spontaneously" in the course of regular classes, rather than being separated from the ordinary course of class events. Seeing a teacher consciously take time from a busy curriculum to discuss an issue will automatically convey to the students the teacher's belief in the subject's importance. Students also enjoy the experience more, since it is so clearly a break from the ordinary routine.[12]

ASSEMBLIES AND SOCIAL ACTION

The value of bringing in speakers and setting up social service projects that involve an encounter with others, Rabbi Bieler's last two recommendations, largely depends on how those plans would fit with the overall practice of the school in these areas. If a school already has regular assemblies to broaden students' horizons by hearing outside speakers, then certainly some of those speakers ought to be non-Jews or Jews who achieve dramatically in the non-Jewish world. The program of assemblies that the Yeshivah of Flatbush had during my attendance was certainly an added facet to my education, and some of those speakers made an indelible impression. Handled carefully, then, an hour out of class time can provide elements of an education that several hours in class could not.

But if the only (or even the majority) of such speakers deal in not specifically Jewish issues—with few or no speakers on directly Jewish topics—we run the risk of conveying an opposite, equally undesirable, impression. Students who see that assemblies are generally dedicated to non-Torah issues will quickly realize that in the "real world" we value non-Torah activities and achievements. Depending on the school, then, watching the balance of speakers who are presented to the students would be vital to ensuring that we do not accidentally send confusing messages about our values.

Similar concerns should govern our social action projects—if the school initiates such projects, or makes some of them mandatory, certainly some of those should engage the outside world. If, however, students are simply encouraged to involve themselves in social action (such as through a *hessed* requirement), the school's role is more passive, and there is less room to actively encourage broad involvement. Further, the question of encounter, whether with students from other Jewish denominations or from completely different religions, involves serious educational issues that are beyond the scope of the current discussion, but should be carefully considered by each school.

MAKING IMPLICIT MESSAGES MORE EFFECTIVE

After reviewing all of the suggestions, I am left feeling that we have not yet conceived a way of attacking the problem set forth. Side discussions, for all their value, cannot dominate a curriculum, nor can assemblies or social action. It may be that we do not have a serious problem and these more minor correctives can deal with it fully and effectively. However, to the extent that we worry about the impression our students are currently receiving about the outside world—particularly since they probably need to hear at least some negative messages about the general culture from their teachers—a few muffin sales for the oppressed of the world and a speaker a year from the John Doe Fund are not going to fundamentally alter the picture these students absorb.

A suggestion that strikes me as more effective in coping with all of the issues raised by Rabbi Bieler is to strive to have *limudei kodesh* faculty teach a secular subject and perhaps even to have them join extracurricular activities that engage the outside world. I know that in Flatbush, *limudei kodesh* faculty were part of a cultural enrichment program that brought students to museums, theaters, concerts, and other such events. I know of several *limudei kodesh* teachers who also teach English, History, Economics, or whatever subject attracts their fancy. Seeing their teachers not just mouth a dedication to engagement with the world, but actually be so involved, conveys a message that repeated talks cannot.

The problem with such a suggestion, I suspect, is that many *limudei kodesh* faculty do not wish to teach those other subjects. While theoretically committed to their importance, they are not interested in reminding themselves sufficiently of those subjects so as to be able to teach them to a high school class. This, again, is a problem in our ability to transmit our values to our students. To the extent that such faculty can be convinced that this is a method of educating students in a Torah lifestyle, we could perhaps make some headway in this area.

A similar suggestion, although perhaps more easily accomplished, involves hiring as many Orthodox Jews as possible (or those visibly involved with their Judaism) as secular faculty. This is not out of a fear of non-Orthodox teachers, but out of a desire to send the clear message that the material studied in these classes (and, by extension, the world that produced this information) is also a significant part of an adult Jew's life, and should be approached in that way. I have already mentioned my connection to Dr. Joel Wolowelsky; many of the secular faculty at Flatbush were practicing Jews, and the message was clear, unmistakable, and effortlessly transmitted.

Ultimately, much of what I have said comes down to a deep belief in effective modeling as the primary vehicle of this kind of education. To the extent that we feel our messages are being poorly transmitted to our students, in the question of engagement with the outside world or otherwise, we need to check our modeling. First, our staff must be modeling a unified, although not necessarily unitary, message. Curricular initiatives, outside speakers, and social action can help in these areas, but must be carefully integrated into the school's model as a whole, not just plugged in to meet a specific perceived need. Most importantly, though, we should reconsider the models of the relationship between *limudei kodesh* and *limudei hol* that we have gotten used to, to see whether we can more realistically show students our vision of a well-lived Jewish life. In that way, regardless of mission statements, Jewish schools will come closer to fulfilling their mission, teaching Jewish children how to become Jewish adults.

NOTES

1. If society in general has turned away from the broad version of good citizenship that Rabbi Bieler supports, the issue of how we educate our children on these mat-

ters changes significantly. We would, in that case, need to question whether we wish to add good citizenship to the list of countercultural impulses we try to ingrain in our students. While we may answer affirmatively, that choice would be a matter for separate sustained debate.

Similarly, if someone argued that even forty years ago Jews were not involved enough in society, that, too, would be worth discussing, but it would then be an issue of questioning long-standing values of the Jewish community, not calling for a return to a standard of yore, as Rabbi Bieler does.

2. In one Talmud class I taught, I dealt with a group of young women who were clearly uninterested in serious study of Torah, although they were planning on attending a school in Israel where Talmud would be a central part of the curriculum. When I questioned how they could succeed there when they clearly did not enjoy Torah study here, they said, "Oh, that's different. Everyone knows you have to get serious when you go to Israel." The odds that those students would also be more open to *hashkafic* education during that year are pretty good.

3. Leviticus 23:9.

4. Jeremiah 29:7.

5. *Eichah Rabbah* 2:9. The differentiation between wisdom and Torah, between knowledge and insight that is humanly accessible and that which needs divine guidance, seems to be a useful way to define our attitude towards non-Jews generally. We can respect non-Jews and learn from them on all the former types of issues—which includes a vast array of subjects—but must resolutely walk our own path on all matters related to the latter, which includes a narrower, but more fundamental, group of issues.

6. While I am again working anecdotally, I have for a long time made a practice of asking educators how much ground they actually cover in a given year. It is my impression that in Modern Orthodox high schools, the average student, if lucky, will have seen about 8 folio pages of Talmud (perhaps 10), 10–15 chapters of Torah, and 10–15 chapters of *navi*. Considering the corpus we are discussing, that is so insignificant an amount as to belie the hope that we are giving these students any meaningful grounding in traditional texts.

7. Incidentally, that educator clearly assumed that educating for communal involvement was easier than educating for Torah study; the same is probably true of educating for involvement in the broader community, and would therefore not need the kinds of changes Rabbi Bieler contemplates.

8. The political and social factors that go into the wording of such statements are probably worth a study of its own, and are unexplored by Rabbi Bieler. In the various statements he records, were they meant as he took them or were they possibly phrased in that way to signal to nervous prospective parents that the school did not intend to completely reject the outside world, college, etc.? Did the schools, when speaking of good citizenship, mean the maximalist model Rabbi Bieler endorses, or did they mean the average version of citizenship prevalent among most Americans?

9. Avot 1:11.

10. *Devarim* 21:18. Incidentally, Rabbi Hirsch's comment also speaks to the question of whether teachers should try to present students with a broad range of options from which they choose or if, at least at the early stages of education, students need to master one tradition (and the multiple voices that speak from within that tradition)

before they can reasonably engage, and learn from, the positive elements in other, alien, traditions. Having a teacher who serves as agent-provocateur, who challenges the students rather than helps them see the meaning in their own tradition, may be useful at some stage, but almost definitely not before the students have a sufficient background to be ready for the challenge.

11. In responding to an early draft of this paper, Dr. Wolowelsky took anecdotal issue with this assessment; my second story, from my perspective, makes the same point, so that I am not committed to that view of his course.

12. One complaint about that system is that teachers, pressed to cover the planned curriculum, will simply shunt aside the called-for discussions; monitoring their doing so seems to me to be a simple practical issue, not a theoretical one.

Glossary of Hebrew Terms

avodah zarah the worship or formal recognition as God of an entity that is in fact not God (or even the unauthorized worship of an entity understood to be a servant of God)

avodat elilim idol worship

baal nefesh one with highly developed religious sensibilities

Ba'al ha-Tanya the author of the hasidic work *Tanya* (R. Shnneur Zalman of Liady)

bar bei rav de-had yoma young child

Bava Metzi'a a tractate of the Talmud

benei dat people of religion

derosh ve-qabbel sekhar Study and receive reward (even though no practical consequences will result)

eivah hatred (the fear that an act or statement will arouse enmity toward Jews)

elohim aherim other gods

eshet yefat toar beautiful woman (in Deuteronomy 21:10-14)

ever min ha-hai a limb of a living animal (which may not be eaten according to the Noahide code)

galut Edom the exile under Christendom

gemara Talmud

ger toshav resident alien

ha-adam the human being

hasidei ummot ha-olam the pious of the nations of world

hashkafah religious worldview

hasid pious individual

Hazal the Talmudic sages

humash Pentateuch

iggun the unmarriageable state of a woman whose husband has disappeared or refused to provide her with a divorce

lo taguru mi-penei ish Fear no man (Deuteronomy 1:17)
mah hu qanna af attah qanna Just as He is zealous, so shall you be zealous
mah hu rahum af attah rahum Just as He is merciful, so should you be merciful
mamzerut the status of one born of an adulterous or incestuous union
naval bi-reshut ha–Torah a vile person acting within the parameters permitted by the Torah
nevelah carcass
periqat ol throwing off the yoke of heaven
qiddush ha-Shem sanctification of God's name
***rishon* (plural, *rishonim*)** a medieval rabbinic authority
shinuyei dehikei forced answers
shittuf association (of the true God with something else)
***shiur* (plural, *shiurim*)** a class in a religious text
talmid hakham rabbinic scholar
ve-lilmod anu tzerikhim and we need to learn
ve-naqqeh and cleanse (Exodus 34:7)

Index

About the Editors and Contributors

Mr. Marc D. Stern (Volume Editor) is co-director of the Commission on Law and Social Action of the American Jewish Congress. Previously, he was a law clerk for the United States Court of Appeals. He writes widely on religion and public policy.

Dr. David Berger is professor of history at Brooklyn College and the Graduate Center, City University of New York, and a visiting professor at Yeshiva University. He is the author of *The Jewish-Christian Debate in the High Middle Ages* among several scholarly studies.

Dr. Jay R. Berkovitz is professor of Jewish History at the University of Massachusetts at Amherst, where he directs the Center for Jewish Studies. Professor Berkovitz is the author of *The Shaping of Jewish Identity in Nineteenth-Century France* and a new book devoted to the study of ritual—*Rites and Passages: The Beginnings of Modern Jewish Culture in France, 1650–1850* (University of Pennsylvania, 2004).

Rabbi Jack Bieler is former assistant principal of the Hebrew Academy of Greater Washington and rabbi of the Kemp Mill Synagogue. He has published articles on the integration of Judaism and general studies, as well as on the philosophy of Jewish education.

Edward Breuer received his Ph.D. from Harvard University in 1990. He taught at the University of Pennsylvania and Loyola University Chicago, and is currently a visiting professor at the Hebrew University in Jerusalem. He is the author of *The Limits of Enlightenment: Jews, Germans, and the*

Eighteenth-Century Study of Scripture, and is currently writing *From Haskalah to Orthodoxy*.

Rabbi Michael J. Broyde is senior lecturer at Emory University School of Law, where he is also director of the Project on Law, Religion, and the Family and a member of the Law and Religion Program. Ordained *yoreh yoreh v-yadin yadin*, he is author of *The Pursuit of Justice and Jewish Law: Halakhic Perspectives on the Legal Profession*, as well as numerous other works.

Rabbi Robert S. Hirt (Series Editor) is the senior advisor to the president of Yeshiva University and vice president emeritus of its affiliated Rabbi Isaac Elchanan Theological Seminary. In 1991, he was named inaugural occupant of the Rabbi Sidney Shoham Chair in Rabbinic and Community Leadership at RIETS.

In 1987, Rabbi Hirt—who formerly directed the University's array of Holocaust studies programs—coedited Shimon Huberband's critically acclaimed book on the Holocaust, *Kiddush Hashem: Jewish Religious and Cultural Life in Poland During the Holocaust*. He serves as the series editor of the Orthodox Forum.

Rabbi Aharon Lichtenstein is Rosh Yeshiva at Yeshivat Har Etzion and the Gruss Institute, RIETS. He is a frequent contributor to books and journals of contemporary Jewish thought.

Rabbi Gidon Rothstein was ordained at the Rabbi Isaac Elchanan Theological Seminary (RIETS) and received a Ph.D. in Jewish studies from Harvard University. He is currently the Rosh Kollel at HAFTER High School.

Professor Suzanne Last Stone is a professor of law and director, Program in Jewish Law and Interdisciplinary Studies, at Benjamin N. Cardozo School of Law, Yeshiva University. She was writing and research editor of the *Columbia Law Review* and a Harlan Fiske Stone Scholar. She clerked for Judge John Minor Wisdom of the U.S. Court of Appeals for the Fifth Circuit and was associated with the firm of Paul, Weiss, Rifkind, Wharton & Garrison.